FULLY REMOTE

How to set up, lead, and manage your own successful
all-remote company

By
Shelly J. Spiegel
CEO & Chief Creative Officer of Fire Engine RED, Inc.

Fully Remote by Shelly J. Spiegel

Published by Fire Engine RED, Inc.
P.O. Box 1017
Havertown, PA
19083-1017

www.fully-remote-book.com
www.fire-engine-red.com

Cover design by Jennifer Hauxhurst.

ISBN: 978-0-578-71521-6
ISBN: 978-0-578-71520-9 (ebk)

Dedication

To the fabulous four … my niece, Olivia, and nephews, Ben, Will, and Harrison.

May all of your dreams come true.

Table of Contents

Acknowledgments

As with everything at Fire Engine RED, it took a team to turn *Fully Remote* into a reality.

This book simply would not have happened without Chuck Vadun, my communications director, who was by my virtual side, working tirelessly with me on this book, day in and day out for almost 18 months. Chuck helped me share my nearly 20 years of knowledge and experience in leading one of the first all-remote companies in the U.S. in an easy-to-read, easy-to-understand, and (we hope) entertaining way.

Next, I'd like to thank my copyeditor, Caren Hayden, whom I met on a Backroads trip (www.backroads.com) to Sedona, Arizona, in March of 2019. Caren brought much-needed experience as well as enthusiasm to this project while making sure every "i" was dotted and "t" crossed.

And, thanks to Jen Hauxhurst, designer extraordinaire, for helping to bring Fully Remote—both the book and the website (www.fully-remote-book.com)—to life.

I also want to thank:

My content experts who made sure that the processes and policies that I described were accurate and complete: Akber Pabani, CFO; Jamie Levick, director of people; Joanna Everett, business operations manager; Katrina Masiak, VP of projects; Sarah Kozay, VP of products; and Zach Beerger, director of operations.

My director of enrollment software, Emma McAneny, for her humorous comments and observations and for making sure that the book's content was clear and user-friendly in places where it was easy to get bogged down.

My longtime accountant, Paul Flax, and attorney, Steve Feder, who reviewed the accounting and legal sections of this book to make sure I got things right.

The following Fire Engine RED team members: Bill Preble, VP of search strategies and solutions; Glenna Ryan, VP of search operations; Jeff McLaughlin, EVP of enrollment data, strategy and analytics; Jim Slavin, EVP of enrollment software; Mark Kieran, director of client care operations; Meaghan Conly, copy manager and operations analyst; Mike Matthews, EVP of search services; Molly Erker, director of enrollment data and operations; and Morgan Frederick, quality manager, student search—for reviewing my manuscript repeatedly and suggesting edits and clarifications that made this book better.

Our intern, Ben Spiegel, who also made significant contributions to the early sections of this book and was my top developmental editor. I only wish he hadn't had to return to school and could have worked with me on the later sections of this book.

My friend, Amy Cohen, who gave me the final nudge to write this book—something I had put off for 10 years because I never felt it was the right time or that I had enough to say. Amy was right; I had nearly 300 pages' worth of things to say!

And finally, Andrew Meslow, my redheaded investor and friend, who supported this project and continues to support me and all things Fire Engine RED.

Chapter 1
Introduction

1.1 Why I wrote this book

When people learn I'm the CEO of a 100 percent virtual company, they have endless questions about how we're doing it. How do you find the right people to work for your company? How do you know if they're working when you can't see them? Can you build a company culture without an office? Questions like these are what led me to write this book, the first of its kind, about the unique benefits (and challenges) of *setting up, leading, and managing a successful 100 percent remote company*, in which *all* of the processes, policies, and tools are built around empowering an all-remote workforce.

There are, as of this writing, more than 170 companies in the U.S. that are fully remote, with no central offices.[1] These are businesses that employ people across the country (and beyond) and have done so without the "benefit" of office space. I believe there would be many more fully remote companies if more people knew about the unique benefits inherent in a workplace that's all remote, all the time.

My company, Fire Engine RED, has been operating successfully without an office since I founded it in 2001. In fact, Fire Engine RED was one of the first 100 percent remote companies in the U.S. (according to the first-known list of all-remote and nearly all-remote companies, published in 2014 by FlexJobs, a job site for those interested in remote and flexible work).[2] Today, Fire Engine RED continues to thrive as a fully remote company, providing technology, marketing, data, and consulting services to more than 300 clients in the education market (mostly college admissions offices). Our 80-plus talented team members work in 26 U.S. states and in five countries, including the U.S., Brazil, Canada, France, and Peru. Our annual employee retention rate is 92 percent, and nearly half of our team members have been with us for five or more years.

In *Fully Remote*, I'll draw on my nearly two decades of experience leading a fully remote business to help guide you step by step through building your own 100 percent virtual company. I'll reveal the secrets to our success as a 100 percent remote company and explain how you can put them to work for *your* business. I'll also give you an idea of the costs involved in getting your fully remote company off the ground and point out which vendors we've had success with along the way. Plus, you'll hear from many of my team members about what it's like to work for a fully remote company.

However, before we dive into the how-tos, I'll fill you in on how Fire Engine RED got started. Then, I'll discuss the pros (and a few cons) of being all-virtual from the perspective of the company, its team members, and its clients.

It's important to note that 100 percent remote companies differ from partially remote and "remote-friendly" companies in one critical way—everyone working for a fully remote company is on a level playing field. When a company isn't fully remote, in-office workers may feel that remote workers aren't actually working (and/or resent the flexibility remote workers have), while remote workers may "worry that coworkers say bad things behind their backs, make changes to projects without telling them in advance, lobby against them, and don't fight for their priorities."[3] Conversely, when *all* team members are remote workers, everyone's in the same "remote boat" together. And that's just one of the many advantages of going all-remote.

Fully Remote is for you if you're an aspiring entrepreneur who's open to growing your company in a way you may not have considered. It's for you if you're already running an all-remote company and want to learn new ways to be more efficient and effective. It's for you if you're a leader of a bricks-and-mortar company who wants to get a perspective on how an increasing number of companies are thriving without an office. And it's for you if you're considering joining a 100 percent virtual company and want an inside look at the workings of one.

I hope you'll find inspiration in *Fully Remote*. It's the book I wish I'd had when I started Fire Engine RED nearly 20 years ago!

1.2 How to get the most out of this book

I recommend you first read *Fully Remote* from beginning to end, to get a sense of the "journey" you'll go through as the leader of your own fully remote company. Then keep it handy for quick reference. I've organized the text into modular sections, so when you want a refresher or need specific info, it's easy to find what you're looking for.

Throughout *Fully Remote*, I'll provide detailed, "how-to" instructions based on my real-world experiences. You'll be able to take the lessons I've learned and apply them directly to your own remote business.

As a supplement to the *Fully Remote* book, my team and I have created a companion website (www.fully-remote-book.com). There, you'll find additional resources that can help you as you grow your 100 percent remote company. (I've included a passcode at the end of the book you can use to access exclusive resources for *Fully Remote* readers.) We've also established a discussion forum where you can get answers to your questions about running a fully remote company, provided by our own experts and other members of the remote-work community.

1.3 Terms of endearment

Throughout this book, I'll use the terms "remote," "virtual," and "distributed" interchangeably. All of them apply to companies that don't have an office, and all describe the way we work at Fire Engine RED.

Let's start with "remote" ... Fully remote "means that a company has no physical headquarters and no 'home base.' All members of the company work from a location of their choosing, anywhere in the world."[4] Our team is a good example of this, as we have no centrally located office.

As for "virtual" ... "A virtual team usually refers to a group of individuals who work together from different geographic locations and rely on communication technology [...] in order to collaborate."[5] In addition, "the most extreme type of virtual company is one with only 'virtual employees' and no central office. Everyone works from home, including top management."[6] These definitions also fit us to a T.

And with regard to "distributed" … "[T]eam members and coworkers are ALL distributed away from each other. This could mean working at home from anywhere in the world, or it could mean […] working in an office in a location where no other team members are located."[7] Our "distributed" team members work from their home offices, coffee shops, or wherever they choose.

Here are a few other terms to keep an eye out for …

Most of the time, when referring to the people who work at Fire Engine RED, I'll use the umbrella term "team member," which includes our full-time employees, contractors, and interns. However, when discussing salaries and benefits, I'll use "employee," which refers specifically to someone who works for our company full-time and receives a salary and benefits.

At Fire Engine RED, our human resources department is called People, Places, and Perks (P3). However, I'll use "HR" throughout the book to avoid any confusion.

"Slack" (noun) is the name of the collaborative tool we use most at Fire Engine RED. However, "Slack," used as a verb, has become part of our language here, as in, "Can you Slack?" or "Let's Slack with Zach and Jen." I'll be using both forms of "Slack" in the text.

Finally, I'll use the term "clients" because we serve colleges, universities, and other schools in a business-to-business context. If you're starting a business-to-consumer company, you may refer to the people you serve as "customers." Again, think of these terms as interchangeable for the purposes of this book.

1.4 How I started my 100 percent remote business

In 1999, I was working as president of Search By Video (a company I founded in 1986 that duplicated and distributed college recruitment videos to high school students). One of my clients, Carnegie Mellon University (CMU), asked me to help solve one of their biggest challenges: managing and responding—in a quick, consistent, and customized way—to the high volume of incoming email their admissions office was receiving each day from prospective students. Bill Elliott, CMU's then-vice president of enrollment, and Mike Steidel, CMU's then-director (now dean) of admissions, knew I had no experience in software development, but they had confidence that I could get the job done.

Essentially, what CMU wanted was an email response system that was affordable and tailored to the unique needs of the college admissions market. Back then, the only solutions available had been created for large business-to-consumer companies with complex needs and six-figure budgets.

I agreed to take on the CMU project, and after months of research, I identified a company that had developed an email response system for consumer companies and was willing to modify its system to meet CMU's needs. Soon, however, I realized that neither CMU nor I would be happy with a product that required lots of work-arounds to be used successfully. The best solution, I decided, was for me to start a new company and develop a product specifically for college admissions offices. And that's how, in December 2001, Fire Engine RED (a company named after my favorite color) was born!

While my new company was starting up, my current one, Search By Video, was winding down. The anthrax scare in the fall of 2001 caused the company's sales revenues to drop by more than 70 percent, as colleges stopped sending unsolicited recruitment videos to students via U.S. mail. By March 2002, Search By Video was out of business and, for all practical purposes, I was personally bankrupt.

Bootstrapping to success

From the outset, there were a few things (beyond its name alone) that made Fire Engine RED unique. The company had:

- A female founder. Nearly 20 years later, only 5 percent of tech startups are owned by women.[8]
- A CEO whose experience was in journalism, law, and business. Most technology companies are founded by people with a technology background.
- Zero startup capital. Closing Search By Video had left me $300,000 in debt. In addition, there was no outside funding available for a startup technology company in December 2001. Nearly all funding for tech companies had dried up after the dot-com bubble burst in March 2000, and the country was in a recession.
- No office. Paying for office space was a non-starter. (See "Zero startup capital" above.)

So, where did the company's startup funding come from? I funded the company by asking three colleges to prepay for the product before it was even built. And they agreed!

I continued to bootstrap the company until 2013. That's when I brought in a private investor to help fund the development of a customer relationship management (CRM) system for admissions offices. This undertaking was simply too big—and too expensive—for the company to go it alone.

Our redheaded angel investor Andrew didn't just appear out of thin air; he and I grew up in the same town, and he'd been my brother Brad's best friend since childhood. In 2013, Andrew was at a point where he wanted to diversify his investment portfolio. Luckily for me, Fire Engine RED represented just the opportunity he was looking for.

All-remote out of necessity

I'd love to say that my decision to start a 100 percent remote company was part of some grand vision (like, "This will be the future of work!"). However, the truth is, Fire Engine RED began operating as a virtual company out of pure necessity.

A few months after I founded Fire Engine RED, I took on a business partner (who has since left the company). She didn't have any money, either, as the dot-com company she had previously worked for had gone bust. Even if we'd had the money for office space, which we clearly didn't, neither of us wanted to commute to an office that, at best, would be equally inconvenient to both of us. I lived in downtown Philadelphia, and she lived in suburban New Jersey, a 90-minute drive from me. We also had one employee, Joe, who lived in the Philly suburbs and had worked for me at Search By Video.

So, in reality, the choice to work from home was our only option.

Timing was everything

The convergence of two factors in the early- to mid-2000s made it possible for our all-virtual company to not only exist but also thrive: (1) the advent of broadband and (2) the development of web-based collaboration tools.

My then-business partner and I were among the earliest adopters of broadband technology. Back then, fewer than 10 percent of adults had a high-speed internet connection at home.[9] Within four years, home broadband usage topped 50 percent, leading to the development of online collaborative tools. This made working remotely not just possible, but *practical*.

Our original lineup of free-to-inexpensive tools included:

1) ACT for managing sales contacts.
2) AOL Instant Messenger for instant messaging.
3) eFax for faxing documents.
4) FogBugz for bug tracking.
5) FreeConference for conference calls.
6) GoToMeeting for screen sharing.
7) ooVoo for the occasional video conference.
8) YouSendIt for transferring large files.

Today, nearly 20 years later, our collaborative tools still serve as our "lifelines" to one another, even though we no longer use any of the tools listed above. Today our toolset consists of 42 tools, which I'll tell you about in chapter

3.13, "Select your collaborative tools," and in chapter 11.1, "Manage collaborative tools and licenses."

Making our first hires

About four years in, when we were ready to hire our first post-startup team member, the person we wanted to hire didn't live in the Philadelphia area. And because our all-remote setup was working well, moving into office space never even occurred to us. Enter Emily S., whom we knew from an education marketing and consulting firm we'd worked with. At the time, she was working in Connecticut but wanted to move to Steamboat Springs, Colorado, so she could pursue her passion of skiing. Unfortunately, the types of jobs available in a small resort town didn't interest her. Hiring Emily S. not only allowed Fire Engine RED to expand our implementation and support hours across multiple time zones but also enabled her to have both the career and lifestyle she wanted.

As the company grew, we identified the next person we wanted to hire. Glenna was working as the director of enrollment operations at Rensselaer Polytechnic Institute (RPI), one of the first colleges to adopt our email response system. We didn't want the responsibility of asking Glenna to uproot her life to move to Philadelphia or New Jersey. She was a single mom with three young children, and the company simply wasn't stable enough yet. Instead, we offered her a position as our director of operations, allowing her to work from her home in

Schenectady—and voilà, we had a New York office. Today, Glenna is still with Fire Engine RED (13 years and counting), serving as our vice president of student search operations.

And so it went. Our company continued to expand, and as new positions became available, we found again and again that the people we wanted to hire lived in places other than Philadelphia, such as Avon, Indiana; Carlsbad, California; Fayetteville, North Carolina; Greenville, New York; Jacksonville, Florida; and Swanton, Vermont. And, yes, we eventually did hire several team members who live in the Philadelphia area. Currently, there are five of us in and around Philly, including our chief financial officer, business operations manager, director of operations, and director of people.

I'll tell you more about how we're able to attract, recruit, and hire top talent in chapter 4, "Attracting top talent: Offer benefits that will help seal the deal," and chapter 5, "Recruiting, interviewing, and hiring: How to do it all virtually."

Fast forward to today

As I write this, Fire Engine RED is still 100 percent remote—and we're still growing. We've gone from offering one stand-alone software product (an email response system) to providing technology, marketing, data, and consulting services to more than 300 education clients.

Here's a quick look at the evolution of our product and service offerings, nearly 20 years after we opened our virtual doors:

Year	Products/Services
2002	Email Response System
2003	Broadcast Email System
2004	Group Chat
2005	Forms
2006	Admissions Applications and Event Manager
2007	Student Search (lead generation)
2009	1-on-1 Chat
2015	Data Services
2016	CRM
2019	Enrollment Consulting

I'm excited to see what our future holds!

1.5 Remote working, then and now

Since Fire Engine RED first hung out its virtual shingle in 2001, remote work has taken off, going from a great option (in our case, the only option) for a cash-strapped startup to a worldwide movement embraced by companies much larger than ours. As of early 2019, "over half of employees globally are working outside of their main office headquarters for at least 2.5 days per week,"[10] and 34 percent of surveyed business leaders predict that more than half of their workforce will be remote by 2020.[11]

How did it all begin? In FlexJobs's "Complete History of Working from Home," the authors write that the first at-home workers were "hunter-gatherers, who foraged for sustenance and brought the fruits of their labor back to the hearth." Medieval homes served as "the first open-plan offices." And, "the working classes often set up craft and trade-focused shops in their homes." The Industrial Revolution and factory work, the authors note, are what eventually pulled workers out of their homes. In a way, remote work has come full circle. [12]

Today, the idea of remote work may evoke images of young people living a "digital nomad" lifestyle—that is, logging in from exotic destinations around the world and working whenever they choose. But remote work isn't just for them. At Fire Engine RED, we have team members representing nearly every age group and generational cohort.[13]

Here's a look at our team's demographics. You'll note that 66 percent of our team members are over 35.

Table 1. Fire Engine RED Team Member Demographics

Age	Generation	% of team members
Under 21	Gen Z	3
21–25	Millennials	4
26–30	Millennials	9
31–35	Millennials	18
36–40	Xennials[14]	22
41–45	Xennials/Gen X	18
46–50	Gen X	17
51–55	Gen X	5
56–60	Boomers	4

Plus, just over half of our team members are parents. So, we don't only have "kids" working for us; we also have team members who are sending their own kids off to college!

1.6 Doing big things, virtually

Forbes reports that the "top industries for virtual companies" include "computer/IT, HR/recruiting, and education."[14] Below are just a few of the 100 percent remote companies out there and what they do.[15]

- **Aha!** - product roadmap software
- **BELAY** - virtual staffing solutions for small businesses

- **Buffer** - social media management platform
- **Collage.com** - custom photo products
- **FlexJobs** - job search site for remote, part-time, freelance, and flexible work
- **Lullabot** - high-profile websites for large-scale publishers
- **MoveOn** - progressive organizing group
- **OnTheGoSystems** - custom WordPress plugins
- **PartnerCentric** - performance marketing agency
- **Time Doctor** - time-tracking software
- **TrustHCS** - healthcare consulting
- **Zapier** - automation of web applications

Finally, no discussion about remote work would be complete without mentioning both **Automattic** (WordPress open-source blogging software) and **InVision** (tools and resources for product design). As of this writing, Automattic has approximately 700 employees and InVision about 800. So, if you "envision" doing big things with your company, there's no reason to "automatically" rule out the 100 percent remote model! (I couldn't help myself.)

For a complete list of all-remote companies, see the Resources section of the *Fully Remote* website (www.fully-remote-book.com).

1.7 And *you* get a job, and *you* get a job, and *you* get a job!

What types of positions do all-remote companies offer? According to FlexJobs's founder Sara Sutton Fell, "half of American employees hold a job that's compatible with telework" (working remotely).[16]

Here are some examples of the job titles held by Fire Engine RED team members:

- Chief Financial Officer
- Client Care Specialist
- Communications Director
- Copywriter
- Creative Director
- Data Analyst
- Designer
- Director of Operations
- Director of People
- Project Manager
- Quality Analyst
- Scrum Master
- Software Engineer

What do the job descriptions look like for these and other positions at Fire Engine RED? The same as if we were a bricks-and-mortar company. The only real difference is that our job descriptions include the following statement,

"This is a full-time, remote position." You can find examples of our job descriptions in the Resources section of the *Fully Remote* website (www.fully-remote-book.com).

Chapter 2
All-remote companies: Just like "real" companies, only better

Just like "real" companies, 100 percent distributed businesses have an organizational structure, a company culture, and regular office hours. However, as you might expect, I believe the all-remote model is better. Let's take a look at how it benefits companies, team members, and clients alike.

2.1 How companies benefit

Ability to hire top talent

One of the biggest advantages of running a 100 percent remote company is the ability to hire top talent. You're not limited to a specific geographic talent pool, so you can hire people no matter where they live.

At Fire Engine RED, we can (and do) hire people from, well, everywhere. Our team members currently work in 26 U.S. states and five countries.

Our lack of a centralized office proved particularly helpful in the hiring of three of our executive vice presidents, all of whom were "unicorns"—highly sought-after education professionals with unique experience, skills, and credentials. The fact that they didn't have to relocate gave us a key competitive advantage over the other companies that were trying to hire them.

Our "virtuality" has also made it possible for us to hire top talent who've worked for industry leaders outside the education field, such as Apple, GoDaddy, Hewlett-Packard, Intuit, and SapientRazorfish. One team member said, "At Fire Engine RED, I still have the opportunity to work with top talent and make a difference, just like I did at my former company, but with much less commuting."

Why is top talent so important to a business? Research shows that top talent is more productive: "In highly complex jobs—those that are information- and interaction-intensive, such as managers, software developers and project managers—high performers are an astounding 800 percent more productive than average performers."[17] I think Steve Jobs, the cofounder and former CEO of Apple Inc., may have summed it up best when he said to "[…] go after the cream of the cream. […] A small team of A+

players can run circles around a giant team of B and C players."[18]

Being virtual also gives companies an advantage in hiring millennials, many of whom "may not even consider a job unless it offers a remote work option."[19] In fact, a 2015 survey of undergraduates, graduate students, and recent college grads found that 68 percent wanted jobs where they could work remotely.[20] This preference rings true with our team members (millennials or not), many of whom have told me that in the unlikely event they started a job search today, they'd only consider remote jobs and companies. Brendan, one of our software engineers, said, "Were I to start looking for a job, 'remote' would absolutely be the first filter I applied."

Finally, I believe our remote structure has helped us to diversify our workforce. At Fire Engine RED, nearly 17 percent of our team members were born outside the U.S., in countries such as Brazil, Canada, England, Greece, Guatemala, India, Iran, Ireland, Peru, the Philippines, Uganda, and Venezuela.

So, it works both ways. Companies that want to attract diverse workers should consider offering fully remote positions because diverse workers are often attracted to companies that offer remote work.

Savings on office space

Office space is typically the third-highest expense for a company, behind only salaries and healthcare. According to Global Workplace Analytics, companies can save up to $10,000 annually per employee by having full-time remote workers, and that amount goes up to $11,000 per employee when factoring in reduced costs for utilities, janitorial services, office furniture, supplies, and equipment.[21] For us, this translates into a savings of approximately $800,000 per year on office-related costs. That's money we invest right back into our offerings and our team members!

Ability to retain top talent

Of course, once you've hired top talent, you'll want to do your best to *retain* that talent. Why? Because, when an employee leaves, it costs time and money to advertise, interview, hire, and onboard a new one. According to *Forbes*, it can cost up to 50 percent of an entry-level employee's salary to replace them. For mid-level employees, that figure is 125 percent, and for a senior executive, it's an astonishing 200 percent![22]

When a team member leaves, vital company, industry, and/or client knowledge may walk out the door with them. New team members, in the meantime, aren't likely to be as productive (and may even make costly errors) as they get up to speed. Employees who remain might experience a dip in morale, especially if they begin to sense their company has a revolving door. This can lead to "greater signs of stress, which ultimately affects company culture and teamwork."[23]

However, when it comes to retaining talent, there's good news for distributed businesses: 46 percent of companies that allow remote work say it helps them retain their employees.[24] Further, "companies that support remote work have 25 percent lower employee turnover than companies that don't,"[25] and remote workers say they are "50 percent less likely to quit their jobs."[26]

The Society for Human Resource Management (SHRM) puts the national average employee retention rate at 82 percent.[27] So, how does our fully remote company stack up? Our annual retention rate is 92 percent, significantly higher than the national average. And, 47 percent of our team members have been with us five years or longer. (See Table 2 below.)

Table 2. Fire Engine RED Team Member Tenure

Years Employed	% of Team Members
Up to 2	24
2–5	29
5–7	12
7–10	23
10–13	12

Note: We made our first post-startup hire in 2006.

I'm convinced our remote structure is among the top reasons we're able to retain our team members, and why so many of them have told me they hope to be "lifers" at Fire Engine RED.

Why is it easier to retain remote workers than employees who work in an office? Remote employees are generally happier at work. In a survey-based study by TINYpulse, remote workers scored 8.10 (on a scale of 1 to 10) on the question, "How happy are you at work?" That's compared to an average score of 7.42 for all workers.[28]

Bricks-and-mortar companies can even have a hard time retaining happy employees. That's because those employees may not be able to take their jobs with them if, for example, they want (or need) to move closer to family, or if their spouse/partner gets transferred to another city or state. As a remote company, Fire Engine RED has been able to retain our employees because they have what's often called "portable jobs." We estimate that we'd have lost at least 28 percent of our current employees to relocation if we hadn't been all-virtual. I shudder just to think of it.

Higher engagement

The *Harvard Business Review* asked, "Is employee engagement dependent on a worker's physical proximity to other team members?" Apparently, it's not. They cited research from Automatic Data Processing (ADP) showing that "people who work remotely at least four out of five days in a typical week are almost twice as engaged as those who do so less than one day a week." The key to this high engagement, it's noted, is whether remote workers feel like they're part of a team (ours do, and yours can too—see chapter 13.5, "Keep them engaged").[29]

Increased productivity

Research has shown that remote workers accomplish more. For example, one Stanford study found that employees who work from home are 13 percent more productive than their in-office counterparts.[30] Another study reported that "employees are apt to work more efficiently and collaboratively when operating remotely."[31] A third study (by FlexJobs) found that "65 percent of workers think they would be more productive at home than working in a traditional office environment."[32]

One explanation for remote workers' enhanced productivity may be that they deal with fewer distractions, such as office politics, endless meetings, frequent interruptions by colleagues, long watercooler conversations, and near-daily birthday celebrations. One team member explained, "I was the birthday and work anniversary coordinator at my last [office] job. We were constantly gathering to celebrate when there was plenty of work to get done."

In fact, nearly three out of four office workers feel distracted when they're on the job, with 16 percent asserting they're *almost always* distracted. The problem is biggest for millennials/Gen Z, 74 percent of whom report feeling distracted in the workplace—one reason so many prefer to have a remote-work option.[33]

The physical workspace itself can be a distraction. Many organizations simply lack truly private areas where employees can work. (Think of the open floor plans enamored by tech companies.) In fact, "chatty coworkers (80%) and office noise (70%) were cited as the top distractors."[34] Chuck, who previously worked in an open-plan office, cited "frequent Nerf gun battles and blaring techno music" as being occasionally fun, but more often distracting.

Another of our team members who previously worked in an open setting, shared, "I had to wear noise-canceling headphones all the time. Not only did I use them to block out the noise but also as a visual signifier that I didn't want to be disturbed. But people ignored them and disturbed me anyway!" He added, "Even worse, every Friday for an hour, I'd have to listen to my cubicle neighbor call in to a status meeting on speakerphone, while she clipped her nails."

In chapter 10, "Maximizing and measuring productivity at your all-remote company," I'll tell you more about how we know that our team members are not just working but working productively.

Fewer sick days

Remote workers take fewer sick days than their in-office counterparts. One survey showed that companies that implemented a remote work plan saw their unscheduled absences fall by 63 percent![35]

Our experience is consistent with this research. The average number of sick days taken by an employee at Fire Engine RED is less than two days per year, compared to the national average of up to five days.[36] You may find this especially surprising given that we provide our employees with an unlimited number of sick days! They can also use their sick days to care for a sick child, spouse/partner, or parent.

One reason remote workers may take fewer sick days is that they aren't working in close quarters with others during cold and flu season. As a result, they don't pick up and spread as many "bugs."

Another reason why office workers may take *more* sick days is, if they're not feeling well, they may decide their commute is too daunting and stay home. When that happens, an entire day of productivity is lost. Distributed team members, on the other hand, have a lower barrier to getting at least *some* work done from home, as they can log in if they feel better later in the day.

Of course, being sick isn't the only reason employees take sick days; other reasons include personal needs and family issues. (One study found that 78 percent of employees who call in sick aren't actually sick.)[37] At Fire Engine RED, we provide our employees with up to two hours of "out time" to take care of these issues, so there's no need for them to use their sick time. On a lighter note, when our team members do get sick, they tend to do so at the same time as coworkers who are closest to them geographically. I kid you not.

I'll tell you more about our sick time and out time policies in chapter 4.4, "Paid leave."

Weather-proof

Like the U.S. Postal Service ("Neither snow nor rain nor heat," etc.), distributed companies don't get shut down by weather. Inclement weather and natural disasters have occasionally knocked a few team members offline, but they've never forced us to close our company completely. For example, we've been able to keep the virtual doors open through hurricanes (Katrina, Sandy, and Irma, to name just a few), wildfires, ice storms, and other events that would most likely have caused a bricks-and-mortar company to close for the day (or even longer).

As Jason Fried and David Heinemeier Hansson of Basecamp put it, "Forcing everyone into the office every day is an organizational SPoF (Single Point of Failure)."[38]

At Fire Engine RED, our remote structure ensures we can continue to serve our clients when the unexpected happens, and in the face of just about anything.

Still, it doesn't always take a natural disaster to bring down a remote worker. Power failures and internet problems are among our more-common obstacles. (There was also the summer day when one of our team members' kids got on Netflix and hogged all the bandwidth, bringing him to a halt.) When interruptions occur, our team members usually just head for the nearest Starbucks until their internet service and/or power is restored (or their kids go back to school).

Savings on salaries (not recommended!)

There's also one money-saving opportunity I hope you *won't* take advantage of. As the owner/CEO of a virtual company, you could potentially pay your employees *less*. Workers, on average, would be willing to take an 8 percent pay cut if they could work from home.[39] But just because you *can* pay remote workers less, it doesn't mean you *should*. I believe that where a person works—whether in a traditional office or from home, a coffee shop, or any other remote workspace—should *not* impact their salary. In fact, given that remote workers are more productive than their in-office counterparts, remote workers should arguably be paid *more*.

In chapter 5.3, "Recruit and interview the all-remote way," I'll discuss salary and compensation.

2.2 How team members benefit

No commute

A survey by Robert Half found that 23 percent of workers "have left a job because of a bad commute."[40] According to our team members, the *lack* of a commute is the biggest benefit of working for a 100 percent remote company. Generally, our team members' commutes require just a few steps, not a car trip or a bus/train ride. Not having a daily commute gives them more time to do the things they want and/or need to do the most.

For example, prior to joining our distributed company, Deb, one of our CRM implementation managers, was what I call an "extreme commuter." She was commuting from her home in Beaufort, South Carolina, to the college where she worked … in Jacksonville, Florida! Because of the commute time (two-and-a-half hours in each direction), she stayed in a dorm room Monday through Thursday. Needless to say, joining Fire Engine RED was a life-changer for Deb: "I get to see my family a lot more! It was a dramatic change—being at home and being able to make dinner and pick up kids instead of trying to 'manage' all that from my office and the road."

Remote companies are also a great fit for people who can do the work, but due to a medical/health condition, aren't able to drive to an office. Jason 1, a designer and one of three Jasons at Fire Engine RED, is legally blind in both eyes and isn't allowed to drive. He said, "Working from home allows me, or any person with a 'disability,' to work and support a family. If I had to go to a traditional office, I'd be very limited in where I could live."

He added, "This is why I left my last job. It was getting harder and harder to drive, and they wouldn't let me work from home." I should mention that Jason 1 has done outstanding work for our clients and our company for eight years. In fact, I wasn't even aware that Jason 1 was legally blind until I interviewed him for this book.

Better work-life balance

People who work from home seem to have an easier time striking a manageable work-life balance. The flexibility of working remotely is also conducive to mental and physical well-being.[41]

Remote workers find it's much easier to stick to healthy eating habits. In one study, 73 percent reported they ate more healthily simply because they were able to do so at home.[42] In fact, many people on our team spend their lunch hours making their own healthy meals, using organic and locally sourced ingredients. One of our team members simply walks to her backyard before putting together a salad, as working from home lets her devote more time and care to her vegetable garden.

Let's look at some more examples based on my team members' experiences.

Brendan loves that his kitchen is right downstairs. "Because I'm at home all day, I'm able to make more complicated meals. I can start preparing a stew at lunchtime and have it for dinner. Also, I make bread, which takes a long time. The longer the rise, the more flavor it has. I'm able to check in on the bread all day and give it the time it needs."

Shalon, one of our project managers, said, "I do meal prep during my lunch hour. This is so helpful to my family, and for me. I am so grateful that I am able to alleviate that stress!"

As an aside, decreasing consumption of processed foods helps to cut back on the energy-intensive processes of freezing and packaging. Buying food produced on a nearby farm lessens the carbon emissions required to transport it. So, by adopting better eating habits, our remote team is helping to reduce its carbon footprint![43]

Working remotely can also make it easier for employees to exercise and/or take on fitness challenges. One of our team members has lost more than 90 pounds since she began participating in our wellness program and taking regular walks at lunch. She said, "I feel empowered by the company and my manager to take a longer lunch to get my workout in. Plus, I'm always available by phone or Slack while I'm on a walk, and, in case of emergency, my husband, who also works for the company, could come to pick me up!"

Molly, our director of enrollment data and operations, is a triathlete who's continually training for her next half-Ironman competition. She explained, "I get up at 4:30 a.m. to work out and then take a power nap at lunchtime. I really appreciate not having to hurry from an early workout to an office and not having to stuff my work clothes, makeup, and hair products into a gym bag."

Alaina, one of our copywriters, said, "I set up a treadmill desk, which would have been too distracting in an office setting. When I'm archiving projects or doing something fairly straightforward, I can get steps in while I work!"

Lunchtime at Fire Engine RED is a popular time for team members to check things off their to-do list. Mark (director of client care operations) said, "I eat on and off all day long, so I don't need the 'traditional' time to eat. In fact, I'd have a hard time if I were required to eat a 'meal' during one hour in the middle of the day! At lunchtime, I'll prep dinner, do laundry, etc. unless there's an outdoor activity to be had, such as kayaking nearby. If I'm spent from the morning's work and don't feel like doing any of those other things, I can take a nap on my lunch hour. Try getting away with all that at an office!"

Greg, our director of student communications and strategy, said, "In fall and winter, it gets dark early. So, on my lunch hour, I'll do some gardening, go for a 45-minute bike ride, and run errands. Anything to get outside in the sunshine and get away from my desk." Alaina said, "At lunchtime, I'll make a 40-minute grocery store trip, 10 minutes there, 10 minutes back. No lines, no hassles." And Emma, our director of enrollment software, said, "Because I can do my gardening and weeding during lunch in the summer, I'm able to be a full-time, soccer-crazy mom on the weekends!"

Emily R., our quality manager, rescues and fosters dogs in her spare time. For a bit about her lunch hour, well, I'll just turn it over to her! "I'm able to take our foster dogs for walks during my lunch hour, when we're not as likely to encounter a bunch of other dogs. Also, when I pick up dogs from the shelters, they're usually nervous, and there's a lot of dog poop and vomit around. Sometimes I get covered in it! Those are times I think, 'I'm really glad I don't have to go back to the office after this.'"

A happier home

A study by Manchester Metropolitan University in England found that remote work can even increase the happiness of married couples! Not surprisingly, this is because spouses/partners who work from home are able to spend more time on household chores. The researcher, Dr. Eleftherios Giovanis, wrote, "Teleworking has been helping to reduce social inequalities by rebalancing domestic duties in the UK," noting specifically, "When men work from home, they tend to help more around the house. This increases the value that women place on their own well-being and frees them to work more themselves."[44]

Fire Engine RED team members—men and women alike, married or not—said they have happier homes because of the remote nature of our company. Mark mentioned, "There are a lot of little tasks and chores around the house that only take a moment, like rotating laundry or letting a contractor in. If you're home, you can do these things and be back at your desk in minutes. If you're not working at home, it could take you hours just to head home, complete a tiny task, then return to the office."

Katrina (vice president of projects) said, "I placed a grocery order this morning and picked it up between meetings!" Glenna, our vice president of student search operations, said, "I use the hour after my kids get on the school bus and before work starts to get a specific chore or chores done around the house."

Emily R. told me, "Pretty much all chores are done during the workweek, with small breaks during the day or before the kids get out of school, leaving the weekends free for fun and volunteering. So, instead of the weekends being full of work, they're actually restorative and allow for family fun!"

Savings galore

In addition to reclaiming their commute time and helping the environment, remote workers can save lots of money — to the tune of up to $5,168 a year, according to FlexJobs.[45]

Table 3. Annual Savings for Remote Workers

Commuting- and office-related costs	Estimated average annual savings ($)
Gas	686
Car maintenance	767
Dry cleaning/laundering	1,000
Lunches and coffee	1,040
Professional wardrobe	925
Tax breaks	750
TOTAL	**5,168**

In a similar study, Global Workplace Analytics found employees who work from home save between $2,000 and $7,000 per year.[46] Our team's experience has been consistent with these findings; many of them told me that they save on meals out (and expensive coffee drinks).

In particular, let's take a closer look at the savings generated by not having a commute and not having to "dress up" for work.

Cutting commuting costs

My team members are thrilled to spend less on gas, insurance, and maintenance for their cars. Several told me that they used to fill up their cars once a week before joining Fire Engine RED. Now, they say they do it about once a month. Greg said, "My car insurance is lower now compared to when I was commuting. I chalk it up to driving a fraction of the total annual miles compared to my pre-Fire Engine RED years—3,000 to 4,000 miles per year now, compared to 10,000-plus per year previously." Another team member has taken it even further: "Now we're able to be a one-car family."

Jeff, our executive vice president of enrollment, data and analytics, is saving in the short and long term: "We still have our second car, but almost entirely to cart kids around or get me to the airport. Provided the second car doesn't get wrecked in the meantime, it will be our now-12-year-old's first car (it's a year older than she is), which will result in enormous savings for us."

It's not just drivers. Mass transit users save too. "The annual cost to take the Long Island Railroad to New York City for work is $2,616. The annual cost for an unlimited MetroCard to use the subway in NYC for work is $1,452," according to Jason 2, another of our three Jasons, who considers these savings "enough of a reason not to work in an office."

Wearing whatever "suits" them

Remote workers also get the benefit of being able to wear whatever "suits" them—so if they choose, they can save a lot of money on buying and maintaining a professional wardrobe.

While Steve Jobs was known for his turtlenecks, Barack Obama for his blue or gray suits, and Mark Zuckerberg for his gray T-shirts and hoodies,[47] I, and many of our team members, have adopted athleisure wear as our work "uniforms." This type of attire is comfortable, and it costs much less to buy and maintain than traditional work attire. It also makes it quick and easy to go for a walk between meetings, as many of our team members do, and even *during* meetings when they don't need to be in front of their computers.

Other types of savings

Our team members also told me about a few other things they save money on because they work from home. Katrina said she spends two-sevenths of what she used to on makeup. ("I only wear it on the weekends now.") Jim, our executive vice president of enrollment software, says he saves money on haircuts and shaving cream and wears (cheap) flip-flops rather than real shoes year-round. Yet another team member said, "I wash clothes far less often than when I worked away from home." (I'm sure it's obvious why I haven't included his name!)

A change of scenery

Remote workers have the added advantage of being able to change their work location, often by choice and sometimes by necessity.

At Fire Engine RED, we've had great success in allowing our team members to work from anywhere for an extended period of time, and that includes our team members who hold client-facing positions. All we ask is that, before embarking, team members meet with their manager and our director of people to discuss their plans for how they'll work from their temporary location(s).

Here are some examples of how our team members changed up their surroundings while continuing to work remotely:

One team member, an avid skier, relocated to Colorado for a month during ski season, and another spent six weeks working while traveling through Spain with a group of remote workers from other companies.

Jason 3 (yes, another Jason; this one is our director of enrollment data, strategy, and analytics) went to Mexico for a month two summers ago. He explained, "This never would have been an option if I weren't working for Fire Engine RED. What an experience for our kids. So, thanks for leading a company and a culture that I'm proud and happy to work for."

Recently, Nicole, one of our designers, let us know that she wanted to travel to Uruguay. She found a coworking group that caters to remote employees, offering a quiet workspace with reliable Wi-Fi during the day, and serving as a base for exploring the country at nights and on weekends. She told us she'd be working her regular (EST) hours. Of course, we approved her request. As long as it doesn't impact our clients, we love to provide our team members with the opportunity to see the world while they work.

Mark's job at our all-remote company has enabled him to relocate, first permanently, and then temporarily each winter. A whitewater kayaking enthusiast, Mark moved from Florida to Tennessee to pursue his paddling passion. He also spends three months a year working from Ecuador, which offers world-class conditions for kayaking. As a result of working remotely, Mark is able to kayak in the Ecuadorian summer while it's winter in the U.S. He explained, "Not only does my place there have excellent internet access, but I'm still in the same time zone as Tennessee."

Greg has made it to a number of exotic locales, which he says he could never have done with a traditional office job. He went on a trip to Sri Lanka and did his Fire Engine RED job there for a week before volunteering with Habitat for Humanity. He noted that Sri Lanka is "a half hour off from the rest of the world," so when meetings would start at the top of the hour in the U.S., he'd be calling in at half past. Greg also spent time in Singapore, where he worked nine to five—that is, 9:00 p.m. to 5:00 a.m. U.S. time. And a few years back, he went to the World Cup in Brazil, working most days and using vacation time to attend the games. While there, he completed the entire process of hiring a new team member—including screening resumes, conducting interviews, and making an offer—all while providing the candidates with a firsthand perspective on the travel-related benefits of remote work!

Melissa is one of our CRM implementation managers. She's an avid runner and usually works from home in Ohio. However, for the past few years, she's spent a good amount of time in Florida—two months the first time and four months the second. She said, "I stayed in an Airbnb, joined running clubs, and basically created a life for myself there." Last year, she headed west, driving to Las Vegas and staying for a few weeks, getting all the way to California, and then making her way back east across the U.S. "I got to sleep in a little bit more whenever I crossed into a new time zone!"

One Fire Engine RED team member who's almost always on the road is Maria, our client care project manager. "Once my husband also started a work-from-home job, we said, 'why do we need to stay in Delaware?'" Maria and her husband bought a pickup truck and travel trailer and set off to visit all 50 states, which they eventually did! (They flew to Hawaii and Alaska.) Maria added, "I always work from 9:00 a.m. to 6:00 p.m. (EST), whatever time zone we're in, so my team always knows when to expect me." And, whenever she crosses a state line, she changes her Slack avatar to the state's welcome sign, so her team always knows where to find her. Maria added, "Technically, we're now also a one-car family. That car just happens to pull our house!" Amber, one of our project managers, until recently, was another RV-er. She and her husband now live on a boat in a Florida marina.

Caroline, a software engineer, laughed at the idea of being called a "digital nomad." ("Oh, that term," she explained, "it just screams, 'millennial!'") But it's hard not to describe her as exactly that. As of this writing, she was nearing the end of five weeks in Alaska (preceded by five weeks in Oregon) and was busy planning her next trip, this time to Peru. The previous summer, Caroline had spent time in Barcelona, Spain: "Most of my team is on the [U.S.] East Coast, so I would spend the morning exploring the city, and then I'd work from 2:30 p.m. to 10:30 p.m.," right in sync with her team.

Deb, who lives in South Carolina, is able to see more of her parents (who have homes in St. Louis, Missouri, and Punta Gorda, Florida), by working a few days a year from each of their residences. She told me that both parents are respectful of her time and space while she's in the virtual office: "I get pampered. My dad brings me food!"

Alaina, one of our copywriters, was living in Austin, Texas, with her husband, who wanted to start a business in California. Alaina's job at Fire Engine RED enabled her to spend time with him there as they worked toward an eventual move. "We spent two years going back and forth between Texas and California, most of the time in our car. Fortunately, I was able to work while he drove!"

Another benefit of remote work is that it affords employees the ability to use their vacation time for an *actual vacation*. Unlike the getaways of their in-office counterparts, remote workers' vacations don't have to be all or nothing. Several of our team members have continued to work while visiting their in-laws. (I'm looking at you, Chuck and Jeff—how convenient for you!)

And speaking of Jeff: As an executive vice president and the head of our data team, he's vital to our company's success. And yet, because we're all-virtual, he'll soon be changing up his surroundings in a big way. As of this writing, Jeff is making plans to move his family to Paris for a year! Jeff's thrilled that working for our 100 percent remote company enables him to have this adventure now. Before joining our virtual workplace, he'd thought he would have to wait until retirement!

As you can see, remote workers can easily do their jobs "virtually" anywhere—for a day, a week, a month, a year, or even an entire career.

Taking care of others

"Family" at Fire Engine RED doesn't just mean spouses/partners and kids. Our 100 percent remote environment has made it possible for our team members to, for example, move closer to an aging relative who needs care.

When his grandmother was diagnosed with a form of ALS, Jason 2 was living about a 35-minute drive away from the home where he grew up. His family didn't want her to move to an assisted living facility; they wanted her to stay in the family home. It so happened that Jason 2's apartment lease was up, so he moved back home. There, he was able to provide his grandmother with another layer of security and comfort. (Even though his family hired an in-home nurse, he said it helped for him to be there with her at night.) "I didn't think about this situation coming up when I started working remotely, but when it did, I was glad it worked out for me to be at home."

Jason 2 added that, even though his design team is spread across the country, they're "all able to step in for each other when needed."

One-of-a-kind workspaces

Once your team members have spent some time at a 100 percent distributed company, they'll discover there are a lot of things about office life that they simply don't miss.

For example, Robert, our assistant controller, told me how not having, yes, control over the thermostat/office temperature left him too cold in the summer and too hot in the winter. Amy, a designer, was glad to leave behind the annoying side conversations happening right outside her office, and Glenna said she doesn't miss the smell of burnt coffee or popcorn.

Of course, there can be an adjustment period when transitioning to your own virtual workspace. Bill, our VP of search strategies and solutions, said, "As an old-school guy and a 25-year veteran of working on college campuses, I wasn't immediately comfortable with the idea of an employer with no physical office. Well, I am a convert—Fire Engine RED is FER-real!"

In a virtual work environment, of course, employees can create whatever kind of workspaces they wish!

Okay, but what about isolation ...

"A feeling of isolation" is often cited as a downside to remote work. However, I see this as a greater challenge for workers at companies that are only *partially* remote. As a company that's gone all-in on remote work, everyone at

Fire Engine RED is in the same "remote boat" together. The result, our team members have told me, is that they have plenty of human interaction at work as well as more time and energy for interaction outside of work.

"With tools like Slack, I feel like each day is a rolling conversation," said Jason 1. "My team jokes around and laughs a lot. But when I need to work, it's easy to just shut it out and work." Some team members even connect with their coworkers outside of their virtual offices. Emma said, "I live on the East Coast, so in January and February, when I get cabin fever, I'll drive about 30–50 minutes to work with two of my teammates in person."

When I asked my team members about the average number of interactions they had with their coworkers on a daily basis, there was even more interaction than I expected. Greg told me he interacted with "maybe an average of 15 to 20 people per day during our 'peak season' of client kickoffs and meetings; probably 5 or so on average during our 'off-season.'" Other team members mentioned ranges of 2 to 3, 5 to 8, and 13 to 17; I usually have 15 to 25 interactions a day.

Surprisingly, several Fire Engine RED team members have told me they speak to more of their coworkers—and get to know them even better—than they did when working in an office setting. What's going on here? In an office, people usually interact and bond with those in close proximity. In a fully remote company, there are no walls, and everyone is just an IM or Slack call away, making it easier to form strong bonds with coworkers no matter where they sit.

Because our team members are in touch so often, they get to know their teammates' children, dogs, and even their delivery people. For example, during our internal conference calls, team members' kids will pop on and say "hi," or in the case of Chuck's daughter, entertain us with her spontaneous singing. Our team members also hear when people are coming and going from their homes. Designer Jen's gardeners and their leaf blowers have made their presence known during marketing calls. And, many people at Fire Engine RED know all about my UPS and FedEx delivery guys, Jimmy and Jimmy. (Competing services and identical names. What are the odds?)

Keep in mind, though, a healthy amount of interaction doesn't happen automatically in a fully remote company. It has to be intentional. Shannon, a quality engineer, said, "I worked 100 percent remote for almost five years before Fire Engine RED, but it was very isolating. I was starved for conversation by the end of the day. It's totally different here for sure, and in the best way! And it's not just about phone calls. We definitely use Slack to build community."

Working from home also requires employees to be proactive about building and maintaining relationships and friendships *outside* of work. Fire Engine RED team members are actively doing so. Nicole said, "Now I actually have more energy to socialize, work out, and run errands after work. Commuting used to drain me." And Joanna, our business operations manager, makes it a point to meet other Girl Scout moms for lunch!

Finally, if your team members want to be in physical proximity to others while they work, companies such as WeWork (www.wework.com) offer the opportunity to mix with other remote workers in shared "office" settings. While none of our team members work from shared office spaces on a regular basis, many do when they travel internationally, with great success.

So, embracing remote work doesn't mean you can't have an office. It's just not a requirement. And, it certainly doesn't mean you have to feel isolated!

… and that whole thing with Yahoo?

In 2013, the CEO of Yahoo, Marissa Mayer, famously hijacked the public conversation about remote work by bringing the company's remote workers back into the office.

Mayer listed a variety of reasons for ending Yahoo's remote work program, such as "better align[ing] Yahoo work culture with customer service,"[48] but reading between the lines, I think it came down to one issue: trust. That is, she didn't trust her people to do what Yahoo had hired them to do without being managed closely. For remote work to work, leaders need to feel confident their employees are doing their jobs, sight unseen.[49]

How did Mayer's edict work out for Yahoo? Not very well. According to Chief Executive, "Within months of Mayer's decision to end remote work at Yahoo, the company's human resources metrics showed a double-digit drop in employee engagement, morale, and trust. It was all downhill from there."[50]

Ultimately, in 2007, Yahoo was acquired by Verizon for $4.8 billion, and Mayer resigned as CEO. That's half of what Yahoo was worth when Mayer was hired five years earlier. However, it wasn't remote work that led to her own and Yahoo's downfall. For that, you could blame a variety of other factors, such as poor acquisitions, security issues,[51] and the company's inability to compete against Facebook and Google for advertising dollars.[52]

Surprisingly, though, other companies followed Yahoo's lead. In 2017, Aetna brought employees back into the office "with the goal of increasing collaboration and driving innovation."[53] IBM also came to the (misguided) conclusion that remote work discourages collaboration.[54] As a result, it decided to discontinue its remote-working policy, supposedly to create a "more collaborative environment for its approximately 380,000 workers around the world."[55] Ironically, IBM had been one of the technology sector giants that pioneered the concept of allowing its employees to work from home.

As the Yahoo debacle shows, distributed workers can become easy targets for companies looking for a quick fix to their problems. Despite these well-known companies trying to turn back the clock on remote work, I believe it's here to stay. In fact, I'll double-down on that: I think the all-virtual, 100 percent distributed model is the way to go.

2.3 How clients benefit

As you'll learn, our "remoteness" is not an issue for our clients. Some actually consider it a plus.

When we first started, we were concerned that our clients might see our remote business structure as a liability. (We were one of the first all-virtual companies, after all.) So, we simply didn't bring it up.

In fact, we kept our remoteness under the radar for 10 years! However, when *Inc.* magazine named us one of the country's 50 Top Small Company Workplaces in 2011,[56] they sort of blew our cover; subsequent media coverage of the award focused on how we'd created a winning culture as an all-remote company. Now, of course, the world has changed, and not only are we completely up-front and transparent about being fully remote but we're also proud of it.

We asked a few of our clients about what it's like to work with our fully remote company. Not surprisingly, several of them mentioned our ability to hire top talent.

Wes Waggoner, associate vice president for enrollment management at Southern Methodist University, said, "I want the best people working on my [student] search program, not just the best people who live or will live in the same city. If that means a team who chooses to live around the world for their own needs, lives, and situations, then that reassures me the best talent will help SMU achieve its goals."

Judith Aaron, vice president for enrollment at Pratt Institute, had this to say about working with Fire Engine RED: "Pratt has been using Fire Engine RED's mass email software and event scheduler for 11 years, and during that time, it never occurred to us that we weren't talking to people in an office, but in actuality, the company was using a virtual office model. In those 11 years, Fire Engine RED has, from the beginning, been the most responsive company we've dealt with." Judith added that she herself is a fan of working from home: "It enables one to focus in a way that does not happen in the office because of daily multiple interruptions, unnecessary large meetings, and sometimes a less-than-comfortable environment. I typically save my harder, more complex, or creative work for the days I work from home."

Byron Lewis, vice president for enrollment management at Lipscomb University, said, "The remote environment has allowed Fire Engine RED to attract great talent across the country. [...] That experience provides real value as we partner with [you] to build our enrollment funnel each year."

Melore Nielsen, interim vice president for enrollment management and dean of admissions at Seattle University, said, "My experience working with the Fire Engine RED team has been positive at all stages. [... You] are extremely collaborative and fully engaged throughout the creative process. [Your] team asks insightful questions and remains equally aware of their clients' desired outcome and also the important details that will inform the project and give it life and authenticity." She added that Fire Engine RED has "built a team with noteworthy talent and one that strives to provide service excellence and exceed expectations."

Jay Jacobs, Ed.D., director of enrollment management and admission operations at the University of Miami, told us, "I think the remote structure has allowed [you] to pull expertise and knowledge from a number of different areas, backgrounds, and institutions." Jay added, "The customer service is great. We hear back from our project manager within minutes or hours if we need something or have questions about our services and campaigns."

Mark Meydam, director, enrollment operations and technology at the University of Wisconsin-River Falls, said, "Our interactions with [your] staff are great, [and you] have systems in place to make it transparent to the client that [you're] actually a remote-based company. I do know that the quality of the staff seems to be much better with Fire Engine RED, and I suspect that because [you're] a remote organization, [you're] able to hire better quality employees because they can live wherever they would like and work remotely."

Gretchen Foster, admissions director at Western Nebraska Community College, said, "I love that the team at Fire Engine RED is focused and efficient. [...] During our project calls, we are laser-focused on the project, as everyone is on a call without [the] visual distraction of each other and the chit-chat that often sends you off track. We get to the agenda and move efficiently through it. At the same time, we've come to know each other and are able to 'tell' from our voices if someone sounds stressed or happy. It's comforting when my project manager, Deb, asks if everything is okay, and I can do the same for her. Thus, the working relationship develops even more."

Monica C. Inzer, vice president for enrollment management at Hamilton College, said, "To be honest, that the Fire Engine RED team all work remotely is invisible to me. Most important to me is that we get excellent quality service from the best possible employees … clearly [you're] able to draw from a larger talent pool."

Michael J. Marshall, Ed.D., vice president for enrollment, marketing and communication at Bellarmine University, began working with us when he was with another university. Mike had this to say about working with us: "Fire Engine RED has transcended our expectations. One example is the team's accessibility. [… You have] made themselves available to answer any questions, troubleshoot or resolve any issues, or facilitate training for [our] team."

I think it's very telling that many of our clients, even when asked about our all-remote model, didn't even mention it; they preferred to focus on what we're able to do as a company, not as a remote company!

Chapter 3
Let's get it started: Setting up your fully remote company

As I mentioned in the introduction, when I founded Fire Engine RED in 2001, there wasn't a guidebook for me to follow with regard to starting an all-virtual company, so I learned by doing (or by *not* doing and learning the hard way!).

In this section, I'll take you step by step through the process of getting *your* 100 percent remote company up and running, based on my nearly 20 years' worth of experience. (I'm going to assume you already have a business idea, a written business plan, and funding in place.)

3.1 Hire an accountant and an attorney

Although this may sound costly, it's actually much less expensive to work with an accountant and attorney as you're getting started than it is to engage them later, after you've gotten yourself into a jam.

An accountant can assist you with choosing a legal structure for your company, applying for business-related licenses, and setting up your bookkeeping system. Accountants are also uniquely qualified to help you with tax and other compliance issues,[57] and, more broadly, can analyze, interpret, plan, and summarize your company's finances to help you make better-informed business decisions.

What should you expect to pay? Accountants typically charge $150–$400 or more per hour. In 2005, after having bad experiences with several accountants, we were referred to Paul Flax at Rudney Smith (www.rudneysmith.com) in Media, Pennsylvania, and we have been with him/them ever since. Not only has Paul provided us with excellent advice and service for more than a decade, but his values are aligned with mine and my company's, which makes working together even easier. (Yes, your service providers should share your values and your company's.)

Attorneys typically charge an hourly rate for their services; amounts can vary from $100 to $1,000 per hour depending on their experience, location, education, operating expenses, and other factors.[58] You may be asked to pay a retainer fee up front, from which the attorney will deduct their fees as you incur them.

Rather than paying for legal services by the hour, it may be more cost-effective for you to hire an attorney to serve as your general counsel (on a full- or part-time basis) for a fixed monthly fee. In our case, Steven J. Feder at GenCounsel, LLC (www.gencounsel.com) has served as our general counsel for nearly a decade. He handles a wide variety of legal issues for us, including contracts, human resources, and more. We've been very pleased with the value, broad expertise, and level of service Steve provides as our part-time general counsel; if we didn't know better, we'd think we were his only client.

How do you find an accountant or attorney you can trust? I suggest you reach out to your professional and social networks for referrals and interview each candidate, just as I did. Again, be sure to hire an accountant and attorney whose values align with yours and your company's.

3.2 Name and brand your business

You'll want to select a name for your business, preferably a name that will stand the test of time. A great name can help you build brand recognition right from the start. Positive associations can help; in our case, the "RED" in Fire Engine RED brings to mind action, boldness, energy, and passion.

When a friend of one of our team members saw her LinkedIn profile, the friend sent her a note saying, "Even before I looked up your company, I assumed it was a tech or web company, with smart, young, dynamic people and 'hot' new offerings." That's exactly what I'd intended!

Naming companies, products, and services has always come easily to me, but if naming things isn't your thing, you should consider hiring a marketing consultant to help you. Such consultants typically charge around $100-$175 per hour.[59]

With all that in mind, I recommend you choose a company name that is:

Short. Preferably, your company name should be no longer than two or three words because shorter names are easier to remember. We've found that most people who hear or read our name, remember our name. And even when they don't, they come pretty close. We've been called Fire Fighters, Little Red Fire Engine, Fire Truck Red, and more. One of my all-time favorites is "the fire truck people," which is how one of our clients, the president of a prestigious university, refers to us. I'll take it!

Attention-getting. Try to come up with a name that's likely to attract people's attention. When people hear the name "Fire Engine RED" for the first time, they ask about it. As a result, my team has learned to start every sales presentation with an explanation: "The CEO named our company after her favorite color: fire engine red." Twice, they tried to eliminate that slide to shorten the presentation. Both times, someone in the meeting stopped them to ask about the origin of our name—and so the slide went back in.

Non-specific. Be careful about choosing a name that limits your company to a specific product, service, or technology. This was a valuable lesson I learned with my first company. When I started the business, we only served colleges, so the name "College Home Videos" made sense. Several years later, when we decided to target independent secondary schools, we had to change the name to something broader, so I chose Search By Video. I believe the name Fire Engine RED has withstood the test of time because it's non-specific.

Once you've come up with a name you like, you'll need to find out if anyone else is already using it. I recommend you start with a Google search, and it wouldn't hurt to plug the name into a couple of other search engines as well.

> *Tip*: I suggest you make sure your company name doesn't result in an inappropriate acronym (for example, "Biologically Appropriate Real Foods" or "Women Take Flight").[60] You'll also want to

trademark your company name (and logo—more
about both below).

Create your company logo

It may be tempting to create your own logo using a free or
inexpensive online program. However, it's worth the
investment to have your logo and branding professionally
designed; "branding" refers to not only your logo but also
all the elements that make up your company's unique
visual style and voice, from colors and typography to
illustrations and photographs. Your branding will visually
represent your company and its offerings, appearing on
everything from your business cards and promotional
materials to your website and trade show booths.

As with the name of your company, you will want to
ensure your logo and branding are memorable so that they
stand out in a world of visual "clutter." I recommend
hiring a design professional to come up with three logo
ideas from which you can choose your favorite. You
should expect to pay $1,500 or more for a professionally
designed logo.

Again, be sure your logo is free of unwanted connotations.
Fans of the HBO TV series *Silicon Valley* will remember the
logo for the "Gavin Belson Signature Box III." (You don't
want to have your logo go "viral" for all the wrong
reasons!) Seriously, though, your logo shouldn't include
symbols or imagery that can be seen as offensive,

insensitive, controversial, or discriminatory. It's especially important to do your homework on this if you're planning on growing your company internationally.[61]

Trademark your company name and logo

Once you have a name and logo for your company (or product/service offering), I encourage you to register them as trademarks or service marks with the United States Patent and Trademark Office (USPTO). If you're the first to register your company name and logo, you'll have exclusive rights to your trademarks or service marks in all 50 states. You can also register words, phrases, taglines, slogans, designs, or any combination of these that identifies your products and/or services and distinguishes them from competing businesses.

I strongly recommend working with an attorney on registering your trademarks and service marks; it can be more complicated than you may think. For example, in 2013, we filed a federal trademark application to use the name "Fireworks" for our CRM product, specifically in the education market. Unbeknownst to us, several months earlier, a certain enormous online retailer had filed for a trademark of "Fireworks" for broad use and was awarded the trademark. Despite the retailer's deep pockets, we weren't intimidated; we challenged the trademark and won on appeal because the retailer had never actually used it, and we were using it in a specific market (education). If we hadn't been working with an attorney from the very beginning, I doubt we'd be using "Fireworks" today.

If you decide not to use an attorney, you can file a trademark application online at the USPTO website (www.uspto.gov/) for a fee of $225 to $400. Keep in mind, for each class of goods or services your business engages in, you'll need to file a separate trademark application and pay a separate fee.[62]

3.3 Choose a legal structure

The type of legal structure you choose for your company will impact the taxes you pay; your personal liability; and possibly your ability to raise capital, should you choose to do so. Therefore, it's best to consider your options carefully with the help of your accountant and attorney because changing the legal structure of your business downstream can be difficult and expensive.

Speaking of options, let's take a look at the most popular legal structures for businesses and how each of them works. (I'll touch briefly on the tax implications associated with each option here and go into a bit more detail on business taxes in chapter 16, "Tax time: Filing your virtual company's taxes.")

Sole Proprietorship. You, and only you, own the business. As a sole proprietor, you're entitled to all of the profits your business earns, and you assume full personal liability for the debts of the business. There's no separate business tax return to file. You simply attach a Schedule C or C-EZ to your Form 1040 personal tax return.[63]

General or Limited Partnership. You share ownership of the assets, profits, and financial/legal liabilities of the business with one or more people. One advantage of a general partnership is that it costs very little in terms of money and paperwork to establish one. However, with a general partnership, you're personally liable for the partnership's obligations; any partner can bind the company to contracts, debts, or other obligations, and any partner can be sued for the entirety of the business's debts.[64] Limited partnerships are required to have a general partner, who bears all of the responsibilities and liabilities, and a separate group of one or more limited partners, whose liability is limited to their capital investment.

If you choose a partnership structure, it's crucial to create a partnership agreement that spells out how the partnership will be run. Such an agreement will specify each partner's ownership interest, role in the business, and initial capital contribution. It also lays out the procedures for exiting the partnership.[65] Again, I strongly suggest working with your accountant and attorney to create the partnership agreement if you decide to go this route.

For tax purposes, the partnership is required to report its income on Schedule K-1 (Form 1065), though the partnership itself doesn't pay federal income tax. Instead, the tax obligations pass through the partnership to the individual partners.

However, if you're interested in limiting your personal liability, you should consider forming a Corporation, an S Corporation, or a Limited Liability Company (see below).[66]

Corporation (C Corp). You shield yourself from personal liability by creating a corporation, which is an independent legal entity separate from you and any other owners/shareholders. One of the biggest advantages of a C Corp is that it allows your company to have many owners/shareholders—so if your ultimate goal is to take your company public, forming a C Corp is likely the best way to go.

You'll have to file a tax return for the corporation itself (using Form 1120) and deal with the dreaded "double taxation." That is, the business pays taxes on its income, *and* you pay personal taxes on the money you receive from the business. This double taxation is most painful when the business's assets are sold—and the double level of tax takes a large chunk away from the net cash you otherwise would receive as an owner.

S Corporation (S Corp). You shield yourself from personal liability and avoid double taxation.[67] Income or losses from the S Corp "pass through" to you and any other shareholders (limited to no more than 100 individuals, and no other business entities)[68] and are reported on your individual tax return. Note that even though the S Corp itself doesn't pay income taxes, you still have to report its income/loss, deductions, and credits to the IRS on Form 1120S.

Limited Liability Company (LLC). You retain the flexibility of a sole proprietorship or partnership and avoid double taxation but limit your personal liability. For federal tax purposes, a single-member LLC is treated as a sole proprietorship (so you'll use Form 1040, Schedule C), while a two-or-more-member LLC is treated as a partnership (you'll use Form 1065 with a Schedule K-1 for each partner). A two-or-more-member LLC can also choose a corporate designation for tax filing. One of the most important advantages of the LLC form is that you can have an unlimited number of members. This may be important if you will be raising capital from investors. Check with your accountant for more details.

According to the National Small Business Association's 2017 Year-End Economic Report, the majority of small businesses surveyed are LLCs (35 percent) followed by S Corporations (33 percent).[69] After discussing the pros and cons with my accountant and attorney, I chose to structure

Fire Engine RED as an S Corp, which has served the company and me well since 2001.

3.4 Determine your company's fiscal year

A company's fiscal year is the 12-month period that the company uses for financial reporting.

If you've chosen to set up your business as a sole proprietorship or a single-member LLC, you must use a fiscal year-end of December 31 to match your personal tax year-end.

If your business is set up as a C Corp, partnership, or multiple-member LLC, you can set your fiscal year to end on the last day of any quarter (March 31, June 30, September 30, or December 31).[70]

The required fiscal year for an S Corp is normally the calendar year (January 1 - December 31); however, there are circumstances under which you could establish any month as your S Corp's year-end.

In any case, I highly recommend asking your accountant and attorney to help you select your company's fiscal year. There are more things to consider than you may think.

3.5 Establish your contact information

Before you can register your company with governmental agencies, you'll need a few things:

A physical mailing address

Even a virtual company needs to have a physical mailing address. For one thing, legal documents generally require one. For another, if you plan to send email campaigns as part of your marketing efforts, government regulations (such as the CAN-SPAM Act) require you to include your street address in the footer of every promotional email.

When I started Fire Engine RED, I used my home address on legal documents and got a post office box (near my home in downtown Philadelphia) for incoming mail. The post office box worked well while I was wearing many hats, but once we hired Joanna, our business operations manager, who lives in the Philadelphia suburbs, it made sense to move our post office box closer to her home.

As we learned the hard way, once you establish a mailing address or post office box for your company, it takes a lot of time and effort to change it. It literally took us two years and hundreds of change-of-address forms to ensure clients, vendors, and government agencies all had our new address. And, to this day, I continue to receive the occasional piece of business-related mail at home.

Fortunately, you can now avoid the hassle of playing musical mailboxes. There are companies, such as VirtualPostMail (www.virtualpostmail.com), that will provide you with a permanent commercial address to use on your business filings. They'll also open your mail, scan/digitize it, and send it to you electronically. Their prices range from $10 to $60 per month, though additional fees may apply based on volume. If I were starting out now, I'd use VirtualPostMail right out of the gate to avoid the hassle of having to change things down the road. (I'd also use them if we had to change our mailing address again, but fortunately, having our post office box near Joanna's home is working fine for now.)

A phone number

Your distributed company will also need a primary phone number to use on legal documentation and to enable your prospects, clients, and vendors to reach you.

Though it may be tempting to use your personal cell phone number or just add another line, I suggest you start using a cloud-based phone system. This way several people can "monitor" your main number and forward calls to the team member who's best positioned to assist the caller.

Although your team members may prefer to use their individual cell phones for conversations with clients and vendors, that usually isn't practical until the client or vendor has established a relationship with them. Having a cloud-based system will also allow you to establish separate lines for, say, client service and/or technical support.

I'd advise you to plan ahead and get set up with a cloud-based system from the beginning! It's much easier to start with a little bit of functionality and scale it as your company grows.

We use Zoom (https://zoom.us/), which costs us $10 per user, per month.

An email/website address

Your company will also need email and website addresses. To streamline the process of selecting a domain name for them, I recommend you use the self-serve tools offered by a managed service provider, such as Google G Suite Business (https://gsuite.google.com/) or Rackspace (www.rackspace.com).

If your company's name is available, you should register it as a domain name immediately. If it's not, or if someone else has the ".com" top-level domain, you can get creative with hyphens, abbreviations, etc. The "fireenginered.com" domain wasn't initially available to us because it was being used by a winery in Sonoma, California. So, I added hyphens to ours and made it "www.fire-engine-red.com"

(which I actually prefer because it helps the company name stand out!).

By the way, don't give up if someone else has your preferred domain name. Choose something else but keep an eye out. Eventually, "fireenginered.com" (without hyphens) became available, and we grabbed it immediately. Now, anyone who enters "fireenginered.com" into their browser is redirected to our website, www.fire-engine-red.com.

Once you've conducted a domain search and registered your domain, you can arrange for the same service provider to host your company's business email account and website.[71] We use Rackspace and pay about $2 per month, per email address; about $40 a year for our registered domain (www.fire-engine-red.com); and about $360 a year to host our external website, intranet, etc. (Rackspace was one of our original vendors; we've been with them since 2001.)

3.6 Register your company

Once your contact information is in place, you'll need to register your company with:

The Internal Revenue Service

If you operate your business as a corporation or partnership, you'll need an Employer Identification

Number (EIN), also known as a Federal Tax Identification Number, from the Internal Revenue Service (IRS) for tax filing and reporting purposes. The IRS provides an online tool (https://sa.www4.irs.gov/modiein/individual/index.jsp), which will enable you to apply for an EIN immediately (and at no cost).

If you're a sole proprietor or have an LLC without any employees, you can simply use your Social Security number as your business tax ID. (There are some exceptions, so be sure to check with your accountant.) However, if you want to maintain the privacy of your Social Security number (and not share it with clients and vendors), you can obtain and use an EIN instead.

Your state

You'll need to form your company with the Secretary of State and County Clerk's office in the state where your "headquarters" is located.[72] In the case of Fire Engine RED, we formed our company (as an S corporation) by registering it with the Secretary of State in Pennsylvania.

To register as a corporation, you'll need to file articles of incorporation and have them approved by the state. The forms you'll need are generally available on your Secretary of State's website, and fees typically range from $50–$300 for a for-profit business. (If you form an LLC or a limited partnership, you'll have to complete and file a similar set of documents called "articles of organization.")

Once your articles of incorporation are approved, your corporation will be deemed a legal business entity. Approval times vary by state. (For example, it takes two to six weeks in Pennsylvania.) In the meantime, you should expect to pay for business expenses using your personal funds. This is why you often hear about entrepreneurs maxing out their credit cards. Of course, down the road, you'll have the option of reimbursing yourself.

While it is possible to register your company on your own, I advise you to work with your accountant and attorney to make sure this important paperwork is done right the first time.

You may also want to set up a "Doing Business As" (DBA) name in the state where your company is located. Why? The reasons can differ depending on whether or not you incorporate your business.

If you *do* incorporate your company, registering a DBA lets you do business under a name different from the one that appears on your incorporation documents. This can be especially helpful if you intend to operate multiple business lines or in a variety of industries. For example, Progressive Technologies, Inc. could register DBAs of "Progressive Software" and "Progressive Hardware."[73]

(DBAs used by corporations may drop the corporate identifier, such as "Inc.," "LLC," etc.)

If you *don't* incorporate your company, registering a DBA enables you to legally use a business name (other than your personal name) to create a more targeted and memorable identity for your company. For example, let's say Catherine Smith, who's a sole proprietor, came up with the name "Cathy's Culinary Creations." I'd recommend she register the name as a DBA, which would allow her to get a bank account with that name. That way, people can write checks payable to Cathy's Culinary Creations, rather than to Catherine herself. This will also make it easier for Catherine to keep her business and personal finances separate (for tax purposes, among other reasons).

Another good reason to register a DBA is that the filing may give you the right to prevent other businesses from using the same name in the same state, which could lead to client confusion (also see "Trademark your company name and logo" above).

Finally, registering a DBA name with the state where your company is incorporated will cost around $50 to $100, depending on your state.[74] There are also online services that allow you to get your DBA without dealing directly with government agencies.

Don't forget about sales tax

Depending on the tax laws of the state(s) where your company is registered, you may be required to collect state sales tax from your clients. If so, you'll need to apply for a state sales tax number. For more information, see your state tax agency's website. In my state, the tax agency is called the Department of Revenue. (As an aside, Fire Engine RED doesn't have to collect sales tax because our education clients are nonprofits.)

Other states

You'll need to register for a state tax ID in each state where you have employees (known as a "nexus"). In some states, you may also need a tax ID if you have an "economic nexus" (significant business dealings) there. Again, registration requirements vary from state to state, and these rules change from time to time, so it's always good to check the rules in every state where you have remote employees and/or are doing business.

There are three things to keep in mind about registering in a state. It takes time, it costs money (anywhere from $10 to $700), and the forms vary from state to state. A few states even require you to fill out their forms by hand and mail printed copies with paper checks. Other states make it easier by letting you register directly on their website.

Keep in mind, you're required by state law to have a local address in every state where you have employees. You can enlist a *registered agent* to receive your legal- and tax-related communications from the state and forward them to you. I suggest you enlist a provider that has a registered agent in every state, such as the one we use, COGENCY GLOBAL (www.cogencyglobal.com). We pay around $2,000 per year for their services.

3.7 Obtain local permits and licenses

Generally, you can't run a business out of your home because of the potential disruption to nearby residents from frequent visitors, noise, etc. However, in many instances, federal, state, and local laws haven't caught up with today's home-based virtual businesses, so there may be some legal gray area here: "Typically, virtual businesses are considered 'no-impact' businesses if they do not disrupt the community, drive more traffic to the neighborhood, or increase resource consumption or waste streams."[75]

So, if you're using your home as your primary business location, you probably won't be stopped from running a home-based business (where it's just you and a computer). Instead, you (and your employees) may have to file what's called a home occupation permit to comply with local regulations. In addition, your local government may require you to have a business license, just as you would if you had office space, a retail shop, etc.

Incidentally, years ago, my condo board took legal action against me for running a business out of my condo. They eventually dropped the issue, and today, nearly 50 percent of the condo owners in my building also work from home. How times have changed!

3.8 Open a business bank account

I recommend that you separate your business banking from your personal banking right from the start. In fact, if you incorporate your business, you're required by the IRS to have a separate bank account for it.

Here's what you'll need to open a business checking account:

1) Some form of personal identification, such as a driver's license
2) An Employer Identification Number (EIN), also known as a Federal Tax Identification Number
3) Articles of incorporation (if applicable)
4) Legal documentation of your DBA name (if applicable)

When choosing a bank, you may want to start by looking into business banking options provided by the bank(s) where you have your personal account(s). However, if you have your personal account at a large bank, it may be worth talking to regional or community banks, which are often more focused on the needs of small businesses than are large, institutional banks.

When I first started Fire Engine RED, my company had bad experiences with two large banks. Neither bank made any real attempt to understand the business, and had constant employee turnover, preventing the company from building contacts that are critical to a successful banking relationship. In 2005, we switched to a small community bank, Penn Liberty Bank in Wayne, Pennsylvania, and built great relationships with people who were eager to understand our business. When Penn Liberty was purchased by a regional bank, Wilmington Savings Fund Society (WSFS) Bank in 2015, we lucked out. That's because WSFS Bank has even more resources, and our original contacts now run the bank!

3.9 Apply for a business credit card

You'll need to choose a business credit card for yourself and your employees, especially those who travel for business. We use American Express (AMEX). One of the big benefits of an AMEX card is that it doesn't have a preset credit limit. In fact, we've been able to charge in excess of $500,000 a month on our AMEX card without any issues. Another benefit of using AMEX for business is their generous rewards program, which allows us to earn free airline travel and more.

However, you should be aware, if your business grows quickly, like ours did, you'll want to be proactive and contact your credit card provider to increase your limit so you don't get stuck in a hotel lobby (or somewhere worse) like I was after a long day of travel! As Fire Engine RED became more successful, we began using our AMEX cards more frequently. Despite paying off our balance each month, my card was declined when I was trying to check in to a Boston hotel. This led to a long conversation with AMEX where they agreed to put through the charges but required me to send them our financials upon our return home to prove that we had the means to pay off our growing balances, in full, each month.

> *Lesson learned:* Just because AMEX doesn't have a preset credit limit, it doesn't mean they won't deactivate your card if they see an unusually high amount of spending activity, even if the spending is a result of your success. So, it's best to be proactive and send them your updated financials to support your increase in spending before they deactivate your card.

You'll also need to keep a couple of other things in mind: Unlike most other credit cards, AMEX needs to be paid off every month. So, if your cash flow is tight, you may want to choose a card other than AMEX. Also, you'll need to personally guarantee your charges until you've established a history as a profitable business.

Who should get a company credit card? According to Akber, our CFO, as few people as possible. At one point, everyone at Fire Engine RED had one, which made traveling to our annual team meeting easier. (Each employee used the company credit card to pay for flights, meals, airport parking, etc.) However, one of Akber's first acts when he joined Fire Engine RED in 2014 was to have everyone turn in their credit cards. Having 60-plus active credit cards (we had a smaller team then), which were mostly used just once a year, was causing him to lose sleep.

Over time, our CFO gave back many of the cards he'd taken away; our leadership team and other employees who travel for business all have a company credit card. In addition, our business operations manager has the one card we use for all company purchases, which makes tracking our expenses much easier.

> *Tip:* According to the IRS, a credit card statement serves as a receipt, as long as it has the transaction date, the payee's name, and the amount paid. Encourage your employees who travel to use their company credit card for all business expenses; this will make it easier for your company to track expenses, and your employees will be happy that

they don't have to include receipts with their business expense reports.

Have we ever had a problem with any of our employees and company cards? Well, there was that one time (many years ago) when someone ran up a bar bill of over $1,000 at a team meeting by buying drinks for everyone in his department. This incident, among others, led us to part ways with this particular employee. Incidentally, our policy is that employees can "expense" one alcoholic drink for themselves per team gathering.

3.10 Purchase business insurance

You may be surprised to learn that, even though you'll be running your company from home, your homeowner's (or renter's) insurance policy will not cover your company (or your employees—wherever they work). Therefore, you'll need to purchase insurance specifically for your business.

Because business insurance is so complex, I recommend that you work with a commercial insurance broker—one who knows your industry as well as the ins and outs of insuring a business with employees in multiple states. You'll want an experienced, responsive broker who will find competitive quotes for you and will review your policies with you on an annual basis. Again, the best way to find a broker is to ask people in your network for a referral. Ours is Oxford Insurance (www.oxfordins.com).

Now, you'd think that companies without an office would be able to take advantage of some kind of overall insurance discount for having fewer physical assets, risks, and so forth. Unfortunately, that isn't the case. I'm hopeful that at some point there will be enough 100 percent remote companies to warrant such a discount!

With all that in mind, here are the types of business insurance you'll need to consider:

Business Owner Policy (BOP). This general policy bundles all the coverage your business is likely to need, including business interruption insurance, liability insurance, property insurance, vehicle insurance, and more. Plus, it's less expensive than purchasing these coverages individually.

The most important part of your BOP is the general liability coverage, which will protect your company against trips, falls, spills, and general damage. (Yes, even companies without an office or other facility need to have this type of coverage.) BOP pricing varies based on location and industry. Typical costs range from $500 to $3,500 a year.[76]

Errors & Omissions (E&O). Also known as professional liability insurance, E&O protects you and your business against claims made by clients regarding negligent actions or inadequate work. When you complete an application for

E&O insurance, you'll want to send along representative contracts to help the insurance companies estimate the risks and exposures your business may have.

For example, E&O insurance can protect you against security and privacy issues (such as breaches and hacks), lawsuits from governmental entities for violating a regulation, cyber extortion, and more. It will also cover the cost of responding to any of these incidents, such as hiring attorneys and/or other advisors.

Your E&O premium will be calculated as a function of the revenue and revenue growth of your company as well as the risks associated with your type of business (size, industry, location, prior E&O-related lawsuits, etc.). Also, when reviewing your options, note the "retention" amount. This is similar to a deductible in that the higher the retention amount you choose, the lower the premium you'll pay. A typical yearly E&O premium for low-risk businesses is around $600.[77]

Commercial Umbrella Policy. Also known as "excess insurance," umbrella coverage extends over your general liability insurance, paying any additional costs related to a claim up to the limit of the umbrella policy itself.[78] Expect to pay around $960 annually for a commercial umbrella policy.[79] (You can also purchase separate umbrella coverage related to E&O.)

Workers' Compensation Insurance. Workers' compensation covers medical treatment, disability, and death benefits should an employee be injured or die as a result of working for your company.[80] Now, you may ask, does workers' compensation apply even if your employees are working from home? In general, the answer is yes, an employee injury or death is covered by workers' compensation if either arises out of and in the course of employment.[81] It's important to note that proving the injury or death was work-related is the responsibility of the *employee*, not the employer.

The cost of workers' compensation coverage is a function of the annual cumulative salaries and a risk rating tied to each employee (if an employee travels often for work, their premium is higher). Workers' compensation is typically required by state law and regulated differently in each state; therefore, costs can vary greatly from state to state. For example, for every $100 in employee wages, "rates range from $0.75 in Texas to $2.74 in Alaska."[82]

As a side note, let's say you hire virtual workers in North Dakota, Ohio, Washington, and/or Wyoming. You'll need to purchase workers' compensation insurance directly from the appropriate state government agency because workers' compensation policies aren't available commercially in those states.

Tip: You've probably seen those Occupational Safety and Health Administration (OSHA) posters that hang in workplace break rooms. What do you do if you don't have an office? The answer is to make a good faith effort to inform employees of their rights—for example, by posting electronic/PDF versions of the posters on your company intranet.[83]

You'll find a list of the nine posters you'll be required to make available to everyone at your all-remote company in the Resources section of our *Fully Remote* website (www.fully-remote-book.com).

Employee Retirement Income Security Act (ERISA) Bond. ERISA was enacted to protect the beneficiaries of employee benefit plans from dishonesty and fraud committed by people who manage the plans (the "fiduciary") and/or those who handle funds or other property of such a plan ("plan officials").[84]

Each plan official at your company must be bonded for at least 10 percent of the amount of funds they handle. In most instances, the maximum bond amount required under ERISA with respect to any one plan official is $500,000 per plan.

You can purchase an ERISA bond through your insurance broker. Premiums start at $100 and go up to $400 for coverage below $500,000. For coverage over $500,000, the bond premium ranges from $400 to $650 per year.

Key Person Insurance. This coverage protects your company in the case of the untimely death of a particular executive or top performer if losing them would catastrophically affect the business. If you have an investor or investors, they will usually require that you have key person insurance coverage.[85]

The company has $3.5 million in key person insurance on my life and pays a premium of $5,360 per year based on my age and health. Incidentally, when I first started out in business, this coverage was called "key man insurance." Someone along the line must have realized that women could be "key" to a business as well!

Our broker for our key person insurance is Alan Fishman at Yorktown Financial Group (www.yorktownfinancialgroup.com).

Other Coverage. In addition to the other types of insurance coverages noted above, you might want to consider purchasing (or be required by your clients to purchase):

- **Business Personal Property** provides coverage against personal property claims.
- **Actual Loss Sustained** provides additional coverage for business interruption, which is unlikely given the remote model, as there's no single point of failure. This coverage supplements your BOP.
- **Employment Practices** provides coverage against a lawsuit brought by an employee for unfair treatment or dismissal.
- **Hired/Non-Owned Auto Liability** provides coverage beyond collision damage in case of death in a hired-vehicle accident.

Typically, you'll want to tap into your insurance only as a result of catastrophic loss/systemic failure. That's because, as with any type of insurance, claiming benefits may make your premiums go up and may even make it harder for your company to buy insurance in the future.

3.11 Implement the right systems

Set up your accounting system

You'll need to choose an accounting software product for your business. We've used QuickBooks (www.quickbooks.com), one of the most popular small-business accounting software products on the market, since 2001, and it's served us well. When we first started, there weren't any cloud-based accounting systems available, so we used the desktop version. When the online version of QuickBooks was first released around 2008, we switched to it immediately, as our accounting workload had grown far beyond what I was able to handle on my own. (In fact, we were one of the first hundred or so companies to use QuickBooks Online.)

Today, QuickBooks Online makes it easy for everyone on our accounting team to access our financials, and it costs us about $600 per year. As your business grows in size and complexity, you may want to consider other solutions, such as NetSuite (www.netsuite.com). We expect to move in this direction within the next two years or so.

> *Tip:* No matter which accounting software you choose, I recommend that you have an expert help you set up your bookkeeping system; most accounting firms have at least one such specialist on their staff. They can set up your chart of accounts as well as your accounts receivable, inventory, accounts payable, payroll, and more. This will save you time and help ensure your books are accurate from the start.[86]

Choose your payment methods and providers

In addition to accepting checks, if your distributed company is a business-to-business (B2B) company, you'll probably need to accept payments via credit card, electronic payment via the automated clearing house network (ACH), and the occasional wire transfer. If you have a business-to-consumer (B2C) company, you may want to take advantage of all the options above, plus online payment platforms (Apple Pay, PayPal, Venmo, etc.).[87]

If you'll be accepting credit cards and other forms of electronic payment, you'll need to select a payment processing company, too. Be sure to shop around and compare fees (for setup, individual transactions, monthly statements, and more). Also, you should get an idea of whether or not they can process all the payment types you wish to accept, and how much time their solution will take to implement.[88] We use TSYS (formerly TransFirst; www.tsys.com) for payment processing and pay approximately 2–3 percent in processing fees.

> *Tip:* If you're going to accept payments electronically, you may want to consider building an additional 2–3 percent into your pricing to cover the cost of the fees.

Select a Human Resource Information System (HRIS)

I can't overstate the value of having a great human resource information system (HRIS)! Our HRIS makes it easier to manage our payroll (withholding, unemployment, etc.), administer our benefits, and handle various other HR processes, such as onboarding, all with just one system. Having an HRIS also gives our director of people more time to assist our employees with tasks that require a more hands-on approach.

A great HRIS can provide you with the analytics and reports you need to help you make better HR-related business decisions. In addition, an HRIS should help you remain in compliance with federal/state/local legal regulations and requirements, which can be a lifesaver if you have employees in multiple states.

> *Tip:* I would also encourage you to consider using your HRIS provider as your employee benefits broker, assuming your provider offers this service. We've found that doing so makes it easier and more affordable to integrate/administer our benefit plans through our HRIS.

When choosing an HRIS, you'll want to be sure it includes an easy-to-use employee portal that will enable your employees to manage their information, request and track time off, access their pay stubs and W-2s, and more. Your HRIS should also allow employees to select their benefits and make changes to them whenever they wish. For example, an employee should be able to adjust their 401(k) and Health Savings Account (HSA) contributions without any assistance from you or your HR team. Finally, your HRIS should also make it easy for your employees to complete and sign forms electronically.

We currently use Namely (www.namely.com) as our HRIS, and we couldn't be happier with it. Namely costs us approximately $26,000 annually.

> *Tip #1:* If you're just starting out, you may want to take a look at an HRIS called Gusto (www.gusto.com), which specializes in serving companies of 50 or fewer employees.

> *Tip #2:* The best way to learn the strengths and weaknesses of any HRIS is to go through a live demo. Then follow up by talking to each provider's references—in particular, companies who have moved from the system you're currently using to the system you're considering. Also, as you do your research, keep in mind that if an HRIS vendor started as, say, a benefits administration provider, their system may not be as robust in other areas, such as payroll, that they've added more recently. In short, be sure your vendor's strengths align with your priorities!

Choose an Applicant Tracking System (ATS)

As you'll find out, "virtually" everyone wants to work for an all-remote company! (We typically receive 100–400 applications in a matter of days for each open position.) Because of the sheer volume of job applications your distributed company is likely to generate, I believe an applicant tracking system (ATS) is a must-have from day one for any remote company.

We currently use an ATS called JazzHR (www.jazzhr.com), which helps Jamie, our director of people (and everyone else involved in the screening/interviewing/hiring process) save valuable time. For example, JazzHR automatically sends acknowledgments to job applicants, enables us to review each applicant's file on a single screen, and makes it easy for us to respond and reach out to candidates in a timely, customized manner. It also provides a scorecard that interviewers can fill out after each interview, which puts the information at the hiring manager's (and our HR director's) fingertips.

Ideally, you should choose an ATS that integrates with your HRIS (human resource information system) like ours does. This way, when a candidate is hired, your HRIS will automatically pick up where the ATS left off, which will simplify your onboarding process. JazzHR costs us $238 per month.

Select a Customer Relationship Management (CRM) system

I also recommend you implement a CRM solution for your fully distributed company as soon as possible. A CRM will make it easier for you to manage, track, and measure your company's relationships and interactions with prospects and clients.

We use Zoho (www.zoho.com) as our CRM. Zoho is powerful, customizable, and affordable. We pay just $35 a month per user for the Enterprise edition.

You may ask, "Didn't I read earlier that Fire Engine RED offers a CRM? Why aren't you using your own product?" Good question! It's because we designed our CRM specifically to meet the needs of admissions offices, and their processes are very different from those of a business.

3.12 Determine your company's office hours

"Remote" and "flexible" shouldn't mean "come and go as you please" or "work whenever you feel like it." That's why you'll need to establish office hours for your fully remote company. For one thing, your clients and vendors need to know when you're open for business! Our office hours are 8:30 a.m. to 5:30 p.m. (EST) because most of our clients are on the East Coast.

When it comes to our individual team members' work hours, most work from 8:30 a.m. to 5:30 p.m. (in their time zone), but we do have a few outliers. Some of our team members work from 6:00 a.m. to 3:00 p.m., and a couple others work from 10:00 a.m. to 7:00 p.m.

Tip: If your all-remote company has team members who work different hours, everyone should have easy access to their colleagues' work schedules. At Fire Engine RED, each team member's work hours are listed in their Slack and Google G Suite profiles. This way, no one schedules them for a meeting outside of their regular work hours.

3.13 Select your collaborative tools

Because your collaborative tools will serve as lifelines between you and your team members, it's crucial to choose the right ones *and* to continually evaluate them. We're always looking for the next great tool!

Even though most of our tool providers offer free versions, we typically opt for the business versions because they're easier to administer and usually provide additional levels of security and control.

Here are a few of the company-wide tools we love and why we love them:

Slack (www.slack.com)
What we use it for: Instant messaging, screen sharing, voice calls, and the occasional video call.
Why we love it: Lets us communicate quickly with each other. It also enables us to indicate our work status, such as "available," "in a meeting," "at lunch," "walking my

dog," etc. More than any other tool we use, Slack helps us feel like we're all in the same office, even when we're states (and countries) apart.

What the business version costs: $8 per user, per month.

Google G Suite (www.google.com/business)
What we use it for: Calendar sharing, document storage, and collaboration.

Why we love it: Enables us to collaborate in a more secure environment and helps us control access to company information. For example, it allows us to easily transfer ownership of documents (and remove access to them) when a team member leaves.

What the business version costs: $5 per user, per month.

Teamwork (www.teamwork.com)
What we use it for: Project management.

Why we love it: Provides a user-friendly interface and customizable features and functionality. Their client support team is also amazing, even reminding us of our own legendary client care team!

What the business version costs: $75 per month for five users; $15 per month for each additional user.

Zoom (https://zoom.us/)
What we use it for: Large conference calls, including high-quality screen sharing.

Why we love it: Lets us have calls with up to 100 people. Plus, it gives our administrator the ability to manage calls as well as record them for future reference. It's also easy to use and makes our slide presentations and demos look great.

What the business version costs: $19.99 per month, per host.

In addition to our company-wide tools, we have several dozen department-specific tools! I'll tell you more about those tools, and how we manage them, in chapter 11.1, "Manage collaborative tools and licenses."

3.14 Secure your vital information

Create a security policy

As a fully remote company with team members working from anywhere and everywhere, information security should be one of your top priorities. A well-thought-out security policy will help safeguard your vital client and company data, even when your team members are using unsecured internet access in coffee shops and hotel lobbies.[89]

Our own Remote Security Policy states that it "should be viewed within the context of Fire Engine RED being a 100 percent remote company with no central office location." With that in mind, the policy applies to all Fire Engine RED employees, contractors, and interns, whether they're working in a home office, cafe, shared workspace, hotel, conference, client's campus, or some other location.

Tip: The best way to ensure compliance with your security policy is to get input and buy-in on it from your executive management team as well as your HR, operations, and software development departments.

Our security policy requires our team members' computers to be equipped with a firewall and antivirus software. It's also mandatory for team members to set their screensavers to lock with password access after 10–20 minutes of inactivity. We also require passwords (a minimum of six characters and a combination of alphanumeric, upper and lowercase, and special characters).

Tip: You should also require your team members to use a password manager, as we do. This makes it easy for your team members to generate varied, difficult-to-guess passwords (and keep track of them). Most of our team members use Dashlane (www.dashlane.com); this is one case where we've found the free version sufficient for our team members' needs. Other free password managers we recommend are 1Password (https://1password.com/) and LastPass (www.lastpass.com/).

We also mandate that our team members use our secure FTP site to transfer client data; back up their computers regularly so they can be up and running within 24 hours if there's an issue; and use only company-approved collaborative tools.

Perhaps most importantly, if our team members are working somewhere other than their home office (such as a hotel, conference, shared workspace, etc.), we also require them to use our Virtual Private Network (VPN) to access internal databases and tools. (A VPN is a service that lets users access the internet safely and privately by routing their connection through a server and encrypting data before their internet service provider—or the coffee shop/hotel lobby's Wi-Fi provider—sees it.)

One thing we *don't* do is require team members to provide us with proof of compliance; rather, we communicate to them the implications of exposing the company to security risks. Nor do we expect/require team members to use their company-issued computers exclusively for business purposes. (That's not realistic because they work from home.) We simply ask that team members take our security policy seriously even when it applies to personal use. Essentially, our security policy is based on trusting our team members to do the right thing … and they do.

You can find our Remote Security Policy in the Resources section of our *Fully Remote* website (www.fully-remote-book.com).

Protect against email scams

An all-remote company can be particularly vulnerable to social engineering attacks, including email scams, because so much of its business communications are conducted online. Therefore, I recommend that you educate your team members about the types of email scams that are common and encourage them to be on the lookout for new ones. We're constantly posting examples of email scams on our company Slack channel, noting that they're from "Fake Naveena," "Fake Zach," and even "Fake Shelly."

Here's a specific example of an email scam to be aware of: Your CFO or another member of your financial team receives an email from "you" (the CEO) telling them to transfer money to a specific bank account. This happens to us a few times a year; however, our CFO has never fallen for it because he knows how I write, and the emails don't "sound" like me. Unfortunately, other companies haven't been so lucky. It's estimated that businesses nationwide lost $676 million in 2017 to email scams.[90] As a precaution, I recommend that you require your financial team to verify *any* type of money transfer with you verbally (and never rely on email) for approval or confirmation.

Don't think large companies are susceptible to financial scams? Think again. Not long ago, a scammer sent phony invoices to Facebook and Google, bilking the companies for a combined $122 million![91]

Here's another type of email scam we've experienced: Our director of people, Jamie, received an email purporting to be from our team member, Greg, which asked her to update his direct deposit bank account information. She thought the request was odd because our team members are able to change their banking details themselves in our human resource information system (HRIS). So, Jamie reached out to Greg to ask if he was having trouble doing it himself, and as you might expect, Greg immediately let Jamie know he hadn't sent her the message! Had Jamie gone ahead and done as "Fake Greg" had requested, his next paycheck would have been deposited into the scammer's bank account.

To minimize our chances of getting scammed, we ask our team members to avoid opening (or acting on) email that appears suspicious or asks for something out of the ordinary. We also advise them against clicking suspicious links or downloading suspicious, unauthorized, or illegal software.

> *Tip:* My best advice for you and your team members is to be skeptical when receiving any financial- or password-related email from another

team member, and to only pay invoices to verified vendors for verified expenses. Also, for your own protection as well as your team members', you should insist that they make any changes to their financial information themselves—which is yet another reason to implement an HRIS.

Establish a social media policy

I also recommend putting a social media policy in place as a supplement to your security policy. Ours is simple: We ask our team members to use good judgment and take personal and professional responsibility for what they publish on social media. We also remind them that anything they post on their social networking profiles could potentially be seen by the company's clients, competitors, and of course, other team members. As the lines between people's professional and personal lives continue to blur, it's important to remind your team members that they serve as "ambassadors" for your company across personal and professional social media channels.[92]

3.15 Define your core company values

In today's business environment, people want to work for companies that share their values. So, it's a good idea to define them as soon as possible.

Here's a look at the 12 values that define and drive Fire Engine RED:

- **Trust.** We trust each other to do the right thing because it's the right thing to do.
- **Integrity.** We're honest, authentic, and transparent.
- **Fairness.** We treat others with fairness and respect, and we believe in opportunity for all.
- **Empathy.** We put ourselves in others' shoes and try to see things from their perspective.
- **Teamwork.** We believe "it takes a team" to do our best work.
- **Simplicity.** We strive to simplify everything we do.
- **Good design.** We believe good design is good business.
- **Innovation.** We're committed to continually improving our offerings and believe that "good enough is never good enough."
- **Client service.** We strive to "wow" our clients and to exceed their expectations again and again.
- **Grit.** We don't get discouraged by challenges and setbacks. We're resilient and stay focused on our long-term goals.
- **Wellness.** We believe a healthy and happy team is a productive team.

- **Gratitude.** We appreciate our coworkers and our clients for contributing to the success of our company.

Keep in mind, it's not enough to have a values statement buried deep on your company's website. It's important that you and your team live those values because they're the foundation of your company's culture. More about company culture in chapter 13, "Building a strong company culture: No office building necessary."

3.16 Create a mission statement, tagline, and motto

Your employees, clients, and vendors need to know why your company exists. That's why I recommend you codify your distributed company's goals in a mission statement, a tagline, and a motto. Like many bricks-and-mortar businesses, Fire Engine RED has all three. We just don't have an office wall to hang them on!

> **Our mission statement:** To surprise and delight enrollment professionals by helping them achieve their strategic goals through our innovative technology, marketing, data, and consulting services.
> **Our tagline:** Simply better.
> **Our motto:** It takes a team.

As you can see, our mission statement, tagline, and motto are all consistent with our company values, and yours should be as well.

3.17 Market your company

Create a website

A great website is a must-have for companies, especially all-remote ones that don't have the instant credibility that comes from having an office. You'll want to create a website for your company as soon as possible, even if it only consists of a single page. (I've seen some great one-page company websites. Just Google "one-page websites" for inspiration.)

When it comes to creating your website, I recommend hiring a web designer or web design firm and having them build your site using a content management system, such as WordPress. This will make it easier for your team members to add and edit content without having to know how to code. A professional or firm with design and coding capabilities can provide you with a great-looking website for $5,000 to $10,000.

Now, if you're on a really tight budget, there are sites such as Wix (www.wix.com) that you can use to design and manage a simple business website. Again, I'm a big fan of hiring a professional, if at all possible.

Tip: I recommend that you post your client list as well as photos of your team members on your website. Doing so can help boost your company's credibility early on. Even if you only have a few of each, it can still help your all-virtual company feel more "real" to the outside world. We've done this since day one, and I'm convinced it helped us gain instant credibility when we needed it the most. In addition, remember that most people will view your website before they apply for a job with your company, so you'll want to include information about your company culture throughout your website.

You'll also need to find a provider to host your company website (and possibly your intranet, if you choose to add one later). More about our intranet in chapter 11.2, "Develop an intranet."

As mentioned previously, we use Rackspace (www.rackspace.com) to host both our email and website. We pay about $360 a year for this service (plus $40 a year to maintain the www.fire-engine-red.com domain).

Choose a broadcast email system

Depending on the type of company you have, you'll probably want to create and send email campaigns to promote your products/services and to keep in touch with your current clients. If your company decides to implement a CRM, it will most likely include a broadcast email functionality. See chapter 3.11, "Implement the right systems."

However, if you're not quite ready to implement a CRM, there are a variety of stand-alone broadcast email vendors out there, such as Mailchimp (www.mailchimp.com). As of this writing, Mailchimp offers three plans—free, $10-plus a month, and $199-plus a month, depending on the level of service you need. Of course, that doesn't include email design and copy, so you may want to consider adding one or more marketing professionals to your team early on.

> *Tip:* Don't underestimate the power of a good email marketing campaign! We send out about 40–50 email campaigns a year through our own broadcast email system and have found these campaigns are our most successful vehicle for lead generation. Every once in a while, you'll see an article or blog post proclaiming "email marketing is dead." I say, don't believe them.

Determine whether you need printed materials

While printed materials can be incredibly valuable to many companies, we rarely use print. On the occasions when we're face-to-face with potential clients at conferences, they prefer to follow up with us electronically. So, the only printed pieces we hand out are business cards at conferences and during campus visits.

Now that your fully remote company is all set up for success, let's talk talent.

Chapter 4
Attracting top talent: Offer benefits that will help seal the deal

When it comes to attracting top talent, I have great news for you—your all-virtual company will have a head start. That's because you'll automatically be providing one of the most sought-after benefits to employees: the opportunity to work from home! Studies have shown that 80 percent of employees consider the ability to telecommute a job perk.[93]

To help seal the deal, I also recommend that you offer a robust employee benefits package (including paid leave)— the best you can afford. But before we discuss voluntary benefits, I want to make sure you're aware of several benefits you'll be required by law to provide.

4.1 Mandatory benefits

There are certain benefits that, by law, all employers are required to offer their employees. As a fully distributed company, you should be aware that some of these requirements may differ from state to state. This can be quite challenging to do on your own, so you'll want to make sure your payroll provider not only keeps up with local, state, and federal laws but also communicates any updates to you in a timely manner.

All employers

As an employer, you're required to pay for the following:

Social Security and Medicare

The Federal Insurance Contributions Act (FICA) mandates that employers (and employees) pay a payroll tax to fund the Social Security and Medicare programs. As a result, both you (and your employees) will need to contribute to Social Security and Medicare, at a rate of 6.2 percent for Social Security (up to the employee's first $132,900 in earnings) and 1.45 percent for Medicare. (These rates are current for 2019.)[94]

Unemployment insurance

You'll also have to pay for unemployment insurance for every employee. This will ensure that an employee who becomes involuntarily separated from your company will have funds to help pay their expenses while they look for a new job. Rates vary by state.

Employers in some states

Depending on which states your employees reside in, there are several additional benefits you may need to provide.

Short-term disability insurance

As of this writing, five states have state-mandated short-term disability requirements: California, Hawaii, New Jersey, New York, and Rhode Island (as well as the U.S. territory of Puerto Rico).[95] Other states are likely to follow suit, so you'll want to stay abreast of developments; your HRIS provider should be able to help you do so.

Workers' compensation

As stated in chapter 3.10, "Purchase business insurance," most states also require that employers (including all-remote ones) obtain workers' compensation coverage.

Employers with 50 or more employees

If you have more than 50 employees, there are two important federal laws you'll need to comply with—the Affordable Care Act (ACA) and the Family and Medical Leave Act (FMLA). Your all-remote company may be exempt from complying with FMLA, even if you have 50 or more employees. I'll explain below.

The Affordable Care Act mandates that employers with more than 50 full-time (or equivalent) employees offer qualified and affordable health benefits to their employees. But remember, offering the best possible health insurance can help you attract and retain more of the types of employees you're looking for. According to survey after survey, healthcare is the primary benefit desired by employees (with flexible work options not far behind!).[96]

When it comes to providing health insurance coverage, the options for a remote company with employees in multiple states are limited. You can choose a single plan (sometimes referred to as a national plan) that covers all of your employees no matter which state they live in, or you can purchase separate plans in each state where you have employees.[97]

A single, multi-state plan. With this option, all employees receive the same group health insurance regardless of where they live. Coverage typically includes healthcare-related essentials such as doctor visits, preventive care, hospital stays, emergency services, and prescription drugs.

As of this writing, there are only four providers (Aetna, Blue Cross Blue Shield, Cigna, and United Healthcare) that offer national plans. You should keep in mind that some national providers may not offer coverage in all 50 states.

In such cases, you'll need to rely on state exchanges to cover your employees who live in those states.

Fire Engine RED currently offers its employees a high-deductible healthcare plan (HDHP). An HDHP is defined as "any [healthcare] plan with a deductible of at least $1,350 for an individual or $2,700 for a family."[98]

Until 2014, we paid 100 percent of each employee's health insurance premium, but the rising cost of health coverage made it impossible for us to continue to do so. We currently pay 66 percent of each employee's healthcare insurance premium, assuming they opt for our coverage. To help offset our employees' out-of-pocket medical costs, we also offer a tax-free Health Savings Account (HSA), and a wellness contribution, which I'll discuss below in chapter 4.2, "Voluntary benefits."

Separate state plans. Another option is to offer separate state plans to accommodate workers in those individual states. However, managing multiple policies can be complicated and time-consuming, especially for a business like Fire Engine RED with employees in 26 states. To keep it simple, I recommend you select a single, multi-state plan from the very start.

> *Tip:* As previously stated in this chapter, you're not required to offer medical insurance for your employees if you have fewer than 50 full-time

employees, but that doesn't mean that you shouldn't.

In fact, if you have fewer than 50 full-time employees, you can provide your employees with what's called a Qualified Small Employer Health Reimbursement Arrangement (QSEHRA), which allows you to reimburse your employees for their medical expenses, including personal insurance premiums, tax-free.[99]

Family and medical leave

The Family and Medical Leave Act (FMLA) makes it possible for "eligible employees of covered employers to take unpaid, job-protected leave for specified family and medical reasons."[100] Here's what eligible employees are entitled to.

- "Twelve workweeks of leave in a 12-month period for:"

    - "The birth of a child and to care for the newborn child within one year of birth."
    - "The placement with the employee of a child for adoption or foster care and to care for the newly placed child within one year of placement."

- ♦ Caring for "the employee's spouse, child, or parent who has a serious health condition."
- ♦ "A serious health condition that makes the employee unable to perform the essential functions of his or her job."
- ♦ Any qualifying urgent need or demand "arising out of the fact that the employee's spouse, son, daughter, or parent is a covered military member on 'covered active duty.'"[101]

Or:

- "Twenty-six workweeks of leave during a single 12-month period to care for a covered servicemember with a serious injury or illness if the eligible employee is the servicemember's spouse, son, daughter, parent, or next of kin (military caregiver leave)."[102]

To be eligible for FMLA:

- The *employee* must have been employed with the company for 12 months and must have worked at least 1,250 hours during the 12 months prior to the start of FMLA leave.[103]

- The *employer* has to employ 50 or more employees within a 75-mile radius of the worksite.[104]

As you can see, the law was not written to account for distributed companies (like Fire Engine RED) that have 50 or more employees who don't work within a 75-mile radius of any company office. Despite this seemingly "unintended" loophole, which may exempt most, if not all, remote companies from FMLA, Fire Engine RED has chosen to provide family and medical leave coverage for our employees, and we've gone *far beyond* what FMLA requires. You'll find more about our family and medical leave policy in chapter 4.4, "Paid leave."

4.2 Voluntary benefits

Even though you're not legally required to provide any of the benefits that follow (that's why they're called voluntary benefits), we've found that by providing employees with a benefits package that's very generous and forward-thinking, we've been able to land just about every job candidate we've wanted to hire.

Before discussing the specific benefits we offer, you should know that every full-time employee at Fire Engine RED is eligible for all our benefits (including paid leave) on their first day of work (as are the employee's spouse/partner and any children). We also keep things simple by having all our benefits run concurrently with the calendar year.

Lesson learned: It's easier for everyone (the company and your employees) to plan if your benefits period runs on the calendar year. We used to have our benefits open enrollment in October. In 2018, we transitioned to a calendar year because people's general mindsets align more with a calendar/tax/payroll year which makes it easier for people to plan.

In addition to health insurance, here's a look at the benefits we offer and why we offer them.

Health Savings Account (HSA)

To help offset the out-of-pocket costs associated with our high-deductible health plan (HDHP), we offer the employees, who are enrolled in our company-sponsored healthcare plan, a Health Savings Account (HSA). Our HSA enables our employees to pay for qualified medical expenses with pre-tax dollars.

Many financial experts say an HSA is like a 401(k) on steroids. That's because employees have the option of receiving a triple tax benefit if they do the following: Pay for their out-of-pocket medical expenses with non-HSA money, invest their money in an HSA investment account, and let their funds grow tax-free. Then, at a later date, they can reimburse themselves for the expenses they incurred.

Even better, they can keep the money invested and use the funds to pay for qualified medical expenses in retirement.

The bottom line: If you have an HDHP, you should also offer an HSA. There's absolutely no downside! (By law, only companies that offer an HDHP are able to offer an HSA.)[105]

Dental and vision

Another great way to distinguish your company from other employers is to provide your employees with dental and vision coverage. That's because only 53 percent of employers provide dental insurance, and even fewer (just 35 percent) offer vision insurance.[106]

Providing dental and vision coverage for your employees can be relatively inexpensive. Our dental coverage costs approximately $35 per month, per employee; and vision coverage costs approximately $6 per month, per employee. Our employees can use their tax-free HSA (or a Limited Purpose FSA, as I'll discuss below) to pay for any of their out-of-pocket dental and vision costs. As you can see, providing dental and vision coverage is a great example of how a little investment can go a long way.

Basic Life and Accidental Death and Dismemberment (AD&D)

You should also consider providing your employees with Basic Life and AD&D coverage. This benefit is usually offered in increments of $25,000 or $50,000, or it's based on the employee's salary rounded up to the nearest thousand. Fire Engine RED provides each employee with $50,000 of Basic Life, which is payable to their beneficiaries if they die. Additionally, each employee has up to $50,000 of AD&D that covers them if they lose a limb, sight, speech, or hearing, or if they suffer paralysis or a coma as the result of an accident (such as a car crash).[107] Providing these benefits is relatively inexpensive. Our annual premium for Basic Life is approximately $2,700 and $775 for AD&D coverage for all our employees.

Flexible Spending Account (FSA)

I also recommend that you offer your employees access to the three FSAs described below. These types of accounts will enable them to pay for various qualified expenses with pre-tax dollars. Depending on their personal tax rate, employees who take advantage of these plans can save between 15 and 40 percent on qualified expenses. Here's a look at the FSAs we provide.

Dependent Care FSA. This benefit allows each of our employees to set aside up to $5,000 in pre-tax dollars to pay for qualified childcare expenses, such as daycare, before/after school programs, summer day camp, and babysitters for children under age 13. In addition, they may use their FSA money to pay for the cost of a caretaker for a disabled spouse or dependent if the person receiving the care: (1) lives with the employee at least eight hours of the day and (2) is claimed as a dependent on the employee's Federal Tax Return.

The one big downside to a Dependent Care FSA is that employees forfeit *all* money left in their account if they don't use it by the end of the plan year. This is one reason why some of your employees who could possibly benefit from this type of FSA may find it too risky to participate. Most employees who use daycare for their kids don't worry about the $5,000 limit (established in 1986, by the way) because they can usually plow through that amount in less than three months!

Limited Purpose FSA. If you want to go above and beyond what most employers offer, all-remote or not, you should offer this little-known FSA. We only added a Limited Purpose FSA in 2018. Until then, we didn't even know it existed!

A Limited Purpose FSA can be used by your employees to pay for qualified dental- and vision-care-related expenses. (In 2019, employees can set aside up to $2,700 pre-tax, per year.)[108] Essentially, what it does is enable your employees to use their Limited Purpose FSA to pay for their out-of-pocket dental and vision expenses with tax-free dollars, while saving their HSA funds for medical expenses. By providing both an HSA and Limited Purpose FSA, you'll be helping your employees stretch their tax-free savings even further.

Another benefit of a Limited Purpose FSA is that it allows participants to carry over $500 of unused funds to the next plan year. (As stated above, some FSAs, such as a Dependent Care FSA, require employees to forfeit *all* money left in their account if they don't use it by the end of the plan year, which is why some people are reluctant to participate in an FSA, finding them too risky.) Therefore, it makes sense for you to encourage employees to set aside a minimum of $500. Even if they don't have $500 in expenses this year, they're highly likely to incur $500 in expenses in another year.

In addition, some of your employees may be able to convert their Limited Purpose FSA into a Full Medical FSA. See below.

Full Medical FSA. There are two types of employees who can benefit from this plan:

1) Employees who are enrolled in an HDHP and have met the IRS deductible for it ($1,350 for an individual; $2,700 for families in 2019) are able to convert their Limited Purpose FSA into a Full Medical FSA and use the money for qualified medical-, dental-, and vision-care-related expenses.

2) Employees who are not enrolled in our health plan can contribute up to $2,700 in pre-tax dollars to a Full Medical FSA and use the money for the same types of qualified expenses as above.

Like the Limited Purpose FSA, a Full Medical FSA lets employees carry over $500 of unused funds to the next plan year.

Retirement benefits

A retirement plan is a highly sought-after employee benefit and can help set your company apart—especially if you're competing against smaller companies, where workers are less likely to have retirement plans offered to them. In fact, about 50 percent of people working for companies with fewer than 100 employees don't have access to a retirement plan through their employer.[109]

If your company employs 100 or fewer people, you'll have two choices when it comes to providing your employees with retirement benefits: A SIMPLE IRA or a 401(k) plan.

The advantages of offering a SIMPLE IRA include, well, simplicity. All it takes is a one-page IRS form to get a SIMPLE IRA up and running. With a SIMPLE IRA, participants can make contributions up to certain annual maximums ($13,000 in 2019 for those younger than 50, with an additional "catch-up" contribution of $3,000 available to those 50 or older, for a maximum of $16,000).

However, a SIMPLE IRA is capped at 100 employees, and we had confidence that we're going to grow beyond that, so we decided not to wait and moved from a SIMPLE IRA to a 401(k) in 2012. In addition, some of our employees wanted the opportunity to save more for retirement (tax-free) than a SIMPLE IRA allowed.

With a 401(k), you'll give up some of the simplicity, as 401(k) plans are covered by ERISA and require a third-party administrator to maintain. However, we've found the benefits (and higher savings limits) to be well worth the additional paperwork and cost. For example, 401(k) participants can contribute up to $19,500 to their 401(k) in 2019. Participants over 50 years of age can contribute up to $6,000 more for a maximum of $25,500 per year.

If you go the 401(k) route, I strongly encourage you to choose a plan with low fees.[110] As Warren Buffett said, "If returns are going to be seven or eight percent and you're paying one percent for fees, that makes an enormous difference in how much money you're going to have in retirement."[111]

For years, Fire Engine RED offered a 401(k) plan through "Vendor A." When our CFO, Akber, joined us in 2014, one of the first things he pointed out was that Vendor A was "killing us with high fees." We shopped around and switched to a plan offered by Vanguard (www.vanguard.com) that's saving our employees thousands of dollars in fees each year.

As part of our benefits package, we make an annual contribution (not a match) to each employee's 401(k) equal to 3 percent of the employee's annual salary. This means that even if an employee isn't contributing to their 401(k), they're still seeing the benefits, which we hope will encourage them to contribute in the future.

At Fire Engine RED, our 401(k) participation and savings rates well exceed national averages. Our employee participation rate is 91 percent compared to the national average of 79 percent,[112] and our employees contribute an average of 9 percent of their salary vs. the national average of 6.8 percent.[113]

How do we get so many employees to participate in our 401(k) plan and save more than the national average? For one thing, we automatically enroll them in our plan, so rather than having them opt in, they have to opt *out* if they don't want to participate. Secondly, I think it has to do with our commitment to educating our employees on the benefits of participating in our 401(k) plan. More on that in chapter 13.7, "Encourage financial wellness."

Healthcare concierge services

Given the complexity of the healthcare system, I highly recommend you include access to a healthcare concierge service in your benefits package. These services can help your employees *and* their families (including parents and siblings) save time, money, and potential stress navigating medical, hospital, dental, mental health, medication, and other healthcare issues.

Our employees use our healthcare concierge service, TouchCare (www.touchcare.com), to find quality doctors, get estimates for treatment costs, and help resolve medical billing problems. I've used our healthcare concierge service myself several times to help me resolve complex billing issues. Without their assistance, I might have just gone ahead and paid the incorrect invoices because I didn't have the time or patience needed to resolve the issues myself. Ray, our director of search client success, has had similar experiences to mine; he shared, "I've used them to verify benefits and find providers. All experiences have been amazing so far!"

Wellness program

Offering a company wellness program is a great way to help your employees stay healthy and promote a sense of community. We began offering a company wellness program in 2015, and that was a good start, but we found that our wellness provider's program had several shortcomings:

- Only employees who were enrolled in our company's medical insurance plan were able to participate.
- Family members (spouses/partners) could not participate.
- The program focused only on physical health.
- The only challenges offered were walking challenges.
- The program wasn't personalized or fun.
- The only financial reward was an HSA contribution.

So, in January 2019, we moved to a different wellness program provider, and much to our delight, our all-new program, offered through WellRight (www.wellright.com), better reflects our company values and addresses all of the above issues. Here are some of the highlights.

Open to everyone. All team members are now welcome and encouraged to participate, whether employees, contractors, or interns, and whether they're enrolled in our medical insurance plan or not. Their spouses/partners and children (over 18) can also participate at no cost.

I'm pleased to say that a whopping 94 percent of the employees who are covered by our medical insurance plan participate. What's more, 80 percent of our team members who *aren't* covered by our medical insurance plan are participating. In addition, several of our employees' spouses/partners also participate, just as we had hoped they would.

Holistic. Our wellness program addresses not just physical health but also the employee's emotional, financial, occupational, and social well-being.

Personalized. Employees earn points by completing our four annual requirements and participating in a combination of annual, quarterly, and personal challenges. There are dozens of challenges to choose from, each designed to foster healthy habit-forming behaviors. Examples include reading 10 books over 12 months; attending 10 classes (of any kind) over a three-month period; and creating a budget using the past three months' worth of bills.

Fun and "rewarding." The more points our team members earn, the greater their rewards: Employees who have our healthcare plan can earn a reward of $500, $1,000 or $1,675 and can choose to receive their reward in cash, or as a tax-free 401(k) or HSA contribution. Even team members who don't have our healthcare plan can win as much as $200 in cash!

While our wellness program is still relatively new, we've received some great feedback on it from our team members: Molly said, "I love that it's more than just physical wellness." And David, our director of client care, shared, "I love our new program because it's interactive and gives me a feeling that I am actually progressing. It gives you legitimate ways to be better and rewards you for it!"

4.3 Disability benefits

Disability insurance, which provides income when an employee can't work due to a disability, is a special perk many job seekers will take note of. This is because short-term disability is offered by only 26 percent of small companies, and long-term disability is offered by just 20 percent of small companies.[114]

At Fire Engine RED, we offer both short-term and long-term disability insurance.

Short-term disability

Our short-term disability plan provides employees with 60 percent of their salary for *up to* 11 weeks, with a maximum benefit of $1,000 per week, should they qualify. Prior to receiving this benefit, our disability plan requires a 14-day unpaid waiting period. For example, after a two-week waiting period, a birth mother (pregnancy is considered a disability) will receive four to six weeks of partially paid leave. The number of weeks depends on the type of delivery.

Long-term disability

Our long-term disability plan provides employees with 60 percent of their salary, with a maximum monthly benefit of $5,000, should they qualify. For disabilities occurring before age 60, benefits will continue to age 65. There is a 90-day waiting period to receive this benefit.

Helping employees get more out of their disability benefits

In 2017, I asked my team to look more closely at our disability benefits. I was concerned that after taxes, there wasn't enough money left for employees to pay their living expenses. I wanted to see if there was a way to make our disability benefits go further for anyone who needed them, including birth mothers, who are covered under short-term disability.

Here's what we learned: Whether a disability benefit is taxable or tax-free to an employee depends on: (1) who pays the premium (the employer or the employee), and (2) whether the premium is paid with pre-tax or post-tax dollars.[115]

As a result, the company no longer pays our employees' short-term and long-term disability premiums (with pre-tax dollars). Instead, we encourage employees to sign up for both short-term and long-term disability and pay the premiums (approximately $500 per year) themselves with post-tax dollars (through a payroll contribution). To help our employees do this, we made a one-time adjustment to their gross salaries to cover the premiums. In 2019, 100 percent of our employees opted for short-term and long-term disability coverage. Again, because our employees pay the premiums with post-tax dollars, these benefits will be tax-free to them should they need them.

Although it's now a bit more work to administer our disability benefits, the advantage to our employees far outweighs the slight hassle. For example, let's say an employee with a medical condition who makes $90,000 annually qualifies for short-term disability for four weeks. Prior to us making this administrative change, she would have received approximately 63 percent of her net salary for those four weeks, due to taxes. Now, she'll receive 92 percent of her net salary while on short-term disability, an increase of nearly 30 percent!

4.4 Paid leave

"Paid leave" is an overall term for holidays, vacation, sick days, etc. A generous paid leave policy is another great way to attract top talent to your company. This is especially true if your budget doesn't allow you to match the salaries other employers are offering.

Before we get into what we *do* offer, though, let's talk about paid time off (PTO) and why we *don't* offer it.

Many employers now lump together vacation time with sick days, and what are often called "personal days," to provide a total number of PTO days. Employers generally like PTO because the amount of days off is basically set in stone, and because they don't have to ask for a reason why an employee is absent.

However, a PTO policy can adversely affect employees who experience significant or repeated illnesses or unexpected emergencies. As a result, employees may end up with less vacation time (or none at all) in a particular year, which is bad for morale and employee retention, and that's why we don't offer PTO.

Instead, our paid leave policies are built around our company values of Fairness, Simplicity, and Empathy. These policies place an emphasis on the holistic treatment of employees, recognizing that they're people with lives beyond the company, and that, yes, "stuff" happens unexpectedly, and they should not be financially penalized for it. The bottom line is, we want our employees to use their vacation time for *vacation*, not for illness, family emergencies, etc.

Now, let's take a look at the types of paid leave we *do* provide.

Holidays

We offer a minimum of 10 paid holidays per year. For 2019, based on how the major holidays fell, our employees got 11 paid holidays:

- New Year's Day – Tuesday, January 1
- Memorial Day – Monday, May 27
- Independence Day – Thursday, July 4
- Day after Independence Day – Friday, July 5
- Labor Day – Monday, September 2
- Thanksgiving Day – Thursday, November 28
- Day after Thanksgiving – Friday, November 29
- Christmas Eve – Tuesday, December 24
- Christmas Day – Wednesday, December 25
- Day after Christmas – Thursday, December 26
- New Year's Eve – Tuesday, December 31

In addition, on the day before each holiday, we close the "office" 90 minutes early so our employees can get a jump-start on their time off. This is such an easy way to boost employee morale; any company could do this. After all, the 90 minutes prior to closing before a holiday is usually not the most productive time, so we're really not sacrificing anything.

Also, once in a blue moon we even invent our own holiday, as we did with "Eclipse Day" on Monday, August 21, 2017, giving our employees a half-day off to enjoy the rare total solar eclipse over North America. And yes, we're planning to do the same for the next one on Monday, August 12, 2045; we even have it on our company website (www.fire-engine-red.com).

Vacation

I strongly recommend that you create a simple, generous vacation policy, one that meets the needs of your employees and is easy to administer. Early on, Fire Engine RED's vacation policy was anything but simple. In fact, I was constantly being asked by Jamie, our director of people, to make exceptions to it, which is a clear sign a policy isn't working.

Our employees received:
- Two weeks of vacation.
- Four days of vacation during the last two weeks of the year when our clients were on winter break.
- Their birthdays off.

However, people would ask, "Is it okay if I switch my birthday day off with a day two days/weeks/months from now?" I was saying "yes" every time, so I started to think, "We need to create a new vacation policy where the exceptions become the rule."

As a result, we instituted our "simply better" vacation policy in 2014, which was more consistent with our company value of Simplicity. Now, everyone gets three weeks of vacation (up from two weeks) right out of the gate, and everyone gets bumped up to four weeks of vacation after just two years with us!

Recently, with so many of our employees hitting the 10-year mark, I decided to take our vacation policy a step further. Now, at 10 years, everyone gets an additional week of vacation for a total of five weeks. It's my way of rewarding our longtime employees for their hard work and dedication to Fire Engine RED.

Under our new policy, employees still have the option of taking their birthday off or working on their birthdays, as some like to do. And if people want to take four days off at the end of the year, there's nothing stopping them from doing so. It's their call, not the company's.

Here's a look at our current vacation policy:

Table 4. Fire Engine RED Vacation Policy

Tier	Years with Company	Weeks of Vacation
Employees		
1	2	3
2	3–9	4
3	10+	5
Leadership: VPs		
1	2	4
2	3+	5
Leadership: EVPs/C-Level Officers		
1	Any	5

Also, our employees no longer accrue vacation time. Instead, they gain access to all of their vacation time for the calendar year on January 1. (New employees gain access to all of their vacation days, prorated from their start date.) So, if a new employee joined Fire Engine RED in April and then wanted to take a 10-day trip to Costa Rica in June, they could. All they'd need is their manager's approval! (Incidentally, most employers require employees to wait six to nine weeks before they're eligible to take vacation time.[116])

One other nice thing about our vacation policy is that employees get to move up a tier on January 1 of the year they're eligible for more vacation. For example, let's say an employee joined in October 2013. They'd have gone from three to four weeks of vacation in January 2016, not October 2016. The reason we do this, instead of prorating vacation time, is that this policy is easier to administer and is consistent with our company value of Simplicity.

Given our generous vacation policy, you might think we'd take the next step and move to "unlimited" vacation time. A study by MetLife found that 72 percent of those surveyed ranked unlimited time off ahead of other benefits like rewards for healthy behavior, phased retirement, and paid sabbaticals.[117] However, when we looked into offering unlimited vacation, we decided it *wasn't* going to be beneficial to our employees! At companies with unlimited plans, employees actually take *less* vacation time, often because they don't want to be seen as taking unfair advantage of the policy.

In fact, the biggest "fear" many of our type-A employees have is that, in an effort to be more generous, we'll move to an unlimited vacation policy! I've talked to them, and they feel just fine about having a limit, so they know exactly how much vacation time to use. With unlimited vacation, they say, they could end up taking less vacation time, or even none at all.

The best thing about our vacation policy, I believe, is that it encourages our employees to take more vacation, not less. And for those employees who for whatever reason aren't able to use all the vacation time they're allotted for a year, we allow them to "carry forward" a maximum of five vacation days to the next calendar year.

> *Tip:* When it comes to vacation time, most states have "use it or lose it" policies. But not all—for example, in California, vacation pay is a form of wages and cannot be forfeited. Under California law, all vacation wages earned must be paid out when the employee leaves the company.[118] Our maximum "carry forward" of five days (see above) helps limit the amount the company has to pay out for unused vacation time.

Incidentally, at Fire Engine RED, "on vacation" means exactly that. We don't bother people on vacation unless there's a true company emergency. One employee said,

"At my last job, you were still expected to work on days off. We called it 'PTO' … 'pretend time off.'"

> *Tip:* If you want people to disconnect while they're on vacation, I recommend that you (as CEO) set the example when you're away on vacation. If employees know that you don't work while on vacation, they'll be more likely to disconnect on their own vacations.

Sick days

Even though I'm not an advocate of *unlimited vacation days*, I do believe *unlimited sick time* is the way to go, especially for a fully distributed company. As discussed in chapter 2.1, "How companies benefit," your employees are likely to take fewer sick days because they work from home.

At Fire Engine RED, our employees can use their unlimited sick days for themselves or to care for a sick child, spouse/partner, or parent.

Our employees also know that they can use sick time for any type of illness, whether it be physical or mental. At Fire Engine RED, we look at wellness in a holistic sense and encourage our employees to take a sick day whenever they need one—no questions asked.

Our unlimited sick policy has worked well for both our company and employees. Again, as I mentioned in chapter

2.1, "How companies benefit," the average number of sick days taken by an employee at Fire Engine RED is fewer than two days per year—less than the national average (up to five days per year).[119]

Medical appointments and procedures

Many companies require their employees to use personal days for medical appointments and procedures. At Fire Engine RED, we don't have personal days. As with sick days, our employees can take as much time for these types of medical appointments (for themselves, their children, a spouse/partner, or a parent).

Out time

Flexibility is the second-most sought-after employee benefit (after better health, dental, and vision insurance).[120] That's why we provide flexibility to our employees through what we call "out time." Essentially, this policy ensures that our employees don't miss "out" on the important things in their lives!

Our employees LOVE our "out time" policy, and many say they simply don't know what they'd do without it. (After learning about this policy, I hope you'll consider offering your own version.) Here's how it works: Our employees can take up to two hours per day of unspecified "out time" without using vacation time. All we ask is that they clear the "out time" with their managers. We trust that our employees will do what it takes to get their work done prior to the next day. We *don't* say that employees who use, say, 47 minutes of "out time" are required to make up exactly 47 minutes later that day or the next. (Also, all of our managers are very supportive of our "out time" policy and use this policy themselves, so there's no reason for any employee to feel uncomfortable about requesting and taking "out time.")

Many of the parents in our company use "out time" for child-related activities, including dropping off and picking up at school, sports practices, and more. (This is also why I sometimes refer to our "out time" policy as our "no child left behind" policy!) As Chuck wrote, "Is it okay to take 'out time' around 4:15 p.m. a lot of my afternoons? I'll make up the time at night after my kids go to bed. Here's why—of all the parents in our girls' high school lacrosse team carpool, the 'work-from-home-guy' is best able to do the drop-off at practice!" Of course, it was okay with me, as the "work-from-home-guy" always gets his work done no matter when he works.

Some other examples of how our employees use "out time" include taking a pet to the vet, picking up a relative at the airport, getting a haircut, going to the gym, and taking a yoga class.

Here's what a few of our employees have said about our "out time" policy.

- "'Out time' makes a huge difference. It's really such a quality of life thing. I feel much less stressed if something comes up; I can deal with it and not be afraid of losing my job."

- "'Out time' is a fantastic benefit, and makes me highly motivated to give plenty of extra time on a regular basis to FER out of appreciation for the flexibility of 'out time,' MD time, sick time, etc."

- "'Out time' is a great benefit, and I love it. It simplifies all the various 'What do I do if …' questions that used to come up when we had more types of absences. I've also appreciated the ability to change my work hours to match the time zone when traveling."

- "This is the first company I've worked for where the 'out time' policy lined up with how I feel employees should be treated. Like adults!"

Family and medical leave

Just 22 percent of professional workers, and only 9 percent of workers at employers with fewer than 100 employees, have access to paid family and medical leave.[121] To help build loyalty among your current employees, as well as attract top talent, I recommend you offer family and medical leave (both paid and unpaid) to your employees, and the more generous, the better.

"Family and medical leave" isn't just about taking time off to welcome a new child. It also enables workers to deal with a serious health condition (their own or a family member's) without fear of compromising their careers or even losing their jobs.

Our previous approach

Up until May 2019, we had two paid family and medical-related leave policies.

- Maternity Leave Policy: Our maternity leave policy provided two weeks of paid leave to women who gave birth, plus four to six weeks of short-term disability benefits, depending on the type of delivery. (These benefits were taxable until January 2019.) See chapter 4.3, "Disability benefits."

- Parental Leave Policy: Our parental leave policy was separate from our maternity leave policy. It gave parents, both moms and dads, three paid days off after the birth or adoption of a child.

However, the more I thought about our policies, the more I felt they were not consistent with our company values of

Fairness and Empathy. I realized that, for our Family and Medical Leave policy to truly be fair and empathetic, it needed to:

- Treat our employees equitably, with regard to paid and unpaid leave, in good times (welcoming a child) and bad (dealing with a personal health issue or having to care for a seriously ill family member).

- Be competitive with the amount of time off (and in some cases, money) offered by the most generous states.

- Provide as much paid leave as possible. Many people are less likely to take unpaid leave because they can't afford to.

An important side note: Family caregiver leave isn't discussed as often as maternity leave, but it should be. That's because, of the employees who take unpaid leave as permitted under FMLA, 75 percent do so to care for *someone other than a new child*.[122] Many people in today's workforce are part of the "sandwich generation," meaning they're not only caring for their children but also caring for aging parents. According to *Forbes*, "about 60 percent of family caregivers work at a paying job and many are trying to juggle full-time careers with time-consuming caregiving responsibilities."[123] Moreover, about 13 percent of family caregivers who don't have any paid time off said they've had to cut their work hours, while 14 percent have had to quit their jobs altogether.[124] The more I thought about this, the more determined I was to make paid family caregiver leave a part of our new policy.

To create a more generous policy that better reflected our commitment to employees and their families, we formed our six-person Family Leave Advisory Group (FLAG), led by Katrina, our VP of projects who was uniquely qualified for this complicated task.

Since joining our company, Katrina's taken three maternity leaves and, in the process, had gained extensive experience navigating California's parental leave policies, which are some of the most complex (and most progressive) in the country. In addition, in 2018, less than six months after Katrina had returned from her third maternity leave, she suffered the loss of three family members—her grandmother, an aunt, and her father—over a period of just five months.

As a result of her personal circumstances, Katrina required more time off than our company policy allowed. As you may have guessed, we insisted that Katrina take all the time off she needed, and we paid her for it, as we would have done for any employee. However, we also realized that it would actually be more reassuring to our employees if we put a formal, yet flexible policy into place.

Our goals

I tasked FLAG with formulating a new *paid* family and medical leave policy that was:

- Simple to administer.
- Aligned with our company values of Flexibility, Simplicity, and Empathy.
- Appropriate for a company of our size.
- Practical for our 100 percent remote workplace.
- Applicable to employees in multiple states.

I'll talk about our *unpaid* leave policy in chapter 4.5, "Unpaid leave."

The challenge

As we quickly learned, creating a family and medical leave policy for a 100 percent remote company is especially complicated because you have to consider federal law as well as the laws in the states where you have employees. (In our case, we have employees in 26 states, so we had to research each of those states' benefits laws to help us create an equitable policy.)

Keep in mind, there's no federal statute mandating that leave time be *paid*, and only six states and Washington, D.C., already have, or are enacting their own, paid leave laws. As a result, some of your employees may not have access to any state-paid benefits, while others may be able to take advantage of up to several weeks of partially paid leave. (There are no states that offer full-pay leave programs.)

Here's what I mean by "complicated." Among the states (and Washington, D.C.) that do have paid leave laws, the benefit period varies greatly. For example, Rhode Island[125] provides employees with four weeks of pay, while the benefit period in Washington, D.C.,[126] differs depending on the situation (two weeks for personal illness, six weeks for family caregiving, and eight weeks for baby bonding). In Washington state[127] and Massachusetts,[128] employees receive 12 weeks of pay for any of the events covered by FMLA. And in California,[129] qualifying employees are guaranteed up to six weeks of paid family leave and/or six weeks of disability leave per year at partial pay (these benefits are administered as two separate programs).

To muddy the waters even further, each state calculates the actual benefit amount differently. Employees in California[130] receive a percentage of their average weekly wage, up to 70 percent, but caps the benefit at approximately $1,200 per week.[131] In New York[132] and Massachusetts,[133] the cap is lower, around $750-$900 per week. And beginning in 2020, in Washington state,[134] employees will receive a percentage of their average weekly wage up to $1,000.

How each paid family leave program is funded also differs from state to state, as do your obligations as an employer.

According to *Forbes*, "Most of the paid family leave states fund the program through an employee payroll deduction (or payroll tax, if you prefer). But D.C. [taxes] employers while Washington [state] and Massachusetts tax both employers and employees."[135]

In addition, when it comes to *unpaid* time off, some states provide employees with 12 weeks of unpaid leave, as required by FMLA, while other states provide more unpaid time off. For example, Oregon provides up to 36 weeks in certain situations.[136]

Got all that? If your head is spinning, believe me, mine was too. Despite the many challenges, after months of research, and more than a dozen lengthy discussions, in May 2019, we introduced our new Family and Medical Leave policy.

The result: A "simply better" family and medical leave policy

We left one aspect of our former policy intact:

Maternity leave (birth mothers). As before, mothers who have given birth are able to receive four to six weeks (depending on the type of delivery) of partially paid leave through short-term disability insurance. This benefit (as of January 2019) is tax-free. As previously stated, prior to receiving this benefit, our disability plan requires a 14-day unpaid waiting period. (See chapter 4.3, "Disability benefits," above.)

However, we dramatically expanded the policy to include:

Parental leave. All employees (female or male, mom or dad) now receive up to eight weeks of parental leave at full salary, paid for by the company. These eight weeks can be used for welcoming a child through birth, adoption, or foster care. Keep in mind, this is in addition to short-term disability for birthing mothers, so for a typical maternity leave of 14 weeks, 12 weeks are at least partially paid.

Employee illness or injury leave. Employees now receive their full salary for up to four weeks. We'll then work with that employee to transition them to short-term disability, and if necessary, to long-term disability.

> *Tip:* Sometimes, an illness or injury doesn't have a clear onset date, and additional paid leave may be required. For example, someone may be attempting to work while balancing doctor visits in search of a diagnosis and treatment. Several weeks may go by before an employee realizes, or is told, they have a condition that qualifies for short-term disability. In other words, four weeks of paid leave can easily turn into eight weeks. This is why you should encourage your employees to keep lines of communication open with their manager and HR.

It's possible they may exceed the limits of your policy through no fault of their own; if so, you may want to consider making an exception in their case, as we did with Katrina.

Family caregiver leave. Employees may take four weeks of paid leave to care for an ill family member. We don't define who is or who isn't the employee's "family" because, in our view, that's up to the employee.[137] In real life, relationships aren't always defined by blood or proximity.

Benefits. Employees retain all of their benefits while on paid leave. Although FMLA only requires that employers provide employees on leave with health insurance coverage,[138] employees at Fire Engine RED continue to receive dental and vision coverage and their full company 401(k) contribution. They also earn vacation as if they were still working.

As you'll see in chapter 4.5, "Unpaid leave," we also introduced a new unpaid leave policy that's even more generous than the 12 weeks provided by FMLA.

We've got an advisory group for that

Because we want our employees to take full advantage of our benefits regarding family and medical leave policies, as well as the policies of the state they live in, we encourage our employees who are considering taking leave to meet with FLAG.

FLAG's current mission is to help employees get the most out of the benefits we offer based on their personal situations, goals, and location. An important part of that is helping employees understand how our policies (and their states' policies) overlap and interact with each other. FLAG helps answer questions like:

- What if an employee's state requires them to exhaust their employer-provided benefits first (as Massachusetts does)? (Our company asks employees who live in states that provide for paid family and medical leave to exhaust their state-provided benefits before tapping into their Fire Engine RED benefits.)

- Should an employee who lives in Washington, D.C., use Fire Engine RED's four-week full-pay family caregiver policy to care for a parent undergoing major surgery and lengthy recovery? Or, should the employee use Washington, D.C.'s six-week partial pay policy?

- How might an employee experiencing an at-risk pregnancy maximize her California and company benefits? (She would need to understand the state's separate disability and family bonding policies, as well as Fire Engine RED's short-term disability coverage and paid parental leave policy.)

In any case, FLAG is available to provide answers and tips on how to optimize an employee's paid leave benefits. However, the way an individual employee uses our paid leave policies is always up to them!

I'm proud to say that, after months of hard work, we now have one of the most progressive family and medical leave policies of any company I know of. In summary, we provide two months of paid leave to parents welcoming babies, one month of paid leave for employees to recover from an illness or injury, and one month of paid leave to care for an ill family member. As you'll see in chapter 4.5, "Unpaid leave," we also provide four months of unpaid leave for any of the circumstances covered under FMLA.

There are many good reasons to offer your employees paid family and medical leave—it's good for employee morale, productivity, and retention. Workers who take paid leave are more likely to return, and that lowers the costs of employee turnover.[139] For example, Katrina has been with us for eight years and is a top performer. My hope is that she spends the rest of her career at Fire Engine RED. Assuming she does, the additional weeks of paid leave she received will have been nominal over the course of a 30-year career. It's a great return on our company's investment in her; as you'll see in chapter 17, "Succession planning: Making sure your all-remote company is built to last," I have big plans for Katrina.

Bereavement

At Fire Engine RED, employees may take up to five days of paid leave due to the death of a family member or someone else close to them, such as a friend or even a friend's parent. And if employees need more time, all they have to do is ask their manager. (Some employees have needed more time because their families and friends live outside the United States.) We simply ask managers to bring these types of issues to our director of people before saying yes. This helps ensure that all employees in all departments are treated fairly. We wouldn't want one manager to say yes and another to say no. (By the way, we've never said no.)

Voting

I also recommend that you give your employees as much paid leave as they need to vote in any election. It's a great way to encourage civic engagement and a sense of community.

Since our company was founded in 2001, Fire Engine RED has always provided paid leave for voting. Prior to the 2018 midterm elections, I learned about Time to Vote (maketimetovote.org), a non-partisan organization of 400-plus companies that encourages voter turnout by making sure employees can take the time to vote. Naturally, we joined the organization, and I would encourage you to do the same. I'll tell you more about how voting has brought our team together in chapter 13.6, "Create bonding opportunities."

Jury duty

The amount of time off employers are required to provide for jury duty varies from state to state. To make things easy, we don't put any time restrictions on the amount of paid leave for jury service, and I'd recommend that you don't either. It's simply not worth the time creating, communicating, and administering different policies for those who live in different states.

Volunteering

Companies with a central office will often sponsor a local charity or organization. Because we're an all-remote company, we provide our employees with up to three hours (in a workday) of paid leave at a time, as desired, to volunteer in their own communities. This allows us to support a wide variety of charitable organizations.

Giving workers paid leave to volunteer is good for business. According to *Fortune* magazine, "By letting employees guide charitable efforts, [...] winning companies create high levels of commitment and pride among their teams."[140]

We encourage our employees to share stories and pictures of their volunteer efforts on our company Slack channel. Glenna recently wrote, "I had an opportunity to volunteer at the middle school this morning to talk to eighth-graders about the importance of reading and writing in my everyday work life. Thank you, Fire Engine RED, for allowing us to volunteer during our workday."

Amanda added, "I have been volunteering for about six months with a 'comfort dog' through my church. I take her to local nursing homes, hospitals, and schools. It has been wonderful to be able to use my volunteering time because the comfort dog team is always looking for more people to help during the day. I usually sign up for a two- to three-hour outing a week and just make up my time one evening a week. Thanks for letting us have the flexibility to go out and help others!"

And Emma shared, "Thank you for the opportunity to volunteer! I have enjoyed so much the opportunity to spend time with the kids in Avary's school, helping with the play production and taking photos of all the performers! My favorite part is getting a glimpse into the day-to-day and seeing Avary interact with her peers. I had a blast and feel very blessed!"

Life happens

Finally, when "life happens," we're there for our employees. I couldn't imagine asking my employees to use their vacation time to deal with some unexpected (and usually unpleasant) occurrence. Rather, we give our employees the time off they need to get things back on track (and be paid by the company while they're doing so). After all, such events don't meet the dictionary definition of a vacation: "An extended period of leisure and recreation, especially one spent away from home or in travelling."[141]

Nick, who lost power and was unable to work because he was in the path of a hurricane, said, "You have no idea how much stress FER takes off my shoulders when things like this happen." Meaghan said, "I love working for a company that bends over backwards to accommodate all that life throws at its employees, myself included!" And another employee shared, "Where else would you find such an understanding 'life happens' policy—everyone stands behind you and supports you when those events happen."

Employees have also used our "life happens" policy when:

- Their washing machine exploded and flooded their house.
- Their fiancée's car got stuck in a blizzard while on the freeway and had to be dug out.
- They accidently took their child's prescription medication instead of their own and were too "wired" to work the rest of the day.

- The power went out at their house due to a hurricane, tornado, or other natural disaster. (We'll even pay for employees and their families to stay in a hotel room if it's unsafe for them to stay in their home.)
- Their dog swallowed a tennis ball—whole—and had to be rushed to the vet. (Fortunately, the dog regurgitated the ball on the ride over.)

Paid leave summary

Here's a quick summary of the paid leave provided by Fire Engine RED:

Table 5. Fire Engine RED Paid Leave

Type	Amount of Paid Leave
Holidays	Minimum of 10 days per year
Vacation	3 to 5 weeks per year
Out	Up to 2 hours per day, as needed
Sick	Unlimited
Medical Appointments and Procedures	Unlimited
Medical Leave	4 weeks
Short-term Disability	Up to 11 weeks
Short-term Disability (Maternity)	Up to 8 weeks (depends on the type of delivery)
Parental Leave	8 weeks
Family Caregiver Leave	4 weeks
Bereavement	Up to 5 days; more as needed
Voting	As needed
Jury Duty	As needed
Volunteering	Up to 3 hours (in a workday), as desired
Life Happens	As needed

By the way, vacation time is the only type of time off we track in our HR system. With regard to the other types of paid leave, we just ask employees to mark the company calendar accordingly, so we know not to schedule them for meetings at those times!

Do people abuse our flexible policies? No. That's because the people we hire share the company's values; they're *invested* in the company and want to do right by it, not exploit our trust and generosity.

So how do you know you have the right paid leave policy? When people stop asking you for more time off and/or to make exceptions to your current policy. I haven't heard a peep since we implemented ours!

4.5 Unpaid leave

Previously, FMLA served as our "baseline" with regard to unpaid leave, allowing employees to take up to 12 weeks of unpaid leave, as needed. See the "Family and medical leave" section in chapter 4.1, "Mandatory benefits."

As part of our new family and medical leave policy, we offer a total of 26 weeks (equivalent to 6 months) of job-protected leave. This 26 weeks of total leave runs concurrently with our paid leave policies and can be taken over a 12-month time period. For example, let's say an employee were to use our new eight-week paid parental leave policy (described above), they could take up to 18 additional weeks of unpaid leave, for a combined 26 weeks.

Chapter 5
Recruiting, interviewing, and hiring: How to do it all virtually

One of the most important things you can do to ensure the growth and prosperity of your all-remote business is to hire the right employees from the very start. However, building a fully remote workforce can be especially challenging if you have little or no experience in hiring remote workers.

As I've said throughout this book, one of the biggest advantages of a distributed company is that you'll have access to a much larger talent pool because you'll be able to hire people no matter where they live. But how exactly can you best take advantage of this benefit?

In this chapter, I'll share some practical tips on recruiting, interviewing, and hiring remotely, and I'll take you step by step through our time-tested processes for building an all-remote workforce. These processes, which we've developed over the past two decades, have helped us grow and retain our team. I'll also discuss how you can actually assess whether or not a potential hire is a "fit" for your company without ever meeting them in person!

However, you should know that these processes are by no means set in stone. We're continually refining our remote hiring processes based on the feedback we receive from our new hires, hiring managers, and team members.

As I mentioned in the introduction to this book, Fire Engine RED's human resources department is called People, Places, and Perks (P3). However, I'll use "HR" throughout this chapter to avoid any confusion.

5.1 Increase your odds of landing top talent

How do you ensure that the best candidates select your fully distributed company? Here's my advice, based on my nearly 20 years of experience running an all-remote team.

- **Hire an experienced HR professional to head up your recruiting and hiring processes.** As soon as possible, hire an HR pro with recruiting and hiring experience to "own" your processes. Our director of people oversees recruiting, interviewing, and hiring of new employees;

serves as a sounding board for hiring managers; and (when asked) stays in touch with the most promising candidates throughout the recruiting process. Early on, we had a number of different people pinch-hitting in this role, which led to inefficiencies and mistakes that caused us to miss out on the best candidates and extend job offers to the wrong people.

- **Join the Society for Human Resource Management (SHRM).** As a member of SHRM (www.shrm.org), you'll have access to a host of HR-related resources and tools, including an HR helpline. We've found SHRM to be an invaluable resource given today's complex, ever-changing HR landscape. An individual SHRM membership costs just $209 per year. (Our director of people is a member.)

- **Review and improve your website with job seekers in mind.** Your website will be one of the first stops for job seekers who want to know more about your company. Make sure it paints an accurate, authentic picture of your company culture (especially in the About Us and Careers sections); it's a great way to attract candidates who are the right fit for your company culture.

- **Make sure your interview team is ready to focus.** The best candidates go fast! We've found that the ideal length of time for identifying, interviewing, and hiring a candidate is four to six weeks. Therefore, it's better not to start the recruiting process until everyone on your interview team has the time to focus on it.

- **Take job descriptions seriously.** A clearly thought out, well-written job description is an excellent way to make a great first impression on job seekers. And the better the job description, the more likely you are to receive applications from the right candidates. (More about the importance of job descriptions later in this chapter.)

- **Create a recruiting guide.** You should define and document your recruiting, interviewing, and hiring processes in a recruiting guide. Doing so will make it easier for your team to follow your processes and will help ensure you hire the right candidate for an open position.

- **Roll out the RED carpet for job applicants.** Competition is fierce for top talent. To give your company an advantage, you should make sure the candidates feel valued. Here's how:

- **Acknowledge the receipt of each application immediately.** Not only is it easy to acknowledge the receipt of an application with a friendly auto-reply message, it's also the right thing to do. Plus, it's likely to prevent your HR department from being flooded with emails from candidates asking if your company received their application.

- **Send referrals a personalized response.** I recommend that you include a question on your online job application asking candidates if they were referred by someone in your company. Identifying applicants who are referrals will allow you to send them more personalized communications and thank the team member(s) who referred them. As I'll tell you in chapter 5.2, "Consider internal and external candidates," 70 percent of our current employees were referrals from team members.

- **Send a personalized response to applicants who are clients or former clients of your company's.** Again, I recommend that you include a question on your application asking applicants if they are a current or former client of your company. You don't want to overlook current or former clients. Such candidates usually have exceptional industry knowledge and are familiar with your company's business model and culture. Want proof that clients are a great source for talent? Approximately 12 percent of our current employees worked for one of our clients or former clients before they joined our company!

♦ **Have the hiring manager review every application.** Many companies use software to scan job applications and resumes for keywords or have HR take the first pass through them. Because most of our positions require specialized experience and skills, we believe it makes better sense for our hiring managers, who have in-depth knowledge of the job requirements, to personally review each application. In addition, we believe that every application tells a unique story, and our hiring managers may spot something compelling that HR software (or even HR) may miss.

- **Decide and respond promptly.** Most people would rather have a definitive "no" than be left hanging indefinitely. That's why I recommend you get back to each applicant within three business days of receiving their application to let them know if they've been selected for a phone screen.

- **Share your benefits information up front.** I would also encourage you to provide all candidates with a detailed description of your benefits package prior to their phone screen. We started doing this after a top candidate declined our offer because we have a high-deductible healthcare plan. Although this was an isolated incident, we don't ever want to go through the entire process again only to discover there was a deal breaker from the very beginning.

- **Have the hiring manager conduct the initial phone screen.** At most companies, an internal or external recruiter does the initial screen. At Fire Engine RED, not only do our hiring managers screen the applications but they also conduct the initial screen with candidates. This is because the initial screen focuses primarily on cultural fit, and we believe the hiring manager is most qualified to determine if the candidate is a fit—not just for the company but also for the department the candidate would be joining.

♦ **Follow up quickly after the phone screen.** As soon as possible, you should update each candidate on whether or not they'll move to the next round of the interview process. Since our hiring managers determine whether to move a candidate to the next round right after the phone screen, we let each candidate know of our decision within 24 hours of making it.

♦ **Follow up quickly after each interview round.** As candidates move through the interview process, it can take more than 24 hours to evaluate them. So, here's what I recommend. At the end of each interview round, let each candidate know when they can expect to hear back from you. Then be sure to get back to them within that time frame.

♦ **Have HR stay in touch with top candidates.** Because good candidates go quickly, you may want to have a member of your HR team stay in touch with the most promising candidates as interview rounds progress, especially if your process is a lengthy one or somehow gets delayed. Candidates will appreciate the additional communication.

Obviously, you'll have to pass on a great number of candidates. Here are a couple of tips on what *not* to do when saying "no."

- Don't ruin a candidate's weekend by giving them bad news on a Friday.

- Don't mislead them by saying that you'll "keep their application or resume on file in case other opportunities arise" unless you actually mean it. It's always better to be honest.

5.2 Consider internal and external candidates

The Society for Human Resource Management (SHRM) refers to the "build vs. buy" approaches to hiring (build =

hire from within, buy = hire from the outside) and notes that successful companies do both.[142] I strongly agree. Here's my advice on how to think about both types of candidates.

Internal candidates

Whenever we can, we prefer to promote or transfer an internal candidate into an open or new position.

Hiring from within is a great way to show your team that it's possible to advance their careers without having to leave your company. It also costs less, decreases the time your company spends on hiring and onboarding, and boosts employee engagement.[143] Perhaps best of all, it involves fewer risks because you already know that an internal candidate is a cultural fit for your company!

We have an excellent track record with regard to hiring and promoting internal candidates. For example, five former members of our client care team are now working in different capacities than when they first joined our company. (Their current roles are VP of products, director of client happiness, designer, assistant controller, and lead quality engineer.)

In addition, when it comes to our leaders, three of our four vice presidents and 12 of our 15 directors were promoted from within.

So, how do people get promoted at Fire Engine RED? They:

- Continually add to their skill set.
- Ask for more and take on more.
- Identify problems that need fixing, develop solutions, and implement those solutions.
- Contribute to boosting the company's bottom line.

And even though hiring or promoting an internal candidate usually creates another opening that our managers need to fill, our managers are genuinely excited when their direct reports move into new roles or receive promotions. They see it as a win for their direct report, for the company, and for themselves.

So, what happens to team morale and engagement when several team members compete against one another for an open position or promotion? At Fire Engine RED, it's actually quite rare that we have multiple internal candidates vying for the same position. That's because our goal is to provide everyone with their own career path, rather than to pit people against one another. More about career paths in chapter 13.3, "Show them a career path."

The last time one of our team members competed against another team member for an open position was in 2014. And, in a way, they *both* got the job. One person landed the initial opening. Then, several months later, a similar position came open, and we filled it with the other team member!

External candidates

Only if we determine there are no qualified candidates already within Fire Engine RED do we begin the search for external candidates. Some examples of our external hires include our current creative director, communications director, and software engineering manager.

Start with referrals

As an all-remote company, your top source for talent will most likely be employee referrals. In fact, more than 70 percent of our current employees were referred to Fire Engine RED by a team member or "friend" of our company. As Mark, our director of client care operations, put it, "I know I didn't appear qualified 'on paper.' I'm so happy I wasn't automatically eliminated from consideration by software. Instead, you gave me an opportunity because I was a referral. It's an example of how seriously FER takes referrals from team members."

We've also found that even when a team member turns out not to be the right fit for our company, they may still be a great source of referrals. For example, nearly a decade ago, we hired someone who was talented but wasn't a match for our company culture. Still, during her short tenure at Fire Engine RED, this person referred four talented team members to us, all of whom are still with our company today!

We've also had particular success in hiring relatives of current team members. At the moment, our team includes a wife and husband (Meaghan, copy manager and operations analyst, and David, director of client care). We also have two brothers (Blake, lead quality engineer, and Robert, assistant controller) and a mother and daughter (Joanna, business operations manager, and Jaci, database and research intern). We also have two sisters—our director of people, Jamie, is my sister. In addition, Jamie's and my nephews, Ben and Will, have spent the past three summers interning at Fire Engine RED.

A word of advice. If you do hire relatives, you need to consider the consequences of letting someone's relative go. We've only had to do this once, with a team member who was the daughter of one of our directors. After working for us for approximately two years, she wanted to move to Europe full time and continue working for us. However, because of her performance while working overseas the previous summer, we denied her request.

Eventually, we found out that she went ahead and moved to Europe anyway. (The IP address she was using revealed that she was not in the U.S.) We parted ways because we felt we could no longer trust her. As I've mentioned several times, trust between a company and its team members is essential in a virtual workplace. By the way, within a year, her father left our company.

5.3 Recruit and interview the all-remote way

Now let's take a step-by-step look at how we recruit full-time employees.

Before posting the opening

Once the hiring manager has identified a need, they need to complete the steps below prior to posting the job opening.

Determine the title, general responsibilities, and salary range for the position. While it's relatively easy for the hiring manager to have a preliminary title and general responsibilities in mind for the position, coming up with a salary range for a fully remote position takes more time. That's because salaries can vary substantially by location. Therefore, we ask the hiring manager to look at salaries for similar positions within the company (if any exist) and then research salaries for comparable jobs in three to five markets.

> *Tip:* We've found that Glassdoor (www.glassdoor.com), Indeed (www.indeed.com), and Robert Half (www.roberthalf.com) are good external sources for salary information.

However, this can be more difficult than you think. Rarely do the published results of salary surveys go into specifics about job duties. For example, a director of operations position could have very different responsibilities from one company to the next, and as a result, have very different salaries.

Get approval to hire. The hiring manager meets with the director of people, the department's EVP/C-level officer, the CFO, and the CEO (me) to get approval to hire. During this meeting, we discuss whether there's a qualified internal candidate for the position.

Because we're a relatively small company, we usually know if one of our current team members is qualified for the position. If we identify a potential candidate, the hiring manager discusses the opportunity with the team member's manager as a courtesy. Then they reach out to the team member directly. If the team member is interested, we won't even post the job opening.

> *Tip:* If there's a viable internal candidate, we skip to an "abridged" version of our standard interview process—interviews with the hiring manager, the two or three team members they'd be working closely with, and the EVP/C-level officer, in that order. (See the section "Interviewing process" below for details on the steps we typically follow.)

Create a job description. After the position is approved, the hiring manager creates a job description. To ensure consistency in all company job postings, we provide our hiring managers with a job description template. The template requires that each job description include the following:

- Job title
- Position summary
- Reporting structure
- List of responsibilities
- List of qualifications
- List of desired personal attributes

For help with content, we encourage our hiring managers to consult our job description library (on our intranet), which includes job descriptions of more than 50 positions. We also refer them to Glassdoor (www.glassdoor.com), Google (www.google.com), Indeed (www.indeed.com), and our competitors' job postings for examples of job descriptions.

Select team members to conduct the team interview. The hiring manager then selects two to three team members, generally people who will work closely with the new hire, to conduct the team interview.

Get feedback on the job description from the interview team. Next, the hiring manager asks the interview team to provide feedback on the job description. This step ensures that everyone on the interview team understands the role the hiring manager is trying to fill.

Have the communications director review the job description. Once the hiring manager has gathered input from the interview team, they ask our communications director to review and edit the job description for consistency and style. Doing so helps ensure our job descriptions are consistent with our company's branding and messaging strategies.

Get the job description approved by the director of people and the CEO. Next, the hiring manager meets with the director of people and me to get our final approval on the job description.

Finalize the details. Once the job description has been approved, the hiring manager completes and submits our recruiting questionnaire (a web-based form) to the director of people. This form provides the director of people with the final information she needs to post the position and ensures that nothing gets missed in back-and-forth email exchanges.

Our recruiting questionnaire asks for:

- The desired job posting date.
- Any minimum requirements (prior admissions experience, enterprise system experience, etc.) for the position.
- Any additional requirements (writing sample, design portfolio, coding sample, etc.) for the position.
- The names of the people on the interview team.

From there, the director of people customizes the job application accordingly.

> *Tip:* If you want to limit applications to U.S. job seekers, be sure to add "this is a full-time, remote position in the U.S." to your job posting. Even so, you'll probably still get dozens of applications from non-U.S. job seekers, like we do. To save time, we include a question on our application that asks applicants "Do you live in the U.S.?" We then use our applicant tracking system to filter out the ones that say "no." (This is the one instance where we do use our ATS's scanning technology.) This is yet another reason why I encourage you to implement an applicant tracking system as soon as possible.

Have the interview team meet with the director of people. Prior to posting the job description, the hiring manager and members of the interview team meet with the director of people to ensure everyone's on the same page. This meeting is a critical step, especially for those team members who may be serving on an interview team for the first time. It helps ensure consistency and professionalism throughout the recruiting and interviewing process and shows our team members just how seriously we take it.

During the meeting, the director of people then reviews the interview process, provides tips on using our applicant tracking system, and suggests potential interview questions. Most importantly, she shares "lessons learned," with the hiring manager and the interview team, including:

Advice for the hiring manager.

- Cover letters matter, so be sure to read each applicant's. It can demonstrate that the applicant has taken the time to educate themselves about our offerings and culture (or reveal if we're just another company on their list).

- It's okay to pass on a candidate simply because their resume has typos, misspellings, etc. In fact, we strongly encourage our hiring managers to screen out these applicants and not waste time interviewing them. Typos tell us something about a candidate's level of care and attention to detail—two qualities that are must-haves for Fire Engine RED team members.

- Before scheduling a phone screen with an applicant, we ask our hiring manager to search the applicant's name on Google, LinkedIn, and various social media sites. This helps us verify the applicant's basic information and gives us a high-level snapshot of who they are.

- Make sure the candidates are asked different questions at each stage in the process. It's a better experience for candidates when they're asked a variety of questions, rather than the same questions in each successive interview. It's also a more effective way of getting to know a candidate as well as their strengths and weaknesses.

- Job descriptions and positions can "evolve" to suit an exceptional applicant. For example, if we discover that someone is too "senior-level" for an open position, we may want to redefine the position rather than automatically ruling the applicant out. We did this recently with an open position on our data team. When we were interviewing Elizabeth, she was clearly overqualified, so we reworked the job description, added responsibilities to it, and hired her. But just a few months later, she'd outgrown the redefined position. What did we do? We promoted her! In any event, I'm so happy we didn't turn Elizabeth away initially because she was overqualified for the original position; it was much better to redefine the position (twice!) than to let someone so talented as Elizabeth slip away.

Advice for the hiring manager *and* interview team.

- Pay close attention to each candidate's personality and "soft" skills. Think about whether or not you'd want to work with this person every day and also how they might interact with other team members. Someone can have outstanding "hard" skills (coding, for example) and not have the "soft" skills to be a good fit for our company culture.

- Look and listen for qualities that show a candidate will be a good fit for remote work, such as being a self-starter, an effective communicator, and a good team player.

- If you're finding you have to "oversell" the position and/or our company, that's a warning sign that the candidate probably isn't a good fit for our company.

- You should express any concerns you may have about a candidate, even if the hiring manager, or another member of the interview team, thinks the candidate walks on (virtual) water. A couple of times at our company, an interviewer deferred to the hiring manager instead of expressing their concerns about a candidate. Had they spoken up, we likely wouldn't have made the wrong hiring decision. In other words, trust your instincts and speak up if something doesn't feel or sound right.

- Expect the unexpected! We once had a candidate who let loose a long string of profanity during their interview. Needless to say, they didn't get the job.

- Even if you determine that a candidate is not a fit, always be polite and professional. It's always best to follow the Golden Rule.

At the end of the meeting, the director of people asks the hiring manager if they're ready to begin the recruiting, interviewing, and hiring process. If the answer is "yes," the director of people confirms the job posting date and then posts the position.

Posting the opening

As stated in chapter 3.11, "Implement the right systems," an applicant tracking system (ATS) is a must-have. An ATS will enable you to standardize and streamline your screening, interviewing, and hiring processes. Ours (JazzHR) also makes it easy to post our job openings on the Careers page of our website, our Facebook (www.facebook.com/fireengineredinc/) and Twitter (@185red), and 20-plus free job boards, including FlexJobs (www.flexjobs.com), Glassdoor (www.glassdoor.com), Indeed (www.indeed.com), LinkedIn (www.linkedin.com), and ZipRecruiter (www.ziprecruiter.com).

> *Tip:* Although the free job board listings have worked well for us, for a fee you can increase the visibility of your postings on the job sites of your choice.

To help generate referrals from our team members, we also post all job openings internally on our company-wide Slack channel the same day we post them externally. This gives our team members all the information they need about the role to share it with qualified people in their network.

Expect an avalanche of applications

As an all-remote company, you're likely to receive an overwhelming number of applications as soon as you post the position—from everywhere and anywhere. In just a matter of days, we typically receive as many as 400 applications for each open position!

I used to wonder why we received so many applications so quickly, many of them directly through the Careers page on our website. While interviewing team members for this book, I was amused when some of them confessed to "stalking" our Careers page for open positions, and then "pouncing" (my word, not theirs) on any opening that matched (or didn't) their experience and skill set as soon as we posted a position.

Jason 3 shared, "I was working in admissions at a community college. I read some great things about Fire Engine RED and its culture, and knew I had to work here. I liked how much information was shared on the website. No other company I researched seemed as transparent. Although there weren't any job openings that were right for me, I wanted to work at FER so badly I applied for a couple of jobs anyway, and, of course, I didn't get them. After about four months of this, I saw a position on the data team that was exactly the type of position I was looking for and was qualified for. I applied and interviewed and got the job!" He laughed and added, "Yes, I was definitely 'stalking' the Fire Engine RED site!"

I'm so glad that Jason 3 continued to "stalk" our site and didn't get discouraged because he's become one of our data all-stars, with an ever-growing fan base among our clients.

Look for people who fit your culture and values

A key to our success has been recruiting in line with our company values, including Integrity, Empathy, and Teamwork. We've found that a good fit leads to higher retention. So, I recommend you focus on fit first.

The people we've hired who've been the most successful:

- Think like owners and act in the best interest of the company at all times.
- Have exceptional judgment.
- Are self-motivated.
- Take initiative.
- Are willing to step outside their comfort zone and take on new challenges.
- Have excellent time-management skills.
- Know how to prioritize.
- Communicate effectively, both verbally and in writing.
- Are proactive and responsive to clients and other team members.
- Meet client and internal deadlines without "nudges."
- Acknowledge and own their mistakes.
- Speak up when something's not right.

- Are focused on results.
- Share praise and credit freely.
- Keep up with trends related to their expertise and our industry.

As a fully distributed company, you'll also want to focus not only on cultural fit but also on hiring people who are a fit for the all-remote work environment. I think we've done a pretty good job with this. In our nearly 20 years in business, only three people have left our company because they wanted to go back to working in an office.

Keep in mind, cultural fit works both ways. Employees today want to work for companies that share *their* values.

As Nicole shared, "I mentioned in my cover letter that I thought I'd be a good cultural fit based on what I read on the website. When I interviewed and learned more about the culture and then was eventually hired, I was happy and relieved to see firsthand that Fire Engine RED meant what they said about their culture." Russell added, "The big thing for me was your blog post[144] where you made it clear that Fire Engine RED isn't for sale and gave really good reasons why. After working at a company through two transitions to new ownership structures, I found your emphatic 'no' to a sale to be really refreshing."

Brendan said, "There was far more effort put into making sure someone was a cultural fit than I'd ever experienced, and that was particularly poignant coming from a position where my direct supervisor and I were NOT a good 'cultural fit' for each other!" Similarly, Ben mentioned, "I had a number of conversations with Jim [(hiring manager)] during the interview process, in which he was incredibly helpful in making sure I understood the Fire Engine RED culture."

And Bill—a former executive director of enrollment management at Vanderbilt University who later joined Fire Engine RED—had this to say about our culture: "So many companies in our field are staffed and led by executives with little or no experience in education, looking for a way to make money on the frenzy of high-stakes admission. Fire Engine RED is the exception: [We're] led by a team of colleagues from education who have a deep desire to help colleges succeed for the betterment of our educational enterprise and society's common good." And that's exactly why he joined Fire Engine RED!

Generalists first, specialists later

When you're in the early stages of starting your all-remote company, I recommend that you hire generalists who are flexible and comfortable wearing many hats. However, to scale your company, you'll eventually need to hire specialists—people with deep experience in particular areas, such as finance, technology, and data services.

Lesson learned: As your company grows, the generalists you've hired will likely need to transition into more specialized roles. Unfortunately, everyone won't be able to do so. I estimate that approximately 40 percent of our early hires were not able to make the transition.

The more experience, the better

You may be tempted to hire entry-level candidates because their salary requirements can be far more affordable. Remember, though, entry-level candidates will need to be trained and mentored by experienced managers and will have the added challenge of getting up to speed in an all-remote work environment. So, before you make an entry-level hire, ask yourself if your company has the time and resources to devote to their development. As I'll discuss in chapter 10, "Player-coaches: The best kind of remote managers," our managers are player-coaches with many responsibilities of their own and as a result, have little time for training.

In my opinion, the better approach is to hire the most experienced people you can afford. At Fire Engine RED, we typically hire people who have at least five years' worth of experience. This is because we put a premium on productivity and have found that the more experience a candidate has, the more productive they are right out of the gate. More about productivity in chapter 12,

"Maximizing and measuring productivity at your all-remote company."

> *Tip:* You should think seriously about whether or not a degree is truly a requirement for a position. By limiting your search to only people with degrees, you could be missing out on some amazing talent. Given that Fire Engine RED serves the education market, you may find it surprising that we don't require a college degree as a condition of employment. We have several talented team members without degrees who are among our top performers.

Interviewing process

As stated above, we've found that the ideal length of time for identifying, interviewing, and hiring a candidate is four to six weeks.

For most of our open positions, it's simply not cost-effective to interview the front-runners (or even a final candidate) in person. That's because the hiring manager, interview team, and candidates are usually spread across the country. The exception is when we're hiring an EVP or C-level officer. More about how we handle senior leadership hires in chapter 7, "Hiring leaders: Building a fully remote leadership team."

For each open position, we typically conduct five rounds of *audio-only* interviews. Although we've conducted video interviews sporadically over the years, in our experience, audio interviews (conducted usually by phone) work better because people tend to listen more carefully. Another benefit of audio-only interviewing is that it reduces the possibility of an interviewer forming a bias based on a candidate's physical appearance or surroundings.

> *Lesson learned:* As it turns out, many of our team members preferred our audio-only interview format when they were interviewing with our company. As Amy shared, "I'm so happy you didn't require me to get dressed up and situated for a video interview, since there's never been a need for me to do a video call here!"

The final time we did video interviews for a position, the person we hired was a disaster and only lasted 10 days (nine days too long). Jim, our executive vice president of enrollment software, stepped in for a vacationing colleague to interview a candidate for a job in another department. Going into the interview, Jim knew that the person he was about to speak to was the interview team's leading candidate. Actually, let's have Jim tell the story:

"Everyone had interviewed this candidate over video chat and loved him. I only talked to him on the phone. I could tell he wasn't prepared. He said he had to go out to his car while we were talking, and then it sounded like he was walking through a wind tunnel. When I referred to a call he had received earlier in the day from our director of people, he told me he didn't know that it was Jamie who'd called him, asking, 'Oh, was that the lady from HR I talked to?' Anyway, I had a strong gut feeling that this guy was going to be a disaster, but I wanted to be a team player, so despite my concerns, I decided to defer to the rest of the interview team. In hindsight, I should have shouted my concerns from the rooftops about how bad this guy was, but I was reluctant to because I didn't want to be a spoiler." (This is one such occasion when you *don't* want your team members to be team players. It's also a good example of how video interviews don't necessarily yield the right hires.)

> *Tip #1:* To prevent groupthink from setting in, we now ask anyone who's interviewed a candidate to avoid communicating with other interviewers about that candidate. Instead, we ask them to provide a rating and comments on a "scorecard" in our applicant tracking system immediately after each interview. Only the hiring manager and the director of people have access to the scorecards.

> *Tip #2:* There will be times when it's imperative that you meet with a candidate in person. For example, if you're hiring someone for your

leadership team, you, as CEO, should definitely interview the finalist face-to-face. You'll be working closely with them, so it's essential for you to make sure the candidate is a fit for your company in general, and for your leadership team in particular. This may be a bit costly, but I believe it's well worth it in terms of maximizing your chances of hiring a great fit—and minimizing the risk involved with hiring for a C-level, EVP, or other leadership role.

Next, let's look at each of our interview rounds in detail.

Initial screen. The hiring manager screens five to seven candidates to determine if they're a "fit" for our company culture, remote workplace, and their department. The initial screen usually lasts 30 minutes.

During this call, the hiring manager asks the candidate their desired salary range. Note that in some cities (including mine, Philadelphia) and states, it's actually illegal to ask a candidate about their current salary or pay history.[145] So, I recommend you don't, no matter where they live. Plus, basing a candidate's salary offer on their past salary can perpetuate a pay gap. (Some applicants may volunteer information on their salary history or current salary, and that's fine. Just don't ask them for the information.)

Tip: As part of the initial screen, be sure to explain that your all-remote company has actual office hours (assuming it does; see chapter 3.12, "Determine your company's office hours"). Several years ago, one of our new team members never seemed to be available during work hours, and we suspected he thought his job at Fire Engine RED was something he could do in his free time. (Yes, this was the guy that Jim was concerned about, the one who was only with us for 10 days.) So, while we do offer flexibility, we don't offer "flex time" as it's often defined.

Team interview. Next, two or more team members who will work closely with the person who's hired, interview three or four of the candidates. This interview focuses primarily on the candidate's skill set and usually lasts 60–90 minutes.

Tip: Prior to this interview, I suggest you provide each candidate with your company's organizational chart so they can see the reporting structure for the department they'd be joining and who's who on the interview team. You can find a copy of our org chart in the Resources section of the *Fully Remote* website (www.fully-remote-book.com).

Hiring manager interview. During this interview, the hiring manager meets with two to three candidates for an in-depth discussion about the position, their experience, and their skill set. This is the second time the hiring manager meets with the candidate, and the interview typically takes 60 minutes.

Senior leader interview. As another check for overall fit, and for any red flags that might have been missed, the department's EVP/C-level officer interviews one or two candidates. This interview typically takes, well, as long as it takes, because it's such a crucial milestone in the process.

Director of people interview. At this stage, our director of people interviews the leading candidate. This interview with the director of people typically takes 60–90 minutes and is the final interview in our process.

As with the senior leader interview, the focus is on fit and on making sure any potential issues were not overlooked by the previous interviewers because they were overly impressed by the candidate's experience and skill set. The director of people also discusses our benefits package.

> *Tip:* It can be especially hard for candidates who are changing industries or switching from a nonprofit (such as a college) to a corporate workplace (or vice versa) to compare the benefit plan we offer to their current benefits package. This

is where our director of people's strong communication skills have been vital. Our director of people spends as much time as required to make sure each candidate completely understands the benefits package we're offering.

The director of people also tells the candidate during the interview process when and how often they'll be paid. It's especially important that the candidate receive this information during the interview process because we pay our employees once a month, which is the least common time frame for paying people.[146] Although it can take some people time to get used to receiving only 12 paychecks per year, we've found that once they get used to it, they like it because it makes it easier for them to plan and budget. It's also consistent with our company value of Simplicity.

Lesson learned: We used to finish the interview process with our "Why you don't want to work here" call with the leading candidate. The idea was for three or four team members from across the company to tell the potential hire the good, the bad, and the ugly about working remotely and working at Fire Engine RED.

The original idea was to give the candidate one last chance to hear about the downside of remote work from people who'd been through it. However, our ever-positive team members began spinning the call into the "Why you *absolutely do* want to work here" call! They offered helpful tips and advice on how to be effective and happy working from home. All of this was great information, but as the call no longer served as a final "fail-safe" in determining if someone was a fit for the remote-work style, we dropped it.

After the director of people meets with the leading candidate, she provides the hiring manager with her feedback and points out any potential "showstoppers." She then asks the hiring manager if they are ready to make the candidate an offer. Usually, it's a resounding yes!

Before extending an offer

Checking references

Once we've selected our top candidate, we ask them for three references. The hiring manager then contacts their references for a quick phone chat. To make it easier for our hiring managers, we provide them a list of questions to ask. (We skip this step for internal candidates and referrals.)

Doing a background check

Here's why we don't do background checks. For one thing, more than 70 percent of our new hires are referrals. Also, whenever an employee at Fire Engine RED hasn't worked out, it wasn't because of something a background check would have uncovered.

> *Tip:* A background check could raise questions (and/or eyebrows), or even bias someone on the interview team, which could put the candidate's job offer in jeopardy over, say, a youthful indiscretion. For example, while in college, one of our team members was arrested for rioting during a football weekend. Because we don't do background checks, we hired him without knowing it, and today he's one of our company's top performers. How did I learn about this? The team member told me about it a year after he was hired, at lunch during a conference. He even showed me a video of the incident on YouTube!

Sure, we do Google people, but I can't imagine spending the time, effort, and money to do background checks. (And, if we did, we'd have to do them for everyone, no exceptions.)

Determining the right salary

Once we have a finalist, we look at their years of experience and any professional certifications (depending on the position) they may have. We also consider the candidate's desired salary range, as their expectations will likely depend on where they live. For example, it's understandable that a software engineer in New York City would have a different salary range than a software engineer who lives in Billings, Montana. On several occasions, we've even paid people above their desired salary range because they had been working in an industry, such as higher education, where salaries tend to be lower.

Determining the right salary for a candidate is more of an art than a science. When setting a salary, I ask my managers to keep this in mind: If everyone's salary became visible to everyone on the team, could we stand by each team member's salary? This helps everyone get on the same page and puts our company value of Fairness front and center.

As we discussed back in chapter 2.1, "How companies benefit," we do not reduce a new hire's salary by the amount that they're likely to save by working remotely. We hope the potential savings provides the candidate with yet another reason to join our team.

Making an offer

Once the hiring manager receives approval on the salary (from their department's EVP/C-level officer, the director of people, the CFO, and me), we'll proceed to the offer stage.

Verbal offer

The hiring manager contacts the candidate by phone with a verbal job offer. During the call, the hiring manager reviews the job title, salary, reporting structure, and start date with the candidate. If, at this time, the candidate wants to negotiate salary, we ask the hiring manager to consult with the director of people and their department's EVP/C-level officer. (It's possible the CFO and I will be brought into the conversation as well.) Once this discussion has taken place, the hiring manager updates the candidate on our decision. In any case, once a candidate agrees to the verbal offer, the hiring manager lets them know a formal written offer will be forthcoming from the director of people.

> *Tip:* I recommend you provide the candidate with a fair and thoughtfully considered salary offer from the start. We've found that doing so prevents us from having to go back and forth on a salary amount with them. Personally, I want to avoid having to negotiate with a candidate, as it feels to me like we're starting our business relationship on an adversarial note. I also don't want some team members to be paid more simply because they're better negotiators. That's not a skill we're hiring for.

Written offer and employment agreement

Within 24 hours, the director of people will send the candidate a written offer as well as our employment agreement—which defines the relationship between our company and the employee, setting forth the rights, responsibilities, and obligations of both.[147] For example, the offer letter covers the new hire's total compensation (salary, benefits, and vacation). The employment agreement outlines the company's confidentiality restrictions[148] and includes language indicating we're an "at-will" employer, meaning either we or the employee can terminate their employment at any time. In addition, the employment agreement states that the new hire's place of employment is their own home address.

The big finish

We provide the candidate with two business days to sign and return the written offer and employment agreement. We never set a Friday deadline for them; that way, if they decline our offer (which, in the case of Fire Engine RED, happens very rarely), they haven't spoiled *our* weekend!

If they sign, everyone celebrates and congratulates the hiring manager and the interview team. If they don't, the hiring manager discusses next steps with the director of people.

> *Tip:* I strongly recommend you don't say "no" to your runner-up until after the leading candidate

accepts your offer. If the top candidate doesn't accept our offer, we go back and reconsider the runner-up, possibly interviewing them again. A few of the times when it didn't work out with our first choice, we hired the runner-up, and it's worked out fabulously!

5.4 Hiring contractors

From time to time, your company may have a temporary need. In such cases, you may wish to hire a contract worker instead of adding a full-time employee.

What's the difference between hiring a contractor and a full-time employee? Generally speaking, contractors, unlike full-time employees, are supposed to be *temporary* additions to your workforce. Typically, contractors are hired for anywhere from six months to a year.

> *Tip:* Even though a contractor will not be with you for the long term, you still want them to be a good fit for your company. A contractor who's a bad fit can have an adverse impact on your company culture, no matter where, or in what capacity, they're working.

Let's talk about a few of the most common ways to add contract workers to your team. For one, you can hire an *independent contractor* (often referred to as a "1099 contractor") directly. Or, you can add a contract worker through a *professional services company.*

> *Tip:* Many independent contractors and professional services companies will likely want to negotiate terms, so it's best to express your preferred terms at the start of any discussions. Therefore, I recommend that you work with your attorney to create templates for a Master Independent Contractor Agreement (MICA) or a Master Services Agreement (MSA), respectively. You should also have your attorney create a Statement of Work (SoW) template. While the MICA and MSA cover broader aspects of the business relationship, the SoW specifies the terms of a particular body of work to be completed. Keep in mind, you can have multiple Statements of Work under the same terms of a MICA or MSA.

Hiring directly

U.S.-based contractors

When hiring a U.S.-based contractor, you'll want to gather information from them, via a Master Independent Contractor Agreement (MICA). A completed MICA should include the following information about the contractor:

- Contact information
- Business entity information (if applicable)

- Tax Identification Number (EIN if they're set up as a business entity, or Social Security number if they're not)
- Start date (and end date, if known)
- Hourly or project rate
- Notice period for ending the contract (ours is 30 days)

You'll also want to send the contractor a Statement of Work, which lists the services the contractor will provide. As noted above, you can create multiple Statements of Work under the same terms of a single MICA.

> *Tip #1:* The IRS and Department of Labor are particularly critical of the common practice of hiring individuals as "contractors" when they really should be classified as employees. They are aggressive about prosecuting companies that violate these rules, and contractors may also have a claim (or even a class action case) for back benefits. Therefore, it's important to review the proper classification with your accountant and attorney. Ideally, all contractors working for you will be separate legal business entities (such as an LLC).

> *Tip #2:* You should also require contractors to purchase their own business owner's Errors & Omissions (E&O) insurance. We ask contractors to

carry $1 million in E&O because our own insurance coverage requires it. The contractor should also name your company as a "co-insured" on the policy and send you a certificate of insurance coverage.

If you hire a contractor directly, you pay them a consulting fee and provide them with a 1099 form at the end of the calendar year. They are responsible for paying their own federal, state, and local taxes.[149] You can pay the contractor as you would any vendor, via check, direct deposit, or wire transfer.

> *Tip:* Pennsylvania requires that we deduct 3.07 percent from payments to out-of-state contractors. I expect more states to adopt similar regulations as they try to get their "piece of the action" from remote companies and employees! So, be sure to see if your state requires you to deduct state income tax from the consulting fee of any out-of-state contractor prior to paying them.

Non-U.S.-based contractors

Some countries make it easier for U.S. businesses to hire workers in their country than others. Before hiring a contractor in a foreign country, you should review the country's business laws and regulations to find out how they define "contractor" and "employee." Risks and possible expenses and legal liabilities are similar in some non-US countries.

You'll also want to find out if there's a tax treaty in place between the U.S. government and the country where the contractor lives and works. For example, the tax treaty between the U.S. and Canada eliminates double taxation for Canadian contractors. Under the treaty, they are only responsible for paying all relevant individual and business taxes to the Canadian government, not to the Canadian government *and* the IRS.[150]

If a tax treaty exists, you'll also want to ask the contractor to sign IRS form W-8BEN-E (www.irs.gov/pub/irs-pdf/fw8bene.pdf) if they're set up as a business entity, or IRS form W-8BEN (www.irs.gov/pub/irs-pdf/fw8ben.pdf) if they're not. By signing a W-8BEN-E or W-8BEN form, the contractor declares that (1) they're not a "U.S. person" (that is, not a U.S. citizen or green-card holder) and (2) they'll pay all taxes due in their home country. Having this documentation can protect you in case of an IRS audit. It explains why you did not withhold taxes from the contractor's paycheck. If the contractor doesn't sign a W-8BEN or W-8BEN-E, you're required to deduct U.S. payroll taxes from their fee at a rate of 30 percent.[151]

Also, by signing a W-8BEN or W-8BEN-E form, you may be able to have the contractor work for you indefinitely (longer than six months to a year), that is, for as long as it's mutually beneficial.

If there *isn't* a tax treaty in place between the U.S. and the contractor's country, the laws and regulations in the contractor's home country may require that you pay payroll taxes and business taxes to that country. You'll have to assess this on a country-by-country basis.

If you employ international contractors directly, I recommend that you use an international money transfer service, such as OFX (www.ofx.com/en-us) to pay them. The benefit of using an international money service is that you can use it to pay a contractor via direct deposit in the currency of their home country.

Hiring through a professional services company

If you hire a contractor through a professional services company, the firm will invoice you just like any other vendor would. You pay the company a fee, and they pay the contractor a salary because the contractor is their employee.

In our early days, we hired contractors directly, in the U.S. and internationally. Since then, we've established a relationship with Actminds (www.actminds.com), a professional services company that's focused on software development. When we have a need for temporary help, we simply reach out to them; their staffing model involves having (their own) full-time employees, based in several locations, who move from project to project. Based on our working relationship with Actminds, they're able to provide us with people who are a good fit, skill- and culture-wise for our company.

> *Tip:* One thing to keep in mind is whether or not a professional services company has contractors performing their jobs outside the U.S. You'll want to find out because depending on who your clients are, you may have to comply with contractual or regulatory stipulations regarding where the work you're providing is performed. For example, you may have a data privacy agreement with a client that states their data can never go "offshore," and if that's the case, you may have to restrict the professional services company's access to servers that could have that client's data on them.

So, if you have a temporary need, or if you anticipate a fluctuating workload in a particular area, adding contractors to your team may be the best option for your all-remote company.

Note: No matter how you hire contract workers, they don't participate in your company's benefit plan because they're not employees.

5.5 Offer internships

It's true, just like "real" companies, all-remote companies have "real" interns! In 2014, we began offering internships to talented high school students, college students, and recent graduates. It's been a win-win for the interns and for our company. The interns gain real-world work experience, and our company receives an infusion of youthful talent, energy, and perspective.

Our director of people oversees our internship program, which includes assigning each intern to a department that can benefit from their assistance. Each intern reports to a director in their department, who helps ensure the intern develops valuable skills and learns how to be productive in our virtual workplace environment.

> *Tip:* At most companies, interns report to the most junior person in a department. I'm convinced that one of the reasons our interns are so productive is that they're each reporting to the director in the department where they're working.

We currently employ seven exceptionally talented interns; three work for us year-round and four during the summer. Four were referred by team members and three from one of our clients, the University of Miami.

Special note: In 2017, we established a relationship with the "U Dreamers" program at the University of Miami.

The U Dreamers Program is available to exceptional and academically accomplished Deferred Action for Childhood Arrivals (DACA) high school seniors and transfer students in the state of Florida at the University of Miami.[152] I'll have more to say about our commitment to DACA students in chapter 9, "Leading the way: Your life as a remote CEO."

At Fire Engine RED, we don't give our interns "busy" work. (In a virtual company, there's no sending the interns out for coffee!) They're all assigned projects that provide real value to our company and contribute to our bottom line. For example, three of our interns help manage our sales database, and two others assist our CRM implementation team in getting our software up and running for clients. We also help our interns develop new skills. One of our interns has learned how to manage websites using WordPress, while another learned how to analyze and assess client data. At the end of his summer internship, he even presented his findings to our student search leadership team.

> *Tip:* One of the best ways to get the most out of your interns is to pay them well. We pay our interns $15 an hour, and they're worth every penny.

I encourage you to give interns an opportunity and some actual responsibility. Done well, an internship program can increase your team's productivity and provide tremendous value to your company.

Chapter 6
All onboard: Setting up new remote team members for success

Comments like these make me confident in our all-remote company's onboarding process:

Nick, our creative lead, told me, "The process is focused just as much on the well-being of new hires as on the needs of the company. It says a lot that Fire Engine RED is looking to provide a great employee experience from Day One."

Brian agreed. "There was a plan for me on Day One. It helped to be up and running on Slack. Everyone was welcoming, happy to answer questions, so I wasn't having to search for everything myself." He added, "By my third or fourth week, I felt like I was really contributing because

Fire Engine RED is set up to accommodate workers, not the other way around."

And as Micah told our director of people, "I have had an incredible first week and am so excited about my future at Fire Engine RED."

Now I'll share with you our time-tested process for onboarding remote team members. And by "time-tested," I mean it took us a dozen or more iterations to get the process right!

6.1 After the paperwork is signed

As an all-virtual company, it's crucial to provide your new hires with a smooth, comfortable onboarding experience. When your company is fully remote, some onboarding tasks require more time to complete. That's why we begin onboarding new employees as soon as they return their signed offer letter and employment agreement.

Here's a look at what onboarding tasks each new hire must complete and when the tasks need to be completed.

I-9 form

You (as an employer) are required to inspect, *in person*, a new employee's legal documents (driver's license, passport, etc.) and to verify their identity and their eligibility to work in the U.S.[153] Although you're allowed to do so within three days of the employee's start date, I would encourage you to confirm their eligibility *before* their start date.

The "in person" requirement can throw a remote company for a loop because it's certainly not practical to send a member of your HR department to each new hire's location. Fortunately, there's an easy, reliable, low-cost way to solve this problem. You can hire a remote I-9 verification service provider to act as your agent. We use N3 Notary (www.n3notary.net) for this purpose.

Here's how it works: Within one day of us contacting them, N3 Notary has a local agent reach out to our new hire and schedule a time and place to meet. At this meeting, the agent reviews our new hire's supporting documents and ensures their I-9 is completed properly. The agent then uploads the completed I-9 and supporting documents to our N3 Notary portal. We then download the documents from the portal and upload them into our HRIS. Each N3 Notary request costs $65 (for most U.S. cities).

> *Tip:* As an employer, you're required by the U.S. Citizenship and Immigration Services (USCIS) to keep an employee's I-9 form and associated documents for three years after their start date, and for one year after an employee leaves the company (if their forms haven't been disposed of by then).

E-Verify site

In addition to having a completed I-9 on hand, I recommend that you use E-Verify (www.e-verify.gov) and make it a standard part of your employee verification process. E-Verify is a U.S. Department of Homeland Security website that enables employers to confirm that their new hire (whether they are a U.S. citizen or foreign national) is eligible to work in the United States.

Even though the federal government, and most states, do not require that you use E-Verify, some states *do*, so it makes sense to use it for all new hires rather than tracking requirements state by state.

> *Tip:* Some clients may require that you use E-Verify. This is yet another reason to make using E-Verify a standard part of your onboarding process.

The good news is, E-Verify is free and easy to use.

6.2 Two weeks prior to start date

Approximately two weeks before the new hire's official start date, our director of people sends them an email with their temporary HRIS login credentials. She then asks them to log into our HRIS and complete the onboarding tasks below.

Employee profile

The first thing on the new hire's list is to complete their employee profile form. Because our applicant tracking system integrates with our HRIS, some of the basic information will have already been populated in the form, such as their name, email, address, phone, etc. They're also asked to provide some additional information, including their date of birth, Social Security number, and direct deposit information for payroll.

This profile form is also where we gather some fun facts from the new hire for use on our website's Team page, such as who would play them in "Fire Engine RED: The Movie" (for me it's Julia Louis-Dreyfus). We've found that this type of trivia is a great way for our team members and clients to get to know each other better.

W-4 form

We also ask the new hire to complete an electronic W-4 (Employee's Withholding Allowance Certificate) form in our HRIS. This form lets our financial department know the amount of tax to withhold from their paycheck.

Computer equipment

There are four general ways that companies deal with equipping their remote workers. They provide (1) all office equipment from a computer to furniture; (2) a computer only; (3) a budget for employees to purchase their own hardware and software; or (4) nothing—that is, they require employees to provide all their own equipment.[154]

Once the new hire submits their employee profile and W-4, our director of client care operations and equipment specialist extraordinaire, Mark, reaches out to schedule an equipment meeting with them. During this meeting, Mark helps them to choose the equipment that's best suited for their role, so the new employee is in a state of "RED-iness" from Day One.

At Fire Engine RED, we do a combination of these things. We provide all employees with their choice of laptop and peripherals, such as an external monitor, a keyboard and mouse, an external hard drive for backup, a headset, and a printer/scanner if needed for their job responsibilities. We budget up to $4,000 for laptops and peripherals. Our employees are responsible for providing their own internet access, smartphones, and office furniture.

Office supplies

Our equipment specialist also orders whatever office supplies the new hire needs so they receive them in plenty of time for their start date. There are only a few cases where an employee requires traditional office supplies (copier paper, envelopes, etc.) to do their job; in fact, we spend less than $1,000 total per year on office supplies for our entire team.

Tip: To make ongoing orders for office supplies easier, I suggest setting up a business account with Amazon (www.amazon.com). Your employees can then create a "wishlist" with the office supplies they need and "invite" your office manager to view their list and place the order.

Once the tasks that require the new hire's immediate attention are complete, we give them additional time to finish the more time-consuming tasks that remain on the list. We simply ask the new hire to complete the remaining tasks below before their start date.

Team photo

If you post photos of your team on your website, I suggest you ask your new hire to provide a photo *before* they start.

Gathering usable photos from remote employees is harder than you think. We used to end up rejecting half of the photos we initially received from new hires because the composition and resolution weren't in line with what we needed.

So, we created a step-by-step guide to getting a good photo; see the Resources section of the *Fully Remote* website (www.fully-remote-book.com) to view our Website Photo Guide. This guide provides new hires with tips on what to wear, what to have in the background, the type of image file to send, etc. Now, the photos we get from new hires are intranet- and website-ready the first time around, which allows us to have their photo up on our website on their first day.

> *Tip:* As a fully remote company, it can be more challenging to ensure that your team's photos have a consistent look. We handled this simply by converting their photos to black and white. See the Team page on the Fire Engine RED website (www.fire-engine-red.com/team/) to get an idea of how you can achieve a consistent look with regard to your team's photos.

(We also include our employees' photos on our intranet. For more details on getting your intranet up and running, see chapter 11.2, "Develop an intranet.")

Team introduction message

We also ask the new hire to provide some brief introductory information for our director of people to include in the introduction message she posts on Slack at the start of their second day.

> *Tip:* Because our team members are such a friendly bunch, we've found it's better to introduce the new hire to our team on their *second* day of work. This way, the new hire doesn't get overwhelmed with greetings while they're onboarding and just starting to get up to speed.

Here's what our introduction messages look like:

> I'm very happy to welcome Milo to Fire Engine
> RED as a Software Engineer, reporting to Astrid.
>
> Here's a little bit about Milo in his own words:
>
> - I live in Reno, Nevada.
> - I'm married with two kids, two dogs, and a
>   chameleon.
> - I love to paint, go off-roading, and eat
>   chocolate.

Employee handbook

We also ask the new hire to download and read our employee handbook (which is posted on our HRIS) prior to their first day. Once they've done so, we have them log back into our HRIS and sign an acknowledgment that they're familiar with the handbook.

For our first 10 years in business, we didn't even have an employee handbook. But with people constantly asking questions about our policies, we finally put one together using a template from a former payroll provider. As a result, it was about as engaging as you'd expect a document full of dry legalese to be, and no one ever read it closely enough to find (and delete) all the crazy, irrelevant things, like the following examples of "inappropriate behavior" ...

- Sleeping or loitering during regular work hours
- Unauthorized possession of a weapon in a company or client meeting
- Gambling on company time

Another "favorite" was our list of *non-reimbursable* expenses, which included "coat check" and "ferry rides."

So, in 2014, we took our handbook and blew it up—in a virtual sense, of course, and started again! Our new and improved handbook is written in an engaging style that's consistent with our 100 percent remote company's unique culture. The guiding principle we followed in rewriting it was to make it read the way people actually talk, as in:

> "Your virtual office location must be quiet and free of distractions, including background noise and interruptions that are caused by pets, contractors, etc. If Rover starts barking while you're on a call, just put yourself on mute."

And:

> "Employees are required to maintain proper standards of conduct and behavior. Simply put, at some point, you've probably worked with 'that

person' who doesn't exhibit conduct or behavior that's appropriate for the workplace. Generally, just don't act like 'that person,' and everything will be fine."

And:

"A client wants to give you a college T-shirt? No problem. A vendor wants to give you courtside tickets to a college basketball game? That's a problem."

Four of the most important words in our employee handbook are "use your best judgment." We feel confident about using this phrase because we trust our employees to do the right thing. Otherwise, we wouldn't have hired them in the first place!

Finally, one of the most remarked-on sections of our handbook is the very last page. It's about "leaving the RED door open," our term for how employees can part ways with our company while setting the stage for their possible return! See chapter 14.1, "When an employee leaves voluntarily."

Want to take a closer look at our employee handbook? It's available in the Resources section of the *Fully Remote* website (www.fully-remote-book.com).

6.3 One week prior to start date

Because the new hire will be working remotely, it's especially important that you tell them *in advance* exactly what to expect on their first day. You don't want them to sit down at their desk with their new computer and think, "Okay, well, I'm at work. Do they even know I'm here? Now what?"

Brian, one of our software engineers, said that when he worked for a startup in San Francisco, he was "one of a handful of remote workers, and there, it felt like I was on an island." His experience with Fire Engine RED was quite different: "This was my first time working remotely that the company had everything in place when I came in."

About a week before their start date, a new hire receives three friendly email messages. The first is from Jamie, our director of people, with the agenda for their first and second days. By providing the new hire with an agenda in advance of their start date, we hope to communicate that our company is focused on them and prepared for their virtual arrival.

I've provided examples of the agendas below.

First day:

- 8:30 a.m.–10:00 a.m.   Set up company-wide tools with FERst Friend
- 10:00 a.m.–12 p.m.   Complete HR action items with director of people
- 12 p.m.–1:00 p.m.   Eat lunch
- 1:00 p.m.–2:30 p.m.   Set up departmental tools with Second Friend
- 2:30 p.m.–3:00 p.m.   Break
- 3:00 p.m.–4:00 p.m.   Meet with direct manager
- 4:00 p.m.–5:30 p.m.   Catch-up time

Second day:

- 8:30 a.m.–10:30 a.m.   Tour of our intranet with director of people
- 10:30 a.m.–11:00 a.m.   Break
- 11:00 a.m.–12:00 p.m.   Meet with direct manager
- 12 p.m.–1:00 p.m.   Eat lunch
- 1:00 p.m.–5:30 p.m.   To be determined by direct manager

Jamie's email is followed by emails from their "FERst Friend" and "Second Friend." These are the team members who will welcome the new employee on their first day and help them set up their company-wide and departmental tools. Typically, these Friends are people who work in the same department the new hire will be joining.

The FERst Friend's email to the new hire is particularly important. In this email, the FERst Friend introduces themselves and lets the new hire know to expect a call from them at 8:30 a.m. (in the new hire's time zone) on their first day. The FERst Friend also tells the new hire that they will help them implement their company-wide tools and that they're available to answer any questions (big or small, serious or not) the new hire has about the company and working remotely.

Later that day, the new hire hears from their Second Friend, who will help the new hire implement their department-specific tools.

> *Tip:* You may find, as we did, that certain people are better at setting up your company-wide and departmental tools than setting up department-specific software, or vice versa, which is why we've found two "Friends" are better than one. In addition, it's less of a burden for each Friend when we split up the responsibilities.

Essentially, being a FERst or Second Friend all boils down to following the Golden Rule. In other words, we ask them to be the Friend they had (or wished they would have had).

> *Lesson learned:* Not everyone has the time, patience, and/or technical skills to be a new hire's FERst Friend or Second Friend. We've had a couple of fiascos, such as when one Friend never called (they were waiting for the new hire to call them), and when another called just to "chat" and didn't remember that they had actual responsibility for helping the new hire set up their tools! In each case, the new hire was left hanging. To help avoid such mishaps, we've learned to (1) not ask relatively new employees to be a Friend, (2) not pair a new hire with a Friend in a far-off time zone, and (3) not

ask a team member who is on a critical deadline to serve as a Friend.

6.4 The day before the new hire starts

One day out from the new hire's start date, the director of people invites our tool administrators to join a Slack group chat, where she asks them to provide the new hire with access to our company-wide and department-specific tools.

> *Tip #1:* Make sure there is a backup administrator for each of your tools. Remember, people get sick, go on vacation, etc.

> *Tip #2:* Make sure someone at your company "cleans out" the new employee's email inbox, so it's not flooded with junk email and auto-generated messages on their first day. Our director of people does this the day before the new hire starts to ensure the new hire only sees the emails they need for activating their tools.

> *Tip #3:* To avoid email from piling up in the first place, you may ask your systems administrator to wait as long as possible before enabling the new employee's account.

The director of people also resends the email with their first- and second-day agendas (in case they've misplaced it) to the new hire's personal email address. This email also includes the new hire's temporary login credentials for our company-wide tools. Again, the director of people lets the new hire know that we're excited for them to start the next day.

6.5 The new hire's first day

Meeting with their FERst Friend

The new employee's first day begins at 8:30 a.m. (their time zone) with a call from their FERst Friend. The FERst Friend walks the new hire through the steps required to connect to the company's virtual private network (VPN) and then directs them to the "new hire" section of our intranet, where they'll find step-by-step instructions for setting up each of our nine company-wide tools. It usually takes the new hire about 90 minutes to get their tools implemented and ready to go.

> *Tip:* If something goes wrong, and the FERst Friend can't solve a technical problem within five minutes, we have the FERst Friend stop and contact the director of people, who will bring in the right people to solve the issue immediately.

Meeting with the director of people

Once the new employee has implemented our company-wide tools, they meet (via Slack, audio) with the director of people to complete the human resources-related items that remain, including enrolling in medical benefits, the company's 401(k) plan, and our wellness program.

During this call, our director of people, Jamie, tells the new employee who's related to whom at our company. This includes mentioning that she and I are sisters. Although Jamie and I are both professionals and would never violate HR guidelines by sharing an employee's private information or confidential conversations with each other, we wouldn't want anyone to be caught off guard, having confided in one of us and only later learning that we're related.

Breaking for lunch

We also schedule a one-hour lunch break for the new hire on their first day. This is to help them get into the habit of taking an hour for lunch, whether it's to eat, run errands, or just enjoy a break.

Meeting with their Second Friend

After lunch, the new hire's Second Friend takes over and helps them implement their department-specific tools (there are about six to 12 of these, depending on the department they're joining). The Second Friend directs them back to the "new hires" section of our intranet, where they'll find step-by-step instructions for downloading and installing their department's tools. The Second Friend and the new hire generally complete the process in 90 minutes.

Meeting with their manager

Once the new hire is up and running with their company-wide and departmental tools, and they have completed all of their HR-related tasks, the next step is for the new hire to meet with their manager to talk about what's next. For example, it might be to meet the other members of their team, listen in on a demo, or review documentation.

6.6 The second day, and beyond

On the second day, our director of people provides the new team member with a comprehensive tour of alfRED, our company intranet, which includes a wealth of vital information for new *and* current team members. This tour serves as our new employee orientation, with our director of people telling the new person about the history of our company, our company values, our products and services, fun stats about our team members, and more.

Our director of people also shows the new hire (via screen share) how to schedule meetings and time off on our company's Google Calendar and introduces them to our company's calendar codes (MTG, OUT, SICK, JURY, etc.) for indicating why they're out of the "office." We want to make sure the new hire gets this right so they don't get scheduled for meetings when they'll be absent.

The director of people also speaks with the new hire about some of the critical remote-work-related policies we have in our employee handbook, such as having a dedicated workspace, and our policy regarding childcare arrangements during work hours.

Here's what our handbook has to say about creating a dedicated workspace: "The idea of being able to work from your favorite coffee shop every day is tempting, but it can often be impractical, especially if you're on calls (background noise and other interruptions). While it's fine for you to change up where you work, we do recommend that you have a dedicated space in your home where you can be productive and work undisturbed."

Our childcare policy states simply, "You're expected to make appropriate dependent and childcare arrangements during your work hours." That's it, you might ask, one sentence? Yes, and here's why: We believe our team members can be trusted to make the right judgment calls when it comes to having children around.

There are two reasons we created our childcare policy. First, we want our team members to be able to focus on their work. Second, we want to help ensure children remain safe while their parent (or parents, in the case of Meaghan and David) is working. Do the kids have the supervision required to keep them safe and the team member(s) uninterrupted?

We also asked ourselves if there should be an age cutoff. Let's say hypothetically that team member Astrid has an 8-year-old and a 10-year-old. The 10-year-old helps to make sure the 8-year-old doesn't disturb Astrid during work hours. So, does Astrid need to have childcare? What about hypothetical team member Milo, whose children are 12 and 14?

We concluded that our policy should be "child-focused" and not "age-focused." Again, because we hire people with good judgment, we trust them to know at what age their kids are "independent" enough.

Okay, so what if an employee's kid gets sick and has to stay home from school? As I've mentioned previously, the employee can use our company's unlimited sick time to care for a sick child. Or, they can work a partial day; it's up to the employee.

Also, you should keep in mind that snow days at a 100 percent virtual company are more like "bring your kids to work day" at a bricks-and-mortar company, because remote workers (unlike their kids) don't get the day off. To keep things moving, we sometimes need to get creative and find ways to keep kids occupied. During a recent snow day, I had a Slack video meeting (yes, video! Anything for the kids!) with Sean, the four-year-old son of one of my team members. I gave him some fun "assignments," including drawing pictures of fire engines, to keep him occupied and amused, so his mom could get her work done. I also scheduled a "show and tell" with him for later in the day where he proudly showed me his drawings (which were great, by the way!).

In addition, two winters ago, I scheduled a conference call with a bunch of kids and had them write me a song about—brace yourself—diarrhea. (Hey, it's said you have to "know your audience.") Then at the end of the day, we jumped back on Slack and the kids performed their songs! I also sent them each a "paycheck" for their efforts. Things have gone so well when I've given some attention to my team members' kids that I've encouraged my other managers to do the same on snow days! It's fun, helps team members and their kids get to know each other, and puts stressed-out parents at ease.

I would definitely recommend that you put a childcare policy in place. But don't feel like you have to get into too many specifics. You've hired the people on your remote team for their ability to make good decisions independently of close supervision. Trust them![155]

6.7 HR pop-ins

It's important to address any issues a new employee has immediately. We've found that the best way to do this is to have our director of people check in with a new employee several times during their first month with our company. We refer to these check-ins as "pop-ins." My intention was that new hires wouldn't get stressed out about talking to HR if these meetings had a friendly name!

FERst Friday pop-in

On the "FERst Friday" after the new employee starts, the director of people asks the new hire how the onboarding process went, including their experiences with their FERst and Second Friends.

By the end of their first week, we want the new hire to feel "connected" to our 100 percent remote company and not take any unresolved issues with them into the weekend.

Two-week pop-in

During this call, the director of people asks the new hire about:

- Any issues they've experienced with their equipment, software tools, and benefits.
- Any issues with their manager or other team members.
- The training (including documentation) they've received to date.
- Their overall onboarding experience.

The director of people also reminds the new hire to register or create accounts on our benefits providers' websites, so the new hire can track and manage their benefits online. Without this nudge, new hires were forgetting that each provider had its own online portal where answers to their questions could be found quickly and easily.

30-day pop-in

At the end of the first month, our director of people reaches out to the new employee to see how things are going and to ask for specific suggestions on how we can improve our recruiting, interviewing, hiring, and onboarding processes. She then uses the new employee's input to make improvements, which helps us show how seriously we take their ideas and feedback.

> *Tip:* If you want your employees to bring you ideas, you need to show them that every idea is considered and, when appropriate, implemented within a short time frame.

Based on what we've heard from new employees, we now:

- Provide each new hire with a plan for Week One with achievable goals.
- Provide clearer instructions on setting up our VPN.
- Recommend that the new hire and their FERst and Second Friends use the same browser (Google Chrome) during their onboarding sessions, so if there's an issue, it's easier to troubleshoot.

- Have more (and better) documentation available for training.

Our director of people also asks the employee what has surprised them the most about working at Fire Engine RED. Answers have included:

- There's a lot of communication in general, and specifically on Slack.
- There's much more structure than I expected.
- The CEO is really involved.
- The CEO is really transparent, especially when it comes to the company's financials.
- I'm really tired at the end of a day working from home!
- Our onboarding process is very structured and organized.
- We use a lot of tools.
- Everyone's really supportive and friendly.

Our director of people doesn't stop engaging with the new employee after 30 days. In fact, she reaches out to every team member at some point during the year to set up a 30- to 60-minute pop-in to ask how things are going and get their ideas on how HR and/or the company can do things better. The ideas she gathers aren't just filed away; if they're great suggestions (and they often are), we'll implement them as soon as possible.

6.8 Onboarding contractors and interns

Our onboarding processes for contractors and interns include many of the same tasks as our process for onboarding full-time employees. They're just streamlined a bit! Let's take a look ...

Contractors

Onboarding U.S.-based independent contractors

Two weeks prior to their start date, we ask the contractor to sign into our HRIS, fill out a contractor profile, complete a W-9 form, and provide information for their team introduction message. (They don't need to read our employee handbook because the policies and processes described in it only apply to employees. Also, we don't ask them to provide a photo because we don't include photos of contractors on our website or intranet.)

Just as with full-time employees, one week prior to their start date, the new contractor receives the same three email messages: one each from our director of people and their FERst and Second Friends.

The day before the contractor starts, they also receive a welcome message from our director of people with temporary login credentials for their tools.

Their first-day agenda is similar to that of a new employee, though their discussion with the director of people is streamlined, with no benefits information or handbook policies. However, they do get a scaled-back tour of our intranet to get an idea of our company history, culture, and offerings.

Onboarding contractors through a professional services company or an agency

Typically, the hiring manager works with the agency and then provides our director of people with the information she needs to start onboarding the contractor.

As with contractors we hire directly, the day before an agency contractor starts, they receive a welcome message from our director of people, which provides them with their temporary login credentials and asks them for information for their team introduction message. (We don't have our agency contractors log into our HRIS.)

On their first day, the contractor meets with their FERst and Second Friends, the director of people, and their manager. They also get the same tour of our intranet as our U.S.-based independent contractors do.

Interns

When an intern joins us, the onboarding process is a highly streamlined version of the one our full-time employees go through. It starts as soon as they return their offer letter and signed employment agreement.

From there, they log into our HRIS to set up an employee profile, fill out a W-4, download and read our employee handbook, set up timesheet access, and provide their direct deposit information for payroll. Interns also go through the same I-9 process that full-time employees do (see above). We also ask them to provide us with a photo of themselves for our website and intranet.

Interns don't have designated FERst and Second Friends. Instead, their direct manager helps them set up their company-wide tools. (Interns typically don't use department-specific tools.)

As with full-time employees, the director of people also meets with the new intern on their first day. The call is shorter because interns don't receive company benefits or need to use the company calendar. However, the director of people does provide interns with a tour of our intranet.

Chapter 7
Hiring leaders: Building a fully remote leadership team

One of the most difficult things about building a business (all-remote or not) is determining *when* to start building your leadership team. As with many startup companies, my then-business partner and I initially divided the company's leadership roles. I oversaw the vision and strategy, marketing, sales, and bookkeeping, while she was in charge of operations, finance, human resources, and software development.

As the company grew, it became obvious that we couldn't continue to do it all, nor did we want to; there simply wasn't enough time in the day. More importantly, though, we needed experienced professionals with specialized skills to help take our company to the next level.

Today, my leadership team includes our chief financial officer, Akber; our executive vice presidents, Mike, Jim, and Jeff; three vice presidents, Glenna, Katrina, and Sarah; our director of people, Jamie; and our software engineering manager, Russell. Like the rest of our team, the members of our leadership team are scattered throughout the U.S., so our quarterly management team meetings are, and always have been, virtual.

Here's a look at why and when we made some of our key leadership hires. Spoiler alert: We didn't get it right the first time, every time. As you'll see, referrals played a crucial role in many of our successful hires.

7.1 Nailed it

It's important to identify the leaders in your industry and build relationships with them. In 2011, nearly a decade after we started, we hired Mike and Jim, who were in leadership positions at the College Board (www.collegeboard.org), a not-for-profit organization that serves students and educational institutions. You may know the College Board best as the organization that administers the SAT and AP tests.

We brought in Mike to lead our student search efforts, and Jim to head up our enrollment software department. The complexity of these two offerings demanded that we hire people with a wealth of experience in leading successful teams that serve the education market. Both Mike and Jim had served in similar roles at the College Board—with Mike as director of Student Search Service and Jim as director of admission and enrollment software for the College Board's CRM product (which was sunset in 2010). It also helped that Mike and Jim were both referred to us by people we respected in the industry (each other!).

Our first two leadership hires went so well that I thought finding our next leader would be just as easy. Well, I thought wrong. Our next hire was much more challenging, in part because the position evolved quite differently.

7.2 Failed badly but then lucked out

In late 2012, we wanted to take our student search offering to the next level, and we believed that the way to do it was to create a data services department. We needed someone to build this new department (and create its offerings), rather than take an already successful department to the next level. Because we didn't know of anyone in our network who had the right experience and skill set, we hired an executive search firm.

From the beginning, we had a long list of "must-haves." We were looking for a person with:

- Experience launching, managing, and growing a data department with new and innovative offerings.
- Senior-level college admissions experience.
- Expertise in technology.

- Excellent communications skills (they needed to be able to communicate complex results to clients and provide them with actionable strategies).

Oh, and we also wanted the person to share our company's values and be a great fit for working in our 100 percent remote environment. (I told you we had quite a few requirements!)

As it turned out, the executive search firm also had a tough time finding someone who met our long list of job requirements. Because we couldn't get it all, we settled and hired someone who had much of the experience we were looking for, but who (as it turned out) wasn't a good fit for our people-centric, values-driven all-remote culture and workplace.

> *Tip:* If you decide to go with an executive search firm, make sure they provide you with enough added value to justify what they charge, which is typically 30 percent of the new hire's first-year salary.

We eventually parted ways with this executive and decided to leave the position open until we found someone who had the whole package—no matter how long it took.

Tip: Even in a 100 percent remote company, a "bad fit" can impact your entire company culture, just like it would at a bricks-and-mortar company. If that happens to you, I suggest you cut ties with the employee immediately. You don't want a bad attitude or bad habits to spread.

Much to my shock, it didn't take long. We filled this formerly impossible-to-fill position immediately. That's because, unbeknownst to us, the ideal candidate for the position had recently joined our company! Jeff had been hired as our vice president of enrollment software in June 2014, the same month the previously mentioned data executive had left our company. Jeff, a former dean of admissions and financial aid, was referred to our company by Mike and Jim, who had known Jeff from their time at the College Board. Although they knew Jeff had data and analytics know-how, what they didn't know was that he was a data "savant" until he volunteered to run the data team in the interim, and immediately began "wowing" us and our clients.

As it turns out, Jeff was (and is) that rare talent who can do everything well, with the right knowledge, skill set, and communication style—not only to lead our data department but also to grow it into what I believe is now the finest in our industry. Plus, his values are completely aligned with our company's. I still marvel at how well it's all worked out with Jeff.

Lesson learned: Never settle, and never compromise on cultural fit, especially when hiring a senior leader. You're always better off waiting until the right candidate comes along. They are always out there; you just need to discover them.

7.3 Waited (two years) too long

In the early years, my then-business partner oversaw the company's finances. By 2009, there was more work than she could handle. So, we brought in a "quarter-time" CFO to lead our finance and accounting team, which then included our assistant controller and business operations manager.

This arrangement worked well for about three years, but as it turned out, we had stayed with it two years too long. The problem was, there were too many cooks in our all-remote financial kitchen. It would literally take weeks, sometimes months, for me to get the information I needed to make the best financial decisions for the company. After my business partner left in December 2013, I knew it was time to hire a full-time CFO.

Because my brother, Brad, has the best professional network of anyone I know, I asked him for recommendations. He sent me only one resume: Akber's. According to Brad, Akber was the one CFO candidate who had the right experience, skill set, and values that aligned with our company's (especially our company value of Simplicity, which I believe is a rare quality in a CFO). My brother was right: Akber was, and continues to be, the perfect fit for Fire Engine RED. We benefited from Akber's financial expertise so quickly that one of my few regrets is that I didn't hire a CFO two years earlier.

An aside: Like me, Akber lives in the Philadelphia area, so I was able to meet with him in person. As you might expect, we chose to meet at a coffee shop. I was so nervous (after all, my brother had told me Akber was the only CFO that fit our requirements and culture) that within the first five minutes of the meeting, I spilled an entire cup of coffee onto the white pants I was wearing!

> *Tip:* Don't wear white to an in-person interview, especially when you rarely interview people in person.

7.4 Found a common thread

The other five members of our leadership team—vice presidents Glenna, Katrina, and Sarah; director of people Jamie; and software engineering manager Russell—were all promoted to their leadership positions by being exemplary performers. There's one other key quality these five leaders share: they were all referred to our company by other Fire Engine RED team members! This is yet another example of why we take referrals from our team members so seriously.

Chapter 8
Your virtual org chart: Structuring your fully remote company for success

Now, I'll share with you some tips on determining the best organizational structure for an all-remote company. You can find our org chart in the Resources section of the *Fully Remote* website (www.fully-remote-book.com).

8.1 The flatter, the better

Like bricks-and-mortar companies, most all-remote companies have a defined organizational structure. In my opinion, the flatter the organizational structure, the better.

I believe a flat structure allows employees, especially those who are attracted to a virtual environment (self-starters), to thrive and do their best work because they feel more empowered, trusted, and respected. A flat structure also ensures that you, as CEO, get the most up-to-date, accurate information from your senior leaders. With this information, you'll not only be able to make better decisions but also innovate and resolve issues more quickly.

I currently have nine direct reports—the three EVPs who head up our product and service divisions (student search, data services, and enrollment software) as well as the leaders of our "functional" teams (finance and accounting, human resources, marketing, operations, and product management). Our flat organizational structure has allowed me to stay in close touch with all of my direct reports and still get my own work done; that's why I recommend that you not have more than 10 people reporting to you.

8.2 Three departments that should report to you

Now, even if you prefer a more hierarchical organizational structure, I strongly encourage you to have three particular departments, which don't always report to a CEO, report directly to you: HR, marketing, and (if you're a technology company) product management.

Human Resources

The Society for Human Resource Management (SHRM) notes that 36 percent of HR leaders report to the CEO, 26 percent report to the president/owner of the company, and just 11 percent report to the CFO/finance department.[156]

Initially, our director of people and our HR department reported to our CFO. After a while, though, it became clear that this was not the best structure, especially for a 100 percent remote company with a strong values-driven, people-centric culture.

As I've mentioned previously, a remote CEO is responsible for creating and maintaining the company culture; sometimes that requires making decisions that aren't necessarily the ones the finance department would endorse.

So, it made sense to shift the reporting structure of HR to me, and now, all decisions with regard to our employees are made in line with our company culture and values.

Marketing

I also encourage you to have your most senior marketing leader (in our case, our communications director) report to you, the CEO.

My full title is CEO and chief creative officer; as such, I shape the company's brand and culture. So, it makes sense for both marketing and HR—who communicate the company's culture and brand—to report to me.

Our marketing team uses the same voice—friendly yet professional—in our external communications to clients (website, promotional email, and blog) and in our internal communications and presentations to team members.

Product Management

If your all-remote company is a tech company, I recommend you remain closely involved by having the people responsible for the product vision—and the processes involved in bringing it to life—report directly to you.

At Fire Engine RED, we develop software using Agile methodology, which requires that we have people in the roles of "product owner" and "scrum master" (Sarah and Katrina, respectively). The product owner is responsible for holding the vision of what's to be built and communicating it to the development team. The scrum master is responsible for serving as a mediator between the product owner and the development team.[157] As these roles evolved, I promoted Sarah to VP of products and Katrina to VP of projects, and now they both report to me.

I've found that working closely with these leaders is the best way for me to stay up to date with this area of our company and to share what I know about the needs of prospective and current clients. Plus, because we have a variety of stakeholders that rely on our product management leaders—including client care, data services, enrollment software, and student search—it's best that the product owner and scrum master don't "live" within any of those teams. By having them report to me, they aren't unduly influenced by one department or another.

As Katrina (VP of projects) shared, "If we report into a particular business unit, it gives more weight to requests from that team, which can take us away from working toward the overall company vision." And Sarah (VP of products) noted, "It's best to have both the product owner and scrum master report to the CEO. If Katrina and I reported to two different people, it could result in a power imbalance."

I'll say more about Agile in chapter 12.1, "How to create a culture of productivity."

Chapter 9
Leading the way: Your life as a remote CEO

In this chapter, I'll discuss the unique challenges of being a remote CEO and how to lead an all-remote business. I'll also share some of the lessons I've learned during the nearly two decades I've led Fire Engine RED, one of the country's first 100 percent virtual companies.

9.1 Create and communicate your vision

Just like the CEOs of bricks-and-mortar companies, you'll be responsible for creating and communicating your vision for the company, and you'll need to help your employees understand how and why their work is meaningful to the company and the clients you serve. As *Inc.* writes, "The CEO is the one person accountable for keeping all company functions aligned and moving in the right direction."[158] However, because your team members all work remotely, you'll have the added responsibility of inspiring and motivating them—*without ever being in the same space as them!* This is no easy task, and it's not for everyone. It takes energy, passion, and lots of practice.

9.2 Build a strong virtual culture

As the CEO, you'll need to build the culture for your all-remote company. Doing so will take you countless hours, so you'll need to learn how to be a great multi-tasker, if you're not already. That's because when you're just starting out, you, like most CEOs, will need to be actively engaged in just about everything—from sales to operations to finance.

In chapter 13, "Building a strong company culture: No office building necessary," I'll go more in-depth and provide you with nine ways to build a strong, all-remote company culture. But for now, let me start by saying that you'll need to establish your company's core values, communicate them (repeatedly) to your team, and make sure the decisions you make are aligned with your personal values. You'll also need to work closely with your HR team to make sure your company's recruiting and hiring practices as well as your HR policies and benefits (including vacation and paid leave) are consistent with your company's values.

Whether or not you'll be successful in creating a strong, virtual culture will depend largely on your communication skills, the frequency of your communications, and whom you choose to hire. You'll make plenty of mistakes, but how you rectify them (and how quickly) will be more important than having made the mistakes in the first place.

9.3 Empower your executives

As CEO, it's also especially important that you empower other executives in your company. Here's something you've probably never heard a CEO say: When I go on vacation, I appoint two "acting CEOs" (Sarah, our vice president of products, and Mike, our executive vice president of search services) who are not only empowered, but encouraged to make decisions, big and small, while I'm away. And I'm proud to say they do!

For example, while I've been away, they've authorized the starting salary for a new hire, parted ways with one employee, and approved updates to the employee handbook. On a lighter note, team members try to hit Sarah and Mike up for all sorts of things while I'm gone, serious or not. For example, while I was away recently, our client care team petitioned them for hot tubs!

Among the many reasons I feel so comfortable having Sarah and Mike make decisions while I'm away on vacation, is that they both understand our values-based culture and how I make decisions. As I tell Sarah, Mike, and the rest of my team, if they make a decision based on our company values, the decision they make will be right nearly every time.

9.4 Be visible, be available, and participate

As the CEO of a virtual company, it's critical that you have a "visible presence" and be accessible to your team throughout the day. From the time I log on to Slack, usually around 7 a.m. (EST), my team sees that my online status is, yes, "available." (I usually log off around 6 p.m.)

In a distributed work environment, you can't lead from the sidelines. You have to be right in the thick of the action. That's because, when you don't have a central office, you need someone to keep your team connected and give them a sense of unity. And there's no one better suited to that role than you, the CEO.

I serve as "presenter-in-chief" on our all-company conference calls and lead our team-building activities, including Walking Wednesday, which I'll talk about in chapter 13.6, "Create bonding opportunities." I'm also an active, daily participant on our Slack channels, weighing in on everything from the best meal kit companies to international travel insurance. I also post articles that get lots of attention from my team. In fact, I recently shared an article about online security that Perry, our senior system administrator, hadn't seen. Perry wrote in response, "One of THE best articles I've read in a long time. What I'm most happy about is that it was you who posted it." When my system administrator's happy, I'm happy.

So, does it really make a difference when I'm away from my office, traveling on business, or on vacation (that is, anytime my Slack light isn't green)? My team members say that, yes, it just "feels" different. Why is my virtual absence so obvious to everyone? Emma said, "It's funny, but when Shelly is out of her virtual office, things just aren't as exciting."

9.5 Reach out and Slack someone

Your company's remote structure doesn't have to limit the information you have access to.

If you were to ask any of my team members, they'd tell you that I somehow seem to know "everything" that's going on at Fire Engine RED. In fact, as Emma explained, "Talk about having her finger on the pulse! There's nothing happening around the company that Shelly doesn't know about, even if she is presenting or tied up in another meeting. It's spooky!"

Here's how I do it. On a typical day, I'm very active on Slack. I communicate with as many as 20 members of my team, through "pop-up one-on-ones," that is, impromptu Slack audio calls. (I rarely use email because writing and responding to email creates extra work for me and my team members, and I find it also slows things down.) Similarly, I encourage my direct reports, and others, to reach out to me on Slack as issues arise throughout the day, rather than wait to brief me at a scheduled meeting. I'm happy to say that they actually do, which helps us to keep things moving and get a lot done each day.

In addition, I usually have two to three internal conference calls a day. Many of the calls are with my marketing and sales teams.

> *Tip:* Make sure your team knows that they're not to "manage" or "spin" their communications to you. If you don't have all of the facts, it's impossible to make good decisions.

Emma had this to say about how I communicate: "Shelly encourages open communication in real time. There's no sugar-coating or putting off a necessary discussion until later. She never sits around waiting for the time to be right." She added, "Shelly creates a sense of urgency and energy, so we get her the information she needs, and she makes decisions in a very agile fashion: quickly and with no fear of change."

9.6 Share information freely

One way to gain trust from your all-remote team members is to be transparent. That means sharing information with your team early and often.

Every other Friday, at 4 p.m. (EST), I host the "SS (Shelly Spiegel) Feed," an all-company call during which I share information with the team. During this call, I brief the team on the latest happenings at Fire Engine RED; this includes providing information on new hires, organization updates, and policy changes. I also talk about year-to-date sales, margins, and third-party costs.

While many leaders aren't comfortable (or interested in) sharing this type of information, I tend to err on the side of sharing more than necessary (even though my full transparency can sometimes stress out my CFO, which is understandable). I believe having this information helps our all-remote team feel more connected and trusted—and enables them to do even better work.

Rather than say more about the SS Feed myself, I'll turn it over to Mike, one of our EVPs. As he put it, "The SS Feed is Fire Engine RED's version of an 'all-hands' meeting. It's a way for the team to stay connected with the state of the company, understand what's happening with our clients, and hear about trends in our industry."

Mike added, "In these meetings, our CEO discusses everything from sales, to new HR-related policies, to light-hearted company-wide games that help team members feel a direct connection to Fire Engine RED (and even win a little prize money). It's also a great way for our team to experience our CEO 'in person.' Her focus in the SS Feed is about building a unique culture, helping team members feel like an integral part of the company, and sharing her vision."

We also record every SS Feed, so if a team member can't attend, they can download the audio file and get caught up later.

> *Tip:* If you do decide to record the calls with your team, archive them in a place where they're easy to find (ideally on your intranet) and urge your team members to listen to the recording of any call they miss as soon as they return to their virtual office.

9.7 Get to know your team members

Everyone wants to feel appreciated and secure in their jobs. Showing your team members that they're valued can be even more challenging in a virtual environment. Because you won't be passing your team members in the halls, it's vital that you're intentional and deliberate about building relationships with them. As a virtual CEO, you don't want your team members to ever think that out of sight means out of mind. Here are some of the ways I stay connected to my team members, especially with those I don't talk to every day.

I try to schedule a one-on-one meeting or virtual walk with a team member nearly every day (including new team members, once they've settled in and have been with Fire Engine RED for about 45 days). The calls help me get to know my team members better. We often talk about their families, pets, travel, and even politics. And I'm always looking for recommendations on the next great television series to binge-watch. I also get a better view of what's going on at the company at all levels. These calls usually last about 60 minutes.

In addition, when I'm traveling for work, I'll try to get together with any team members who live nearby. And when my team members are passing through Philadelphia, I ask them to let me know so we can have dinner together; family members and friends they're traveling with are welcome, too. Just this week, I heard from Megan, who wrote, "I wanted to let you know that my husband and I will be in Philadelphia next month! I'd love to get together while we're there! Will you be in town then?" My answer was an enthusiastic, "Yes," and I'm looking forward to dinner with Megan and her husband. I'm thrilled when team members include dinner with me on their vacation itineraries!

… And know what they actually do

In 2018, I took a big step toward getting a better understanding of how my team members spend their time. For several months, I worked with my 60-plus team members (and their direct managers) to update their job descriptions.

It turned out to be a win-win for my employees and for me. My employees appreciated that I'd taken the time to understand how they were contributing to the company, and I gained a new appreciation of how each of them was contributing to the bottom line. In addition, because I was able to gain a deeper understanding of what each employee actually does, it led to a variety of promotions, title changes, and salary increases.

9.8 Be empathetic

I also believe it's especially important for a CEO, especially a virtual one, to be empathetic, that is, to be able to put themselves in the shoes of their employees and try to see things from their perspective. In fact, 96 percent of employees think it's important for their employers to show empathy![159] Being empathetic can help you gain the trust, respect, and loyalty of your team members, which makes it good for business and employee retention.

However, demonstrating empathy can be even more challenging for a distributed company's CEO than for a bricks-and-mortar company's executive. That's because you don't have visual cues (facial or body language), which can make reading the room more difficult. To compensate, you'll need to listen more carefully on calls and read written communications more thoroughly. And, yes, this does take practice.

9.9 Don't just tell them, show them

Many CEOs give lip service to all sorts of things, but in practice, they do little to show their team they actually mean what they say. If you want your team to believe what you say, you'll need to back up your words with action.

For example, how many times have you heard CEOs tell their employees the idea that "we're a team and we're all in this together?" I do this too, but in 2011 (our tenth year in business), I wanted to *show* my employees that I meant it and valued their contributions to the company equally. After all, our motto is, "It takes a team." So, I rewarded each individual team member with a $10,000 bonus (real dollars, not virtual ones), regardless of their position or how long they'd been with the company.

In addition, I've always told my team that client "fit" matters more than making a sale to a client. In 2017, I had the opportunity to demonstrate to my team that I meant it. Here's what happened: A small group of us had traveled to a college campus in Connecticut to meet with a prospective client. During our presentation, the college president was disrespectful (and at times outright hostile) to me and my leadership team. After 45 minutes, she told us she had to leave, but asked us to continue the presentation for her colleagues. Once she was out of the room, I stopped the presentation and told her team that Fire Engine RED wasn't the right fit for their school, and that we couldn't take them on as a client (even if they wanted to work with us). Then it was our turn to walk out, and that's exactly what we did.

On the train ride home, I sent my *entire* team an email, letting them know what had happened, and I explained to them that no amount of money would have been worth bringing on a client who was likely to treat them badly, were we to win the business. Here's the silver lining—this unpleasant incident gave me the opportunity to *show* my team that I had their backs.

9.10 Thank them

One easy way to show appreciation to your team members is to simply say "thank you" for a job well done. (It helps when you have supportive managers, like we do, who tip me off!) For example, I've written the following notes to recognize and thank my team members:

- Thank you for helping the company move forward!
- I LOVE your idea. It's very consistent with our values!
- Your name has been coming up repeatedly recently. You're dazzling people with your wizardry!
- Thanks for continuing to take on new challenges and mastering them!

And sometimes the situation calls for a bit more. When several of our quality analysts helped find and resolve a whole host of software bugs in record time, I sent them a note of appreciation, along with an animated GIF of Oprah Winfrey celebrating. The note said, "And *you* resolved a bug, and *you* resolved a bug, and *you* resolved a bug!"

A little gratitude can have a big impact. As Justin shared, "I was plenty motivated already, but this little note definitely gives me renewed energy!"

9.11 Manage change through education

I've found that the best way for me as a CEO to manage change effectively is to educate my team. I find that the more I've done so, the easier it's been for me to make the changes necessary to protect the well-being of the company, and ultimately, their jobs.

For example, during our first 13 years in business, we had a low-deductible health insurance plan and paid 100 percent of our employees' health insurance premiums. In 2014, due to skyrocketing healthcare costs, we moved to a high-deductible healthcare plan, where employees were asked to contribute to the cost of the premiums. As you can imagine, my team wasn't happy about it.

However, as I shared information about healthcare trends and costs, they quickly realized that it was the right thing to do to ensure the company's long-term financial viability as well as their job security.

9.12 Speak out and act

Given the current political environment, I believe CEOs, remote or not, have a special obligation to speak out against policies that aren't consistent with their company's values or that could negatively impact their team members and/or clients. Even better, act! It's good for your team to know where you stand.

I can still remember the day—Tuesday, September 5, 2017—when President Donald J. Trump ended the Deferred Action for Childhood Arrivals (DACA) program, which allowed undocumented immigrants who came to the U.S. as children to remain in the country.[160]

More than any other issue, the DACA decision had the most dramatic effect on the morale of my team. This made sense, as 87 percent of people want DACA recipients to stay in the U.S.[161]

How did I know that the decision to end DACA had upset so many of my team members when we all work virtually? Well, I couldn't miss it. My team members were sending me Slack messages, initiating audio calls with me, and sending me emails. They were talking about it on the departmental calls I participated in and on my walks with

them. What was upsetting the most was that they felt powerless to do anything.

I knew I had to act but wasn't sure what to do. Then the idea hit me. Several months earlier, one of my team members, Ray, had told me about the U Dreamers Program at the University of Miami.[162] As a show of solidarity, I asked Jamie, our director of people, to contact the program's administrator and have them recommend two students for (paid) internships. We interviewed and hired Albany and Mathi within four weeks of the DACA decision. Being an all-remote company made it possible, and easy, for us to hire these students. How have things worked out with our DACA interns? They've done so well that we brought on a third intern, Dinora, in January 2019. (See chapter 5.5, "Offer internships.")

As I had hoped, hiring these interns helped boost my team's morale. One team member wrote, "Thank you so much for making these hires. I appreciate this effort and am proud to work for a company that would take this step."

Recently, I took it a step further, and turned over the SS Feed to two of our DACA interns.
I thought my team members would benefit from hearing about the reality of DACA from people who are living it. On this call, our interns told stories of adversity and hardship the majority of us will never have to endure, and

the rest of our team members had much to say on our company-wide Slack channel:

- "You ladies are extraordinary. Thank you so much for sharing your stories with us; it is humbling to say the least." – Meaghan

- "I certainly learned a lot from the call. It's another reminder of how much we take for granted. You both should be so proud of how far you have come! It makes me happy to be a part of a company that can help you both get a little closer on your journey." – Amy

- "Just a note to say thank you so much for making these hires. I am among those who appreciate this effort, and I am proud to work here." – Morgan

Between our interns and our other team members, I feel like we have very solid alignment with our company values of Grit and Empathy.

If doing what I can to support DACA students makes me an "activist CEO," then I'm proud to be one!

9.13 And, use humor

Finally, I've found humor to be one of the best ways to connect with my 100 percent remote team. I want them to know that, yes, I'm a real person who has a sense of humor and doesn't take herself too seriously. Whenever possible I try to interject some humor into my team's workday.

For example, when someone on my team gives me good news (usually via Slack), I often respond with a "Woo-hoo!" or a virtual "High kick!" Several years ago, I shared with my team a marketing email I received, in which the writer addressed me not as "Shelly," but as "Shitzy." I'm also not above passing along awful photos of myself to get a laugh. One Halloween, I emailed the entire team a selfie of me having an allergic reaction (my puffy face looked pretty scary) with the subject line "Boo!" Nearly as scary were the "big hair" photos from high school that I showed to my team.

But, perhaps, my most memorable stunt, according to my team, was at our 2013 annual team meeting. I dressed up as singer Katy Perry, cupcake bra and all, to announce that our new customer relationship management (CRM) product would be called "Fireworks" (a name inspired by my favorite Katy Perry song). I could go on and on, but you probably get the picture. At Fire Engine RED, CEO also stands for chief *entertainment* officer!

As you can see, being a CEO of an all-remote company takes a lot of work and requires that you assume multiple roles beyond chief executive officer, such as chief *communications* officer, chief *culture* officer, and even chief *entertainment* officer. I simply can't imagine having a better job!

Chapter 10
Player-coaches: The best kind of remote managers

Your managers will play a key role in whether your distributed company is successful or not. Just like managers at bricks-and-mortar companies, remote managers of virtual teams need to (1) hold department meetings, (2) ensure their direct reports' job descriptions are up to date, (3) provide their direct reports with feedback, (4) work with their direct reports on their career paths, and (5) make recommendations regarding promotions and salary increases.

So, what makes remote managers different? At Fire Engine RED, our managers act as "player-coaches." They're doers, not just delegators. That is, they work on projects of their own as well as manage other team members. This is why no manager at Fire Engine RED has more than 10 direct reports.

Let's take a look at what your managers can do to help their direct reports stay engaged, happy, and productive. (I'll also have more to say about productivity in chapter 12, "Maximizing and measuring productivity at your all-remote company.")

10.1 Know their direct reports' jobs

I believe that managers who have previously done their direct reports' jobs get the most out of their team members. At Fire Engine RED, the overwhelming majority of our managers previously held the same jobs their direct reports do, either at our company or at a previous employer. I find such managers are better able to define the positions on their team, determine each direct report's responsibilities, and ensure their team's processes are efficient and that their team members are productive. Someone who's done the job is also more credible and more likely to keep their expectations and deadlines reasonable.

10.2 Build relationships with their direct reports

At a 100 percent remote company, it's especially important that managers and their direct reports have a good relationship.

Mandy, our creative director (who manages a team of six designers) noted, "Our team chat in Slack is very active and is only directly work-related about 50 percent of the time. Everyone on the team is a huge fan of *The Office*, so there are a lot of jokes going back and forth on any given day about the show and lots of other topics we find funny or interesting."

Mandy further explained, "I make an effort to also have individual, personal conversations with my team members often, making it a point to not be work-related. Getting to know your team on a personal level makes them comfortable to approach you with requests they might find difficult."

Shannon told me that managers should "make the effort to establish a good one-to-one relationship with each team member." Jeff, one of our EVPs, has done this to the extreme! Every time a new person joins his team, Jeff travels from his home office in Minnesota to meet with them in person. He's traveled to Missouri, Ohio, Oregon, Pennsylvania, and Wisconsin, and I expect he'll soon be headed to South Carolina to meet Ashley, the newest member of his department.

Despite the distance, many of our team members have grown so close to their managers that they even make their wedding guest list. Chuck, who lives and works in

California, used to manage another team member, Zach (now our director of operations) who lives 3,000 miles away in Philadelphia. Chuck and Zach worked well together right from the start, and they bonded through instant message conversations about beer, hockey, and obscure heavy metal bands. So, it was only natural when Zach invited Chuck to his wedding; Chuck and his wife made the cross-country trip to attend! (I was invited, too, and made the trip across town!) What surprised Chuck the most when he finally met Zach in person? "He was much taller than I had expected."

10.3 Treat their direct reports like adults

It's been said that "people don't leave companies, they leave managers." I completely agree, and that's why I believe that managers of fully remote teams should be "good manager[s] of people who don't need to be managed."[163] As Jason 2 shared, "A good manager should treat their direct reports like adults and expect them to act like adults in return."

Nick added, "People who are attracted to and thrive in virtual environments tend to want more freedom to follow their own workflow, so allowing for that is a big plus."

When I asked Shannon what makes a great remote manager, she suggested we "clone Emily R.," her manager. Shannon said, "Emily makes the effort to establish a good relationship with each team member with regular one-on-

ones and team check-ins." Erica, another one of Emily's direct reports, agreed: "What Shannon said. Emily doesn't micromanage and trusts us to do what needs to be done to make the company great. She has it down!"

Your managers should also focus on results rather than hours worked. That is, what their direct reports are actually getting done, not on how many hours they're online. It all comes back to our company value of Trust. As Jason 2 shared, "Our team has client success/happiness as the primary goal, so we all do what is needed to make that happen." And Nick added, "*That* the work gets done is usually far more important than *how* it gets done."

I should mention there are a couple of things we *don't* do. For one, we don't have people "clock in" or track how they spend every minute of their workday. For another, we don't access team members' computers remotely. Doing so is, unfortunately, a go-to for some managers who begin supervising remote employees and fear a loss of control.

10.4 Be supportive

It's one thing to have policies in place that enable employees to take time off for personal or family reasons; however, employees also need to feel supported by their managers with regard to actually taking the time off. For example, our unlimited sick time and "out time" policies wouldn't be helpful if our employees felt like their managers (subtly or not) didn't support our policies.

As David, who manages our client care team, shared, "It's important for a remote manager to understand that they are leading a group of human beings, not worker bees. Each with their own wants, needs, goals, specialties, and limitations. They have complete lives outside of the office, which are equally as important to support as the lives inside the office."

Following up on David's point, Amy talked about the support she gets from her manager as well as the other designers on her team: "It's been super vital over the past year. On our team, almost all of us have had something personal come up, but we've all been there to help support one another if we needed to be leaned on. What's important is the person's well-being. The work is something another one of us can handle, and we're happy to do it."

10.5 Help their direct reports prioritize

Your managers should make sure that their direct reports are focused on your company's top priorities, and they should be aware of any side projects their direct reports take on. However, this can be easier said than done.

Here's an example. Early on, before we defined processes for developing software features and functionality, team members would reach out to developers directly to request "small" improvements. Developers, who were eager to please, did the work. Now, as you might expect, priority items got bumped for these side projects, many of which even our director of technology didn't know about! Even though the developers had their hearts in the right place, these stealth projects would end up getting in the way of our prioritized projects and, therefore, conflicting with our company goals.

Don't get me wrong—collaborating across departments can lead to higher employee engagement and big wins for your company. The only caveat is that any side projects should first be cleared with the collaborating team members' managers.

10.6 Communicate frequently and effectively

Your managers should also be in frequent communication with their direct reports. Research has shown that when the manager/team member relationship is strong, and the leader communicates frequently, the virtual team member is more likely to contribute to team decision making, which in turn increases innovation.[164]

Because fully remote managers don't have the luxury of "managing by walking around,"[165] it's critical that they are comfortable using multiple channels to communicate, including instant messaging and audio-only conversations (that is, using a variety of technologies to stay in touch).

As Meaghan explained, "In a virtual environment, it's important for managers to over-communicate and be straightforward when setting expectations and providing feedback. This can provide team members with a sense of security, and it lets them know if they're meeting their manager's expectations."

Whenever possible, our managers use instant messaging rather than email to communicate. We simply don't have time for drawn-out email exchanges, especially when a quick Slack IM or audio call will do.

This fits with what Erika shared, "Being open to exploring different ways of communicating effectively—Slack, email, video conferencing, etc.—with your team is extremely important in the virtual work environment."

Managers should always keep in mind that communication is a two-way street. Our team members are expected to communicate proactively and keep their managers up to date on the status of their work or particular projects, rather than wait for their managers to track them down and ask them for an update. This allows managers to focus on the bigger picture instead of micromanaging the information flow. Ben had this to say about how managers communicate: "It's important to note that communication isn't just talking with someone; it's crucial to make sure that you are listening as well." And

Emma added that remote-team managers "need the ability to listen to what has been said or not said because we have no visual cues for how people are feeling about work and/or personal stuff."

Mandy, our creative director, had this to say about her approach (and echoed Emma's mention of visual cues): "From an employee's first day, I make a point to let them know how important communication is, especially in our virtual environment. If they have a question or are stuck, they need to make an effort to speak up because we can't see visual cues if something is wrong. I think this helps to foster the openness we have as a group because no one seems to be shy about coming to me or the team as a whole."

Mandy added, "Our team chat is also a great spot for problem solving. When someone runs into a bug, code issue, etc., they are quick to post it, and other team members are quick to jump in with opinions and ideas to try and find a solution collaboratively."

One challenge of being all-remote is not being able to have serious conversations with team members in person. There's more trust shared when you talk face-to-face, and people can "read" each other better through facial expressions and body language. To compensate, I encourage our managers to try what I've learned to do, and that's to listen actively when talking via Slack audio or by phone.

10.7 Develop future leaders

Managers should help identify and develop future leaders, by (1) serving as mentors and cheerleaders for their direct reports, and (2) by assigning tasks that align with their direct reports' strengths.

For example, Jeff (an EVP) helped one of our data specialists, Jason 3, build on his already-well-developed skill set. When clients began requesting more work from our data department, promoting Jason 3 was a slam dunk for Jeff.

Here's another example. We wanted to have one of our implementation managers (Melissa) move from our legacy à-la-carte software products to our flagship CRM product. So, we paired her with our then-director of implementation (Keith, now our director of client happiness). Keith worked with Melissa on CRM implementations for various clients until he was able to step back. Now Melissa is handling CRM implementations on her own.

Nichole, from our student search team, takes a similar approach. "It's like a bell curve," she told me. Initially the team member shadows her, then at some point we're each doing the same amount of work, and eventually she shadows the team member to help them build their expertise and confidence.

Also, it's easier than you might think for remote managers to help their direct reports grow. At our company, managers may be miles away, but they're always virtually close by to offer support and assistance via our communications tools. As Glenna, our vice president of search operations, shared, "When situations occur that require escalation, it's helpful to know that when you need your boss, they are just an IM or Slack call away."

> *Tip:* Managers in remote companies have a unique opportunity to train their direct reports in real-time situations with clients: Coaching via instant messages. Let's say hypothetical manager Astrid is on a client call with her hypothetical direct report Milo. Both Astrid and Milo participate in the call, with Astrid sending prompts, comments, and feedback "behind the scenes" to steer Milo in the right direction. (We always let clients know exactly who's on our calls with them, and you should, too.)

Chapter 11
Managing business operations:
The all-remote way

Your fully remote company will reach a point when someone will need to take the lead on operations. That person should focus on creating efficiencies and establishing processes that are rooted in your company's vision and strategy.

In 2018, we created a director of operations position and promoted our marketing manager, Zach, into the role. Zach was uniquely qualified for the job. Over his eight years (and counting) with our company, he'd gained deep insight into our company vision, strategy, and culture. He'd worked with both our sales and marketing teams, so he knew the benefits of our products and services inside and out. He'd also worked closely with HR on internal communications and had taken on the additional responsibility of helping HR streamline its policies and operations.

Here are some of the projects that Zach took on when he first became our director of operations, any or all of which you should consider having your operations leader handle.

11.1 Manage collaborative tools and licenses

More and more companies, distributed or not, are using Software-as-a-Service (SaaS) tools to boost their productivity. In fact, "Seventy-three percent of organizations say nearly all their apps will be SaaS by 2020."[166] Before your tool set grows and becomes difficult to manage, I encourage you to implement a SaaS management tool to help you optimize your SaaS usage and spending.

For years, each department at Fire Engine RED had selected and managed their own productivity tools. As a result, we didn't know:

- How many tools we were using.
- The number of licenses we had for each tool.
- What each tool was being used for.
- Which team members were using which tools.
- How much we were paying for each tool.

One of the first tasks Zach undertook as our director of operations was to conduct an audit of our tools, and it turned into a huge project. It was as though he'd embarked on a scavenger hunt with team members providing clues along the way.

Two months later, after connecting with nearly every team member, Zach presented me with a spreadsheet with 30-plus columns and multiple sheets of data about our tool usage and costs. And still, Zach and I were fairly certain that the spreadsheet he'd diligently put together had not captured all of the SaaS tools in use, who was using them, how frequently they were being used, and the costs associated with them. It was clear to us that we needed (ironically) yet another SaaS tool to manage the 38 SaaS tools our audit had uncovered (and those that had yet to be uncovered). Using a spreadsheet simply wouldn't work.

Zach set out to see if such tools existed. What he found was that SaaS management tools did exist, but the market was fairly new, and there were only a few early-stage products available for small companies like ours.

It took Zach several tries to find a solution that not only works for us but that we can also enthusiastically recommend. The tool, Intello (www.intello.io), has helped us identify all the tools we were using; we also found that we were using more than twice as many tools (85 of them!) as had been captured in our original audit.

Many of the tools that were missing from the original list were ones we weren't paying for because our team members were using the free versions. Because these tools had no cost associated with them in our QuickBooks account, they'd gone undetected by our audit. As a result of implementing Intello, we found we were actually paying for 42 tools and were using the free versions of 43 additional tools.

Once we knew what tools we were paying for, which team members were using the tools, and how frequently they were using them, we were able to eliminate six tools that:

- We weren't using or were using infrequently.
- Were redundant (including a variety of project management and screen-sharing tools).
- We'd outgrown.
- Were used only by people who were no longer with our company.

In other cases, we opted to keep the tool but reduce the number of user licenses. For example, we found that many team members weren't using (and didn't need) Office 365. They were able to use G Suite (one of our company-wide tools that has the same functionality) instead. By dropping a bunch of those Office 365 licenses, we saved a good deal of money.

Another big benefit of implementing a SaaS management tool relates to onboarding. Because we now know the specific tools each department is using, we're able to ensure our new hire implements the right tools (based on their role) during their onboarding session with their Second Friend. (For example, our software development team has a total of 16 department-specific tools.)

Similarly, when a team member leaves our company, Intello helps us identify what tools they were using, so we can remove access and stop paying for those particular licenses immediately. Also, when a team member shifts to a new role, Intello helps us identify the tools they don't need anymore as well as any new ones they do need.

I encourage you to get a good handle on your tool set before it becomes too unwieldy, like ours did. A SaaS management tool is one tool that you absolutely shouldn't run your virtual business without!

11.2 Develop an intranet

At an all-remote company, it's especially important that your team members are able to "serve themselves," which is why I would encourage you to put an intranet in place for your company as soon as possible. An intranet can serve as your company's cultural hub, provide easy access to HR-related information (such as your benefits and paid leave policies), help your team members get to know each other better, and centralize your company's documentation regarding processes and best practices.

What's more, your intranet should be friendly, accessible, and provide information in a simple and easy-to-understand manner. It should also reflect your company's culture and personality. Ideally, it should be fun to use, so your team members *want* to use it, not dread having to go on it.

> *Tip:* Because your intranet will house some of your most important company information, I recommend putting your intranet behind a VPN.

Prior to establishing our intranet, we had what we called "The Big RED Book," which provided new hires with a lively introduction to all things Fire Engine RED. As our company grew, so did The Big RED Book. What had started out as a three-page introduction to our company had grown into a 150-plus-page tome that was difficult to manage and update. Even worse, it had become practically impossible for team members to find the information they needed.

As we quickly learned, finding the right intranet solution for a 100 percent remote company was a challenging one. The off-the-shelf solutions we looked at were mostly ugly, difficult to navigate, packed with more functionality than we needed, and time-consuming to implement. They also required a part-time (or full-time) administrator, lots of user training, and endless support. In short, all of the solutions we found were inconsistent with our company values of Simplicity and Good Design.

So, because we had design, user experience, copywriting, and web development expertise in-house, we decided to build our own intranet using WordPress. Here's what our designer, Jen, had to say about her part in the project: "When I was given the task of designing and developing the brand identity for our intranet, I was so excited! My goal was to build it in a way that not only addressed our company's need for a central location of all company documents but also was friendly, warm, and allowed users to find more delight in using our intranet."

Fortunately, it's easier than ever to create an intranet. Here's why: It used to be that a company's intranet also served as their communications/social hub, and as a result, it needed to include tools for instant messaging, discussion groups, news feeds, and more, all of which increased the complexity and cost of the project.

But not anymore. Employees today don't want to spend their time communicating through subpar tools on a company intranet when there are better tools, such as Slack, in the

marketplace. So, your intranet should be designed to work in tandem with your
company's communications tools. There's no need to duplicate them.

As I've mentioned previously, at our company, Slack picks up the, well, slack in the communications/social area. For example, we have Slack channels for company news, new hire announcements, organizational updates, wellness, and even for this book, *Fully Remote*.

To give our intranet a "personality," I named it "alfRED," after my grandfather, Alfred. As Jen remembered, "The first thing I did was 'sit down' with Shelly to chat and learn about Alfred. During that conversation, Shelly mentioned that he 'knew everything, but wasn't a know-it-all,' which was exactly the personality that we wanted the intranet to have. And then came the kicker: he was an organic tomato farmer."

Jen continued, "After our conversation, I created a style-tile (or mood board) of key images, textures, and colors that communicated the visual story of what alfRED, the intranet, would become. From that point, and pardon the pun, everything came together so organically!" Jen ended up creating a logo (or as she calls it, a "signature character") that's a tomato with a smiling face. I loved it, and so did my team members; many of them asked Jen to create a sized-down version of the logo to use as a Slack status icon. (I also showed the alfRED logo to my mom, Andrea (the real-life Alfred's daughter), who called it "the cutest logo ever." Moms are great like that!)

In keeping with our desire to make an intranet fun, and to reflect the real-life Alfred's personality, any time someone logs onto alfRED, they're greeted with a fun fact or a witty comment. It might be about our company, a team member, working remotely, or even the real-life Alfred.

Here's an example: "G'day! Did you know … Fire Engine RED has been mentioned in *Inc.*, *Entrepreneur*, *Fast Company*, *Forbes*, and *Men's Health*? Mind. Blown."

I recently asked team members for feedback about our intranet. David from client care said, "I love that our intranet was built from the ground up. There are products out there that may have done a halfway decent job, but developing exactly what we need, and having complete control, has made it an incredible tool, which will grow and adapt as the company's needs change."

Robert, our assistant controller, added, "I think the intranet became important as the size of Fire Engine RED grew. Ten years ago, when there were 12 or so of us, we were all communicating with each other on a constant basis. If we needed information, we could just request it 'in person.' Now this isn't feasible or practical, so the intranet is a resource that allows team members to obtain information on their own."

Keep in mind that your intranet will never really be "done," so be sure that there's someone who "owns" your intranet and ensures that HR and other departments keep their content fresh and up to date. At Fire Engine RED, that's Zach, our director of operations.

11.3 Document your processes

Once you have an intranet, you have the perfect hub for storing your training materials. First, though, you'll have to document your processes and best practices. Every department at Fire Engine RED has a playbook, in which their processes are codified and explained.

> *Tip:* If you have a process that isn't efficient, it becomes obvious as soon as you try to write about it! If you're having problems documenting a process, you most likely need to rethink the process. If a process is efficient, it's easy to write a step-by-step guide to it.

How do these playbooks get created? As we say at Fire Engine RED, "it takes a team," and after years of trial and error, we've found that taking an Agile approach works best. A methodology often used by technology companies, "Agile" can be defined as taking an incremental, iterative approach, that is, planning and working to complete projects in small sections, also called iterations.[167]

First, our director of operations works with each department to break down their processes into manageable chunks of work and to produce a timeline. From there, each team member documents their own processes. As sections are completed, they're handed off to Meaghan, our copy manager and operations analyst, who organizes and edits the documentation, reviews the content for accuracy (she actually performs the steps), and applies our company style to it. The result is an easy-to-follow playbook.

> *Tip:* When starting a new playbook, we've found that one of the fastest ways to create content is to ask new members to write down the processes as they learn them. Not only is this a great way to train someone, it's also a way for the new team member to feel like they're contributing to the success of your company from their first day onward.

How long does it take to create a playbook? It depends on how detailed and complex the processes are. For example, it took eight people, including two new team members, nearly *two years* to create our nearly 300-page data services playbook!

Our playbooks provide a variety of benefits. For one thing, they establish "the Fire Engine RED way" of doing things, which helps us deliver consistently excellent client experiences. For example, our student search department has several project managers who handle a total of 125-plus projects a year for clients. They lead efforts that bring together teams that include 10 or more people. The playbooks help everyone working on a particular student search project get on the same page and take advantage of the efficiencies we've put down on (virtual) paper for everyone to see. Put another way, our playbooks include all the ingredients and recipes for producing the "secret sauce" we use to help our clients meet their goals!

The playbooks also serve as handy references when one team member needs to fill in for another, due to a vacation, illness, etc. Each playbook forms the basis of our training and cross-training efforts, so someone can jump in to help with no drop-off in the high quality of service provided.

As Laura shared, "We use our data department's playbook on an everyday basis. Recently, I had to cover for Molly, who was on vacation. This involved following a process that I hadn't done in over a year and couldn't remember how to do. However, because the process was documented in the playbook, I was able to follow the instructions without having to delay or call Molly on her vacation."

Molly herself said, "We all dreaded putting the playbook together because documentation is so time-consuming. But, at one time or another, each person on our team has said how grateful she is to have it. It's been really useful for training new team members and for covering for team members while they're on vacation."

Finally, the playbooks have also helped us retain key knowledge on the rare occasions a team member has left the company and saved us time on training their replacement. Amber said, "In case someone moves on, it's good to have processes in writing. That way you don't have to have 10 people working to bring one person up to speed."

It does take time and commitment to keep our playbooks updated. So, as you might expect, we have processes in place for maintaining the playbooks! Each manager is responsible for the content of their department's playbook and designates a team member to deliver periodic updates to Meaghan, our copy manager and operations analyst. Meaghan, in turn, is responsible for organizing, editing, testing, and formatting the playbook documents.

Emma shared, "Because Meaghan and Zach work with *all* our teams to document their processes, they've been able to find inconsistencies and redundancies from department to department."

Tip: Our playbooks are created in Google Docs. But, when we first wanted to make them accessible and searchable via our intranet, we realized it would take valuable time and effort to reformat all the content into WordPress. Instead, we simply created a new Google account for the playbook content, made the Google Docs read-only, and linked to them from our intranet. When we need to make updates to the playbooks, we simply do so in the Google Doc.

11.4 Create and implement a document retention policy

As your all-remote company grows, each of your departments will begin to accumulate virtual "piles" of electronic documents. These documents will likely be stored in different places, for different lengths of time, etc.

All of this can lead to a big problem—finding a document you need in a timely manner. That's why I recommend you create a document retention policy (DRP) before your documentation gets out of hand. As an aside, I appreciate the need to keep documentation that's useful, informative, or legally necessary, but I also believe in decluttering and deleting whenever possible!

Tip: I also recommend you look at federal, state, and local regulations regarding document retention to see if there are any special requirements for your industry.

Your DRP should basically identify which kinds of documents you need (or just want) to save, for how long, and where you'll store them. Having a DRP in place will reduce the time and effort it takes to find and to retrieve documents as well as free up valuable storage space.

We created our DRP to align our management of documents with our company value of Simplicity. Zach, our director of operations, served (and continues to serve) as the point person. The first step he took was to discuss with each manager their department's needs and current methods of storing electronic documents, including where they were storing them. Next, he assessed which types of documents we were retaining and for how long. He found that, as I suspected, we were basically keeping every document, forever.

Zach and I then began working with each department to determine appropriate time frames for deleting different types of documents. For example, we decided that proposals that weren't accepted would be kept for a shorter amount of time than signed contracts. Zach determined that a tool our development team was already using, Confluence (www.confluence.com), would be an ideal central hub for storing our documents. Using Confluence would help us get documents off people's hard drives and centralize information in a space where the appropriate team members could easily access it. It could also make it easy for us to set up the naming conventions and hierarchies we wanted to establish. Once we decided on Confluence, Zach consulted with our IT team to add an extra layer of security to it, so our Confluence site now resides behind our VPN.

Then we implemented our DRP in an Agile fashion, rolling it out one department at a time (with HR as our "proof of concept" team) and continuing as others were ready. For example, we created "Sales" spaces for our student search and CRM sales teams to store their proposals and contracts. Any team member involved in the sales process (anyone from the CFO to a proposal writer) can access these documents. This makes it much easier for someone who's not the original owner of the document to verify, revise, or otherwise continue with the sales process if the original owner isn't available.

> *Tip:* We found that the best organizational structure for our documents involved creating duplicate page titles. For example, we need to use the word "Proposals" in the hierarchy for our CRM and student search business units to help us stay organized. Here's the thing: Confluence, by Atlassian (www.atlassian.com/software/confluence), does not allow you to create pages with duplicate titles (it

applies a unique identifier to all spaces and page titles). Fortunately, there's a fix for that. To customize the naming conventions and hierarchies for our needs, we found and downloaded a simple, yet powerful add-on from the Atlassian Marketplace (https://marketplace.atlassian.com) called Duplicate Page Titles. This add-on attaches a hidden unique identifier to any duplicate page titles, giving us the ability to create pages and folders with the same title/naming convention.

Part of the rollout included minimal training for our teams on the DRP. From there, we trust our team members to follow our policy accordingly. As I've mentioned before, we rely on the honor system at Fire Engine RED, rather than enforcement tactics.

In summary, when it comes to documents, define and keep the essential ones and make them easy to find. Doing so has made for more efficient operations at Fire Engine RED, and will, at your fully remote company as well!

Chapter 12
Maximizing and measuring productivity at your all-remote company

I'm often asked, "How do you know that everyone at your all-virtual company is working when you can't see them?" My answer is always the same. I'm more concerned about my team working too much, rather than them working too little. What's more important is that I know that everyone is being productive.

Let's look at what you can do to help your team get more done, and how you can keep track of everything they're doing, the all-remote way.

12.1 How to create a culture of productivity

As the CEO of an all-remote company, you must ensure that a culture of productivity is encoded in your business's virtual DNA. (We'll discuss company culture in a broader sense in chapter 13, "Building a strong company culture: No office building necessary.")

Work in interdependent teams

To help your team members be productive in an all-remote environment, I recommend having them work in teams. And at the team level, they should work interdependently rather than independently, so they're accountable to one another.

Alaina, one of our copywriters, shared, "If I don't have the copy ready, the designer can't go beyond a certain point. Also, with our project management software, it's really incremental and easy for the project manager to see if there's a delay somewhere in the process." She added, "It's like we're passing the virtual baton!"

Chad T., a designer, explained, "We have a Slack channel for every client. This helps us focus questions and issues and direct them only to the people who can provide answers and help. We're able to be more productive because we can just type a quick message, get the information we need right away, and move forward."

Greg said, "People reach out proactively about deliverables, which shows they're engaged with what's going on." He added, "If someone wasn't consistently available or meeting their deadlines, word would travel fast."

Jason 3 agreed, and he explained that even in a fully remote environment there's nowhere for an unproductive team member to hide. "I have the luxury of working on a team where it would be really obvious if deliverables and deadlines were not being met. I can just look in our shared documents to see if the data has been entered."

Trust but verify

As with nearly all virtual companies, yours will likely be filled with self-starters who thrive when they feel empowered, trusted, and respected. In most cases, I've found that the more responsibility we give our team members, the better their work, the more engaged they are, and the longer they stay with our company. However, I would caution you against trusting blindly. As President Ronald Reagan said, "Trust but verify." In other words, check in with your team occasionally to make sure they're not just working, but doing things the way you want and getting the results you expect.

Adopt an Agile mindset and approach

When it comes to getting work done, I recommend that teams throughout your company work in an "Agile" fashion. Agile is a methodology that's been embraced by software companies (all-remote and not), including ours. As I mentioned in chapter 11.3, ("Document your processes"), it's about rolling out usable products and services in "chunks" and ensuring continuous delivery and improvement. At Fire Engine RED, we've found that working in an Agile manner can benefit each of our other departments as well. These principles have served us well when creating our intranet, managing our student search projects, and even writing this book.

Below are several of the Agile principles[168] we've adopted. For each project, we:

1) Determine the highest priorities.
2) Identify the minimum requirements.
3) Plan the work to be done in "short" periods of time (one to two weeks).
4) Track progress in a way that's visible to all involved.
5) Hold weekly meetings to check on progress and discuss challenges. (With software teams, these "stand-up" meetings are typically held each day and last five to ten minutes.)

6) Have a "retrospective" meeting at the end of each milestone to discuss what went well, what didn't, and what could be improved.

As you'll find, when you break every project down into small, manageable chunks, you'll feel more productive and that virtually anything is possible!

Make sure every project has a manager

One of the best things you can do to increase productivity is to make sure that every project has a good (or even better, a great) project manager.

A few years after our distributed company was founded, several of our team members were working on updating our company's website, but nothing was getting done. When I mentioned this to my then-business partner, her question to me was, "Who's the project manager?" I immediately realized there wasn't one and that no one owned the project. It wasn't until then that I realized just how crucial a project manager is to a successful outcome. From that moment on, every project (whether internal or client-focused) at Fire Engine RED has had a project manager.

Project managers can also help you avoid one of the biggest time wasters I've encountered—putting projects on hold and trying to restart them later. Without a project manager to keep us focused, we've occasionally "paused" a project to turn our focus elsewhere, and when we've returned to the project, something in the market or with the project has shifted, so we have to go back to the drawing board.

Implement the right tools fully

To maximize their productivity, many of your departments will need to supplement your company-wide tools with department-specific tools. However, selecting the proper tools is only half the battle. The tools need to be fully implemented to maximize your team's productivity. Otherwise, your team members will have to devise complex work-arounds that drag down output (and even result in costly errors).

Ray, one of our project managers, said, "By taking the time to fully implement, especially something as critical as a project management tool, you set yourself up for long-term success. Otherwise, the tool may end up actually being a burden rather than helping your team work more efficiently. It's a big up-front investment in time and resources, but well worth it!"

Glenna shared, "Full implementation means that an individual or team has been very thorough in researching all aspects of the tool and will take advantage of new features and upgrades as they become available. It's great to have a 'tool champion' on your team, so not everyone has to be an expert." And Nichole added, "It's also important to make sure you're getting the most out of the tools you've invested in. If you're not fully leveraging a tool, you're throwing money away."

For more about how we manage our tools, see chapter 11.1, "Manage collaborative tools and licenses."

Make meetings count

Your company should keep meetings to a minimum and hold them only when absolutely necessary. We try to meet only when there's something that actually needs to be discussed or a decision has to be made; when we do have regularly scheduled meetings, they're usually once a week and rarely last more than one hour.

One team member explained, "At my previous company, we'd have meetings on issues that could have been sorted out with a quick instant message. Being all-virtual, we actually do get work done that way at Fire Engine RED."

Another great thing about being 100 percent remote is that we don't have meetings where people just show up to be seen. When we do have a meeting, it's most often a working session with a predetermined agenda, so by the end of nearly every meeting, we've made a decision or created a list of actionable items to advance a project. Amazing, right?

Make decisions quickly

As I mentioned in chapter 9, "Leading the way: Your life as a remote CEO," when it comes to decision making, don't kick the can down the virtual road. I believe that faster is usually better. It's okay for you and your team members to cut short the decision-making process if the decision feels right.

For example, at one point, when we needed to hire a contractor, we knew exactly what we wanted in terms of skills and expertise. The first person we spoke to was a perfect fit, so we hired him. Sure, we could have interviewed at a lot of other people, but because we all felt the same, we hired the contractor without interviewing anyone else.

And when I refer to "we" above, I'm talking about a small group of us charged with choosing the right contractor. Contrary to what some of my employees have seen at other companies, it's not always critical for *everyone* to have a voice or a vote (this can lead to people making suggestions they don't even believe in). Nor do we need a "devil's advocate" in every situation to challenge ideas. Additional ideas, even opposing ones, are welcome; we just get them all on (and off) the table as quickly as possible.

So, what happens if we make a mistake? It's simple: We correct it immediately.

Share client results and outcomes with your team

All of your team members, whether they're involved in strategy or implementation, should be aware of how your company does with regard to helping clients achieve their goals. I've found this increases engagement and productivity.

Here's a specific example. Our student search team, which markets to high schoolers on behalf of our college clients, has a "Search Scorecard" that they use to track the results of every project from start to finish. Early on, the student search leadership team only provided the scorecard to me. In the interest of transparency, I decided to share it with everyone on the search team, so they could all see how well we're performing with regard to our clients' goals. As a result, I believe the search team has become even more engaged.

Cross-train your team

Your managers need to make sure their direct reports are cross-trained on each other's responsibilities. This can help boost your company's productivity in a variety of ways.

For example, because we work across multiple time zones, work doesn't stop when a team member on the East Coast leaves at the end of their workday. Instead, a team member on the West Coast who's been cross-trained can pick up where their teammate left off and complete a time-sensitive task, rather than requiring the East Coast team member to work late to finish it.

In addition, cross-training enables us to keep everything moving even when an employee is on vacation or out sick. It also prevents us from having to contact someone while they're out of the office.

12.2 How to measure productivity

Now, let's take a look at how we track productivity at Fire Engine RED, using several of our departments as examples.

As you'll see below, you (as CEO) and your remote managers will be able to use many of the same types of productivity metrics and reporting data that bricks-and-mortar companies do.

Client Care

Our client care team tracks:

- The number of client implementation projects per team member.
- The number of support tickets successfully completed monthly.
- Response time per request.
- The number of training sessions conducted.

- The number of internal projects completed annually.

However, there's a more subjective measurement we value above all, and that's the answer to the question, "Is the client happy?" Fortunately, the answer is almost always a resounding, "Yes." In fact, we've received hundreds of unsolicited email messages from clients praising our client care team. Visit www.fire-engine-red.com/testimonials/ to see some examples.

Data Services

Our data services team is the only team at Fire Engine RED that uses time tracking. The reason it does so is to ensure that our flat-fee pricing covers the actual number of hours it takes us to deliver the highly customized and complex services we provide to clients. In other words, we use time tracking to make sure we have our pricing correct, not to track productivity of our data team members. (Though every time I see the time tracking information, I can tell that our data team has been very productive!)

Our data team tracks:

- The number of student lists purchased.
- The number of email messages sent.
- The number of customized reports produced.
- The percentage of clients retained.

The data team's scorecard is integrated with the student search team's; again, client happiness is the most important productivity metric.

Finance and Accounting

Our finance and accounting team tracks the number of days it takes to:

- Close our books each month.
- Collect receivables.
- Prepare quarterly and year-end financials.
- Prepare contracts.

Finance and accounting also tracks sales revenue, revenue per employee, the operating expenses for each department, and the number of internal projects completed annually by its team members.

Human Resources

I receive quarterly reports from our director of people (our one-person HR department) with this information:

- Team member retention rate
- Team member tenure rate
- Employee engagement rate (tracked through surveys, Team Feed, etc.)
- Percentage of employees who choose our benefits packages

- Percentage of employees who participate in our 401(k)

Generally, the ratio of HR people to employees is 1.4 to every 100.[169] So, yes, it is possible for just one HR person to support 80-plus team members, even in a fully remote environment. It just takes teamwork on the part of our finance, marketing, and operations departments.

Marketing

When we first established our marketing department in 2013, this small team, consisting of our communications director, marketing manager, and designer, was focused mainly on creating and sending monthly email campaigns to prospects and keeping our company website up to date.

Today, this same team:

- Writes, designs, and sends marketing email campaigns to prospects and clients.
- Creates and sends internal communications.
- Creates, designs, and manages our intranet content.
- Keeps our company website up to date.
- Designs trade show booths.
- Coordinates conference events.
- Creates social media posts.
- Develops content for webinars.
- Takes care of all things *Fully Remote*.

I don't need any fancy metrics to see my marketing team is incredibly productive. I can tell that from the sheer number of campaigns and other projects they handle.

Sales

The sales team stays focused on its goals by tracking:

- Annual sales vs. year-over-year.
- The percentage of likelihood a sale will close.
- The number of software demos and data/student search discussions we conduct.
- The number of proposals we provide vs. the number of sales we close.
- The number of RFPs we respond to vs. those we are awarded.
- The number of days it takes to close a sale.
- The number of days to receive a signed contract (the fewer, the better).

Software Development

As discussed previously, our software development team follows the Agile methodology that's been embraced by software companies everywhere. Our development team works in two-week "sprints" and tracks the following:

- Average number of story points completed per sprint

- Sprint burndown (total work remaining vs. time left in the sprint)
- Feature burndown (total sprints needed to complete feature work remaining)
- Number of bug tickets closed per sprint
- Working functionality at the end of each sprint

Our development team also holds daily stand-up meetings to discuss:

- What they completed yesterday.
- What they expect to complete today.
- Anything that's impeding their progress.

While they're at it, they use this meeting to communicate how they can best work together to ensure their goals for the current sprint will be met.

Student Search

As I wrote earlier in the book, we partner with college admissions offices on their student search efforts. That is, we help them identify and market to the students that are the best fit for their institutions. Every year, we manage 125-plus highly customized, large-scale marketing projects for our clients.

To measure the productivity of our search team, we look at:

- The number of projects handled by each member of our search team (including project managers, copywriters, designers, QA data specialists, and print managers).
- The number of electronic messages created.
- The number of print pieces created.
- The percentage of clients retained.

As mentioned above, I also receive a monthly scorecard from our student search team that provides the status of every project and indicates how well we're performing with regard to our clients' goals. The scorecard also tells me how happy (in the form of a happiness rating) each of the project's four stakeholders (the client, the project manager, the senior strategist, and the data strategist) are with the project to date.

So, what's the difference between the productivity metrics remote companies use and the ones that "real" companies use? As you can see, there really isn't any!

Chapter 13
Building a strong company culture: No office building necessary

I believe our company culture has been instrumental in helping us achieve a 92 percent annual employee retention rate.

In fact, in 2011, Fire Engine RED became the first 100 percent virtual company to be named as one of the country's 50 Top Small Company Workplaces by *Inc.* magazine.[170] We received this honor for our talented team, innovative culture, and core values.

And Jens Larson, a blogger who's well known in the college admissions market, summed up our company culture this way: "Fire Engine RED is sort of a 'Google meets Apple yet no one gets stabbed in the cafeteria' sort of place."[171]

In this chapter, I'll show you some proven ways to create a strong, positive company culture for your own all-remote business.

13.1 Start with an inclusive leadership team

When it comes to your company's leadership team(s), make sure women have a seat (or, better yet, several seats) at the table. Distributed companies have a true advantage here. In fact, according to FlexJobs founder Sara Sutton Fell, "compared to traditional companies, remote companies have nearly three times more women in leadership roles."[172]

For example, approximately 28 percent of distributed companies have a female founder or cofounder, and 19 percent have a female CEO.[173] As the founder and CEO of Fire Engine RED, I'm proud to say we're able to check both boxes.

At Fire Engine RED, women make up 50 percent of our company's leadership team. In addition, 75 percent of our vice presidents are women, as are 36 percent of our directors. I'm also especially proud that women hold three of the four leadership positions on our software development team, which is highly unusual, considering the technology field is largely dominated by men.[174]

So, why do remote companies have so many women in leadership roles? As Sutton Fell put it, "Remote work eliminates some of the obstacles that tend to throw women off the traditional leadership course: Inflexible schedules, long hours away from home, and long commutes."[175] Katrina, our VP of projects, a member of our leadership team, and a mother of three children under the age of six, shared, "Working remotely gives me more hours in my day. If I didn't work here, I couldn't work, period."

When women see other women in leadership roles at your company, they'll be more energized, knowing they can grow into a leadership position themselves. And, they'll be less likely to take their talents elsewhere.

At Fire Engine RED, women have seen firsthand that they won't have to choose between parenthood and a leadership position. They also saw Katrina promoted to vice president when she was eight months pregnant with her third child. They saw Sarah promoted to vice president several months after returning from her second maternity leave. (Incidentally, the first time Sarah was promoted was shortly after she returned from her first maternity leave.)

Mandy, our creative director, put it this way: "It all boils down to a culture of mutual respect, equal for women and men. Integrating this culture and demonstrating it, starting at the top, shows employees that you truly walk the walk."

It also helps that we employ men who "get it." Jeff, one of our EVPs, sums it up like this: "Half of our clients are women. More than half the people going to college are female. Heck, half of my children are girls. It seems pretty logical that half of our leadership team should be women."'

13.2 Be family-friendly

Another way to help retain employees is to create a family-friendly workplace. Our company's all-virtual environment goes a long way toward providing the work-life balance that our employees and their families appreciate.

At Fire Engine RED, 51 percent of our team members are parents, and as of this writing, the company "family" includes 94 children! Because our employees don't have to commute and generally work from home, they can remain in close proximity to their school-aged kids. And as we've discussed, our "out" time policy makes it easier for parents to be there for their children.

In fact, our all-remote work environment is a hit with parents and kids alike.

- Chad T. told me that he's "basically an Uber driver" for his children. "If I were in an office, I don't know how I'd make this work. [Being remote] makes it easier to meet with my kids' teachers, and it helps when they're doing plays and other activities."

- Jeff said his son told him, "I like it when you're here when I come home from school. Even if you're on a call, I get a hug."

- Glenna shared, "From a personal perspective, my kids have benefited from having my physical and emotional presence during the most important time of their lives."

- Sarah sent me a picture of her then-three-year-old son Grady in which he had set up his own virtual office, complete with toy computer and headphones! Grady loves, as he puts it, "Doing the bizmus on the computer."

13.3 Show them a career path

As mentioned previously, our company culture doesn't pit team members against each other. Instead, we've created a win-win environment that I think would have impressed even Stephen Covey (of *The 7 Habits of Highly Effective People* fame). There are plenty of opportunities for recognition, growth, and advancement for everyone.

For a while at Fire Engine RED, we had what we called the "Un-review," an annual meeting between our employees and their direct managers. The direct managers would ask:

1) What were your top three accomplishments in the previous year?
2) What lessons did you learn in the previous year?
3) What are your top three goals for the coming year?

What was missing from these meetings was a discussion about the employee's career path. So, we changed our focus away from the "Un-review" to a conversation on how direct reports can "climb the RED ladder" at our company. Here's how it works:

1) The manager speaks with their direct report about the direct report's career goals.
2) The manager then discusses the direct report's goals, skill set, and desired career path with their EVP, the director of people, and me.
3) If the employee's goals and the company's needs are aligned (and in most instances, they have been), we create an official career path in our HRIS that enables the employee to track their progress as they reach their goals.

4) If the employee's goals and the company's needs are not aligned, the employee may have to leave the company down the road. (For example, let's say someone wants to be the CFO; our CFO is likely to be with our company for a long time.) Even if it looks like the person will need to leave Fire Engine RED at some point, we'll help them build their skills accordingly.

The bottom line is we're committed to helping our employees grow, whether or not it's realistic for them to get the role they want at our company. The way to do this is through frank, honest conversations.

> *Tip:* While many companies use a performance improvement plan (PIP) to address performance issues, we don't—unless we honestly believe the employee can improve.

> I believe many companies, rather than using PIPs to help an employee improve, use them to document the employee's performance issues before terminating them. Because your employees are "at will," I don't believe there's any reason to mislead an employee with a PIP if you know it's not going to work out. I think it's simply better to part ways with the employee.

13.4 Provide salary increases

Here's how we determine salary increases at our company. We have a group of six people that meets quarterly to discuss raises for employees company-wide. It's called "R6," short for "raise six." This name was inspired by the former R6 Regional Rail line in Philadelphia. The group consists of the CEO (me), our CFO, three of our executive vice presidents, and our director of people.

Prior to each R6 meeting, our director of people meets with our senior leaders to come up with a list of candidates who should be considered for raises. The leaders consider any recent changes to an employee's actual responsibilities, their current salary, and how long it's been since their last increase.

When R6 meets, each leader brings the names of candidates they would like to be considered for a raise (and an idea of how large an increase to give them). We then decide to increase, decrease, postpone, or simply approve the raises based on the company's financial performance at that time.

Once we've identified which individuals will receive increases, we let them know immediately, even though raises usually take effect in the next quarter. It's hard for me to keep quiet about good news!

13.5 Keep them engaged

Here's how we keep our team "together" even though we're miles apart.

Year in Review

Each year, our marketing team puts together a Year in Review presentation, which we share with our team the first Friday of the New Year. Set to music, it commemorates our business-related achievements from the past year. But that's not all. It also celebrates our team members' personal milestones, including adding new spouses/partners, kids, and pets to the Fire Engine RED family. It's a great way for us all to acknowledge the contributions of team members, reflect on the successes of the past year, and get pumped up to face the challenges of the new year.

SS Feed

As mentioned in chapter 9.6, "Share information freely," every other Friday, at 4 p.m. (EST), I host the "SS Feed," an all-company call during which I share information with the team. I've found that the SS Feed is one of the most effective ways of keeping our team engaged.

Team Feed

And I'm not the only one with a "Feed." The team has one as well, and as you may have guessed, it's called the "Team Feed." Essentially, the Team Feed acts as an electronic suggestion box where team members can share a concern, suggest a way we can do better as a team, or simply ask for clarification on a particular company policy.

Submissions are totally anonymous and sent directly to me. Since 2015, I've received more than 275 submissions from team members!

Why is the Team Feed so popular? I think there are four reasons:

1) I share all submissions with the entire team.
2) I respond to every submission within 24 hours of receipt.
3) I take quick, and sometimes immediate, action when it's appropriate.
4) Our team members know that their submissions are completely anonymous. (To make sure they feel secure about using the Team Feed system, I asked our team's data privacy experts to vouch for it, and they gladly did.)

Here's an example of how the Team Feed works. Several years ago, I received a Team Feed suggestion that we remove employees' phone numbers from our website because some team members were getting unwanted calls from recruiters and spammers. Within minutes of receiving the submission, I sent a copy of the submission to the entire team, told them I agreed with the request, and let them know that we would be removing everyone's phone numbers within 48 hours. We did so for everyone but our leadership and sales teams, who opted to keep their phone numbers on our website.

Team Feed case study

One of the best cases I can make for the Team Feed is that, even when it seems like
everything's working just fine, there can be issues beneath the surface. Fortunately, we had the Team Feed in place to alert me to a potential issue I was unaware of at Fire Engine RED.

Here's how it started. In January 2019, I received this anonymous submission through the Team Feed:

> "It seems that many team members would benefit from training on gender bias in the workplace. Many of my own interactions with team members here suggest the existence of gender bias against females. I doubt (and hope) many of these interactions/experiences have been intentional, but I think accountability and awareness of behavior should be taken into consideration."

Though I was surprised by the submission, I appreciated the anonymous team member's willingness to share their feelings about an uncomfortable issue and to make a constructive recommendation that we consider implementing a gender bias training program. As always, I immediately shared the anonymous submission with the entire team and asked if anyone else at the company had experienced anything similar. When the sentiment of the original submission was echoed by a few team members, I let everyone know that we'd be addressing the issue, and that I'd get back to them soon with a plan.

After spending several days researching gender bias, I created an anonymous survey to get a better handle on how our team members were experiencing (or perceiving) it.

More than 90 percent of our team members completed the survey, with respondents split almost equally between females and males. The survey found that, over the past six months, several of our team members stated that they'd experienced some gender bias, mostly in the form of "small slights." Examples of gender bias cited by our team members included interrupting, talking over, mansplaining during work calls, and being treated as less competent than male colleagues.

Interestingly, 100 percent of the respondents said Fire Engine RED was supportive of their family life, due to our family-friendly policies. I was especially happy to see this; I had learned from my research that gender bias is often an issue at companies that don't support work-life balance.

In any event, I wanted to move quickly to address this issue, and there didn't seem to be any facilitators with experience doing so for fully remote companies. Therefore, as CEO, I decided to take action myself in a manner consistent with our company values, and I developed a process for raising awareness about the issue of gender bias in our virtual workplace. Here's what I did:

1) Scheduled an all-team meeting to watch a TEDx talk on gender bias (https://www.youtube.com/watch?v=eCknUJJc3qU).

2) Had the team break into discussion groups (each with a mix of genders drawn from various departments) and asked team members to share instances of gender bias they'd experienced at Fire Engine RED or other companies.

3) Had each discussion group document the examples on gender bias. (I then shared them with our entire team in the hope of raising awareness of gender bias.)

4) Required everyone to see the film *On the Basis of Sex* and/or the documentary *RBG* on the life of Supreme Court Justice Ruth Bader Ginsburg,

both of which address the issue of gender bias. Team members were able to take time during the workday to watch either of the films; the company reimbursed them for buying a theater ticket or watching it on demand. (Several years back, we'd asked our team members to see the film *Moneyball* as we were introducing our Predictive Modeling offering.)

I received lots of positive feedback from my team, especially about how seriously I took the issue and moved on it. So, now that I've raised awareness about gender bias, I plan to survey my team again in a few months to see if our efforts have had an impact.

Surveys

Above is just one example of the employee surveys we conduct several times a year. These surveys cover a variety of subjects, and response rates are always high. Usually, about 80 to 90 percent of our team members complete each survey. I think that's because the surveys are presented in short and simple online forms, the topics are important and of interest to team members, survey responses are anonymous, and I share results with the team within 24 hours. It doesn't hurt that we implement the best ideas from our surveys in a timely manner.

For example, in a recent survey, I learned that a majority of our employees would be interested in having paid volunteer hours. So based on our employees' input, we created a volunteer time policy and it's been very enthusiastically received. (For more about our volunteer policy, see "Volunteering" in chapter 4.4, "Paid leave.")

REDcognitions

We also have a Slack channel where our team members can REDcognize another team member. This is an easy way for one team member to thank another for outstanding performance, dedication, and commitment to our company values.

Here are a couple examples of REDcognitions:

> Mark wrote, "Sometimes it seems silly to REDcognize someone for something small when that person is constantly slaying dragons big and small all year long. Other times you realize that maybe you are so accustomed to their awesomeness that you take it for granted. Big shout-out to Sam and Boris—who are so great at what they do, I sometimes forget!"

> Another team member wrote, "Jared is an AWESOME team member, and I am so lucky to have him on my team. He is always extremely polite and willing to help. I have had a lot of questions lately, and he has been my go-to guy to help me out every time."

It won't surprise you that our director of people, Jamie, gets lots of shout-outs. Jess wrote, "I want to take a moment to REDcognize Jamie. There was a mishap with some insurance stuff, and the insurance company was of ZERO assistance to me, but Jamie personally took it upon herself to rectify the situation today and did an incredible job with it. I know she does wonderful things on our behalf all the time, but I really want to REDcognize her for her work helping me out today in such a great way!"

This channel is also where we share client feedback. For example, one client took the time to send Deb the following thank-you email:

> "I just wanted to take this opportunity while we are over halfway through our build on our new Fireworks system to tell you how much we appreciate you. You have been an incredible project lead in walking us through each step of the process. You have demonstrated unwavering patience and a can-do attitude even during our most challenging days! I know we still have a ways to go before we are ready for 'go live,' but I just wanted you to know how very much we appreciate you, and the work that both you [Deb] and Micah have done.

It's been a true joy getting to know and work with you thus far! Thanks for being you."

13.6 Create bonding opportunities

As a virtual company, we have to be a bit more creative in putting together team-building activities that don't require physical proximity—or a big budget!

Some of the activities we've come up with have been a part of our company culture for years. In any case, we're always brainstorming new ways to help our team stay connected and retiring activities that we've exhausted.

Here are a few of our bonding opportunities that *have* stood the test of time.

Walking Wednesdays

Every other Wednesday from May through November, I lead "Walking Wednesday," which is my way of encouraging team members to stay active, healthy, and engaged, as well as helping them get to know their teammates better. Here's how it works: Wherever they're located, everyone is encouraged to get outside for a walk and to call in to a conference number for an interesting and fun discussion with their team members. I set the table with topics and encourage callers to weigh in. A typical Walking Wednesday attracts between 60 and 75 percent of our team members.

We recently had a series of Walking Wednesdays with the theme, "Better Know a Team Member," which was inspired by *The Colbert Report*'s "Better Know a District." These calls really brought home what a diverse group of employees we have. Here are some of the topics we've had our team members speak to:

- **Growing up internationally.** Our CFO, Akber, told us about what it was like to be a kid in Uganda and about having to flee his home country to avoid ethnic persecution by President Idi Amin. Software engineer Sam talked about his childhood in Iran, and software engineer Ron V. filled us in on growing up in the Philippines.

- **Being digital nomads.** Three team members who've traveled the world (Argentina, Brazil, Ecuador, Sri Lanka, Turkey, New Zealand, and more) while working at Fire Engine RED told us how they've done it, and how we could do it too. Their presentations led to the creation of our Travel Advisory Group (TAG). Now, team members can "know before they go" by asking these globetrotting employees for tips and advice about traveling internationally.

- **Growing up in Alaska.** We have two employees who were born and raised in the 49th state. They shared with us how different their upbringing was compared to those of us who grew up in the lower 48.

- **Working from the road.** Two team members who spent several years working from their RVs told us how they did it and about their adventures traveling to all 50 states!

Our Walking Wednesdays typically occur at 4:00 p.m. (EST), though once in a while an impromptu, midday walk will happen. For example, the morning after the 2016 U.S. presidential election, I could tell by looking at our team members' IM statuses (lots of "sad face" icons and the like) that many (including me) needed something to take our minds off the result. So, we took a virtual walk together and discussed all the positive things we could think of, including music. That led to one of our EVPs, Jim, singing "My Favorite Things" from *The Sound of Music* for all of us! By the end of the call, I think everyone felt better and took comfort in knowing that they worked with people who felt the same way about the election result as they did.

Pep rallies

Every few months, we hold a pep rally to thank our software development team for everything they're doing to make our CRM the market leader. Though attendance at these pep rallies is optional, approximately 80 percent of our team members participate. When we held our first pep rally in January 2019, I had no idea how much our Fireworks team would appreciate the feedback shared by team members (and from clients via our client care team). Here's what a few of our software engineers said:

> "Before this pep rally, I have only had one person, in one company I worked for, once go so far out of their way to give the developers positive feedback." – Brendan, software engineer

> "I was once told something like 'your development team is like the electric company—nobody cares what you do until the lights won't come on.' So, this positive feedback is unusual and very appreciated!" – Russell, software engineering manager

> "During the pep rally, I heard positive feedback about a feature I worked on. It turned out the feature was even more important and helpful to clients than I had thought while I was working on it, which was great to learn." – Drew, software engineer

The pep rally went so well that, last June, we held our first *reverse* pep rally, during which our software development team told our CRM sales team what they loved about our

CRM and why they were so happy about the direction of the product. Given the feedback I received from my team members, we plan to make such pep rallies part of the Fire Engine RED tradition.

Sports pools

March Madness and Fantasy Football (seasonally). What would an "office" be like without basketball and football pools? Keith, our director of client happiness, organizes our online March Madness bracket and serves as commissioner of our fantasy football league. There's no money involved, just bragging rights, and Slack serves the participants well when it comes to gloating and other smack talk!

Politics (sort of)

Election Challenge. In the run-up to the 2016 presidential election, we had a contest in which employees were invited to predict (1) the winner and (2) the electoral vote count. The grand prize was a $200 gift card, and the challenge itself was popular enough that we did the same for the 2018 midterm election. For the midterms, team members had to guess the post-election composition (Democrats vs. Republicans) of the U.S. Senate and House of Representatives. (Much to our surprise, one team member nailed it with a perfect guess!)

For the 2018 elections, we also created an "I Voted" Slack channel to encourage our team to vote, and we asked everyone to share photos and stories related to their voting experiences (in 26 states) that day—which they did, overwhelmingly.

Another team member wrote, "Fire Engine RED has been the best company I've worked for in terms of encouraging civic participation." And a former team member (Emily S.) shared via LinkedIn, "I'll never forget standing in a 3-plus-hour line to vote. Without even consulting you, I knew that you had my back to miss work, stay in that line, and vote."

Glenna, our vice president of search operations, shared, "As I watch all of the camaraderie happening in the 'I Voted' channel, I can't help but think how incredible you are at keeping this virtual team connected. After all these years, I really feel in touch with the team today, even those I haven't met, and it reinforces how important these efforts are toward encouraging these types of interactive chats. It definitely makes for a more cohesive, happy, positive, and productive team!"

I also heard from Mike, our executive vice president of student search, who wrote, "I've been bragging to everyone about how you have made [our participating in] elections a 'movement.' It's amazing how Fire Engine RED can feel like a community and not just a company—and we're VIRTUAL!"

So, even in this age of bitter partisan politics, I've found that encouraging voter participation is a great way for a virtual company to bring people together.

Charitable giving

Each year, we set aside two days for charitable giving as a company.

RED Cross Donation Day. We encourage our employees to donate blood in their local community and then post a photo in Slack to let our team know they did it! This team event typically takes place in February, usually around Valentine's Day.

Donation Drop-off Day. We also encourage our employees to donate unused clothing and other items to organizations that help people in need. This team event typically takes place in December.

Housekeeping (and bribery)

Every once in a while, we need everyone on our team to do administrative tasks that are unexciting (okay, just plain boring) but necessary. So, I try to make getting through these tasks fun and/or (literally) rewarding.

I've discovered two techniques that work for our virtual team: (1) do it together, and (2) offer a reward. For example, when we all needed to load a particular font on our computers, we threw a Friday font-loading party where we all took care of this task while on a freewheeling conference call. And when we wanted everyone to list their computer equipment in our HR system for inventory purposes, I offered to "close" our virtual office early that Friday if everyone did so … and, of course, they did so.

Getting together in person

Although we haven't had a team meeting since 2013 (more about that below), our team members take advantage of other opportunities to get together.

Meet, greet, and eat

We encourage our team members to get together in person and meet up for lunch or dinner, whether it's one-on-one or in a larger group. Fire Engine RED pays for lunch or dinner for each team member attending. All we ask is that they take pictures of the gathering and post them on our Slack channel the next day. Also, when my leadership team and I travel on company business, we try to meet up with other team members in the area. Recently, Jeff, one of our EVPs, and I went to Cleveland for a meeting and had dinner with Mike and Melissa (who live there) as well as Amber (one of our RV travelers who was passing through town at the time!).

Sometimes, we'll have a fellow team member meet a new hire for lunch if one lives close enough. Also, as previously mentioned, some of our team members have even included visits with coworkers (even with the CEO!) in their vacation itineraries. In any case, the team members usually share pictures, and the company always picks up the tab.

Annual team meeting

We haven't had an all-team meeting since 2013 because we've been heavily investing in the development of Fireworks, our CRM product. However, back in the day, our annual team meetings were much-anticipated events, bringing our entire company together each April for four days of business and fun.

Here's what longtime employee David had to say about our team meetings: "Just like at a bricks-and-mortar company, you communicate with a smaller group of team members much more than with people in other departments. With our fully remote company, seeing the people you speak with all the time is like meeting up with old friends right from the get-go. The team meeting also gives you a great opportunity to make personal connections with many people that you may not interact with regularly, which opens up even more lines of cross-company communications going forward."

Mark added, "Team meetings are like a family reunion, but one that you'd attend four times a year if you could!" And Nick said, "Team meetings are like mullets. Business in the front. Party in the back."

Emma noted, "At our first team meeting in 2009, we could all fit around Shelly's dining room table!" As our company grew, we needed more room and eventually decided on an "official" hotel brand for our team meetings: 21c Museum Hotels (www.21cmuseumhotels.com/). Each is a combination boutique hotel and contemporary art museum. My team members and I have found these hotels to be an inspiring setting, as they reflect our company culture, values, and innovative spirit. And, of course, we love their colorful iconic penguins, especially the RED ones!

Former team member (and current strategic partner) Matt M. had this to say about his first team meeting: "I had already been employed for nine months before I 'met' my colleagues; it was striking how diverse our personalities, backgrounds, and demographics were in this first face-to-face. The factions that develop in a bricks-and-mortar office never materialized, and I had established friendships with people I may not have gravitated toward elsewhere."

As of this writing, I've met 52 of our 80-plus team members in person, and I'm looking forward to meeting everyone on our team when we resume our annual team meetings in 2021!

13.7 Encourage financial wellness

We're continually looking for ways to help our employees get the most out of their compensation, and, based on the messages I've received from my team, I can tell they appreciate it.

One thing we've learned is that, as a virtual company, it's not enough to just post links to financial wellness tips and articles on our intranet. We have to work harder to make sure our employees have the information they need to optimize their financial wellness.

Financial Fridays (quarterly). Once every couple of months, our entire team "gathers" for our "Financial Friday" call. This meeting is dedicated to helping our employees optimize their personal finances.

For example, we spent one Friday together implementing Mint (www.mint.com), a personal finance and budgeting software product; on another call, we had a few employees walk us through the benefits of "cutting the (cable) cord." On a third call, we asked employees to share their own tips for saving time and money related to our benefits, so their coworkers could take advantage of aspects of their benefit plans they might not have known about. Here are a few of the best tips.

- **Triple dip on vision benefits.** If you visit an ophthalmologist and need new glasses or contacts, you can use all three of these to reduce the total cost: 1) your vision benefit, 2) your HSA funds or Limited Purpose FSA, and 3) a cash-back credit card. One person saved nearly $300 by doing so.

- **Save money on your kids' sports physicals.** If your child has to pass a physical to play school sports, you can save up to 30 percent off what you would normally spend at a regular doctor's appointment. How? Take them to one of the mini-clinics at pharmacy chains like CVS and RiteAid, or even to an urgent care center at a slow time. Note that the pharmacy chains will take appointments, while urgent care centers are first-come, first-served. In either case, be sure to call ahead to make sure they're able to fill out the specific paperwork you need.

- **Visit GoodRx.com.** You can find coupons and/or discounts on your prescriptions on this website.

13.8 Create advisory groups, not committees

When you think of a "committee," if you're like me, you probably think of a group of people that regularly meets to talk about their *next* meeting, rather than achieve any actual results! That's why we don't do committees at Fire Engine RED. Instead, we create advisory groups. These groups are tasked with solving specific problems and serve as a resource for our team.

In true Shelly J. Spiegel fashion, I've made sure that each of our advisory groups has a punchy acronym. Here's a look at our advisory groups and what they do.

BAG (Benefits Advisory Group) researches and proposes improvements to our benefits programs, and it provides employees with tips and advice on getting the most out of their Fire Engine RED benefits.

FLAG (Family Leave Advisory Group) helped create our family and medical leave policy and helps employees sort through their leave options.

SAG (Security Advisory Group) leads the way in ensuring we maintain a safe and secure work environment with regard to our sensitive client and company data as well as our proprietary software code.

TAG (Travel Advisory Group) made up of some of our most well-traveled team members, helps those who are considering working while traveling get answers to their technical, and even cultural, questions. Their motto is "Know before you go!"

WAG (Wellness Advisory Group) helped create our new wellness program, which included choosing a new wellness provider. They also provide tips on how to get the most out of the program.

13.9 "Speaking" of culture

Like most companies, we have our own lingo. Many of the terms we use include the abbreviation of our company name, "FER," and the word "RED." Here's a look at our company's shared vocabulary. (You may have already seen some of these terms throughout this book!)

2 FER. We use this any time we get two of something, such as two demo requests, two new team members, two new clients, etc.

alfRED. This is our company's intranet, which I named after my grandfather, Alfred, who "knew everything" (in a good way).

Calendar Coaches. This is a group of helpful team members that provides tips on using our team's Google Calendar. For example, they'll help team members determine which calendar code to use to indicate their status ("LH" for life happens, "MTG" for in a meeting, "OUT" for a child's school event, "VACA" for vacation, etc.).

FERst Friend. This is a current team member who helps a new team member navigate our company during their first day on the job.

FERrell. This is the made-up word I use to express feelings of happiness! My dream is to have the musician Pharrell Williams perform at a future Fire Engine RED team meeting. I'm obsessed with him and his song "Happy." As a result, I now use "FERrell" interchangeably with "happy," as in, "I'm so FERrell about client X's results," or "the design of this marketing email makes me feel very FERrell." (You can imagine how excited I was in January 2019 when we hired a project manager named "Ferrell." As I told my team, he had me at "Ferrell!")

Ket-chups. These are one-on-one meetings where I "catch-up" with team members, called so because the color of ketchup is pretty close to the color "fire engine red." I also thought that referring to my one-on-ones as ket-chups would be a great way to put my team members at ease, especially the newest ones.

R6. This is our company's compensation group, named after the former R6 Regional Rail line in Philadelphia. The "R" stands for raises, and "6" is the number of people on the group. R6 includes our CFO, EVPs, director of people, and me; we get together every quarter to discuss salary increases, bonuses, and promotions for employees.

"The Fire Engine RED Way" presentation. This is available on the Careers page of our website and provides job seekers with an inside look at the values and culture that make our company "simply better."

REDheads. These are our company's fans. When it came to choosing a name for them, I was inspired by the band the Grateful Dead, whose hardcore fans are known as "Deadheads." I thought, "Deadheads" … "REDheads" … "yes, let's go with REDheads!"

State of REDiness. This is when a team member has everything they need to perform their job and handle whatever comes their way. For example, once upon a time, there was a team member who needed to fax (remember those days?) a document to a client. Unfortunately, she did not own a fax machine, so she needed to head to a Kinko's to fax the document at the worst possible time. Thus, our heroine was not "in a state of REDiness."

Well RED. This is the name of our company's blog (www.fire-engine-red.com/blog).

Oh, and there's one more we couldn't leave out.

Jim's Rule. This is a rule that requires internal meetings, whenever possible, be limited to 50 minutes. Several months after joining our company, Jim, one of our EVPs, mentioned to me that he had difficulty finding time to use the bathroom between meetings because all his meetings were scheduled back-to-back, and they always began on the hour. Shortly after our discussion, I implemented "Jim's Rule," much to his and other team members' great relief.

Chapter 14
On the move: Parting with remote employees

14.1 When an employee leaves voluntarily

It's inevitable that people will leave your company no matter what you do to keep employee retention high. When people leave Fire Engine RED, it's usually for a new career opportunity. For example, one of our former software engineers, Matt R., left us to take a director of technology position that we simply didn't have at the time. Years after we parted ways, he shared, "I always think about and miss the Fire Engine RED family. Best group of people I ever worked with. I have many great memories." And another Matt, Matt M., left us to become an associate vice president of a business owned by his family. Their company also serves the education market, so we now work with Matt M. in a different capacity, that of strategic partner.

One of the most bittersweet departures, though, was when our "rockstar" employee left Fire Engine RED to pursue a music career full-time. Yes, you've probably seen the term "rockstar" used to describe awesome employees. But what sets us apart from most companies is that we had *an actual rockstar* working for us. Joe, who's also known as Joe Jack Talcum, guitarist and vocalist of the satirical punk rock band, the Dead Milkmen (www.deadmilkmen.com/), started with Fire Engine RED in 2001 as Employee #1! Because we're a virtual company, Joe was able to live a double life for 15 years as a quality assurance/client support guru *and* a rocker, often working from the road. (You may be familiar with two of the Dead Milkmen's big hits: "Punk Rock Girl" and "The Thing that Only Eats Hippies.")

Sadly, in 2016, Joe left Fire Engine RED to dedicate himself full-time to his musical career, but we let him know he's always welcome to return. As Joe wrote in his parting email, "Thanks for all of the opportunities you've provided me with over the past couple of decades, and thanks for leaving the RED door open for me!"

Leaving the RED door open

As stated in the "Employee handbook" section of chapter 6.2, "Two weeks prior to start date," if a Fire Engine RED employee decides to leave the company, and does so on good terms, we're happy to welcome them back if they choose to return. (Of course, there needs to be a position open at the time.) It's all about doing a great job for us while they're here, choosing the appropriate time to leave, and making a smooth transition.

For example, to help team members decide on the right time to leave, our employee handbook suggests:

- If you're working on an ongoing project such as a website, campaign, or product release, please try to wait until the project launches.
- If you're working on something seasonal, please wait until the end of the season to leave, if possible. (Imagine if a tax preparer left an accountant's office in early April!)

We also ask our outgoing employees to:

- Put together a transition plan with their direct manager.
- Document their processes and any other information that will help their replacement succeed.
- Help identify, interview, and/or train their replacement, if possible.
- Share as much as possible with their coworkers before they leave.

One more thing. When an employee does give appropriate notice, we're happy for them to stay with us as long as they're able to. We don't escort employees off the virtual premises the moment they resign! Trust doesn't stop just because someone is leaving.

Bottom line, we want all of our employees (past and present) to consider themselves to be REDheads for life!

Exit meeting

About a week before the employee leaves, they receive an email with a list of to-dos from the director of people. Then, three days or so before the employee's last day, our director of people meets with them (via Slack audio) to conduct an exit interview and go over their exit to-do list.

Exit interview

During the exit interview portion of the exit meeting, our director of people asks the departing employee these four questions:

1) What's the primary reason you're leaving the company?
2) Are there other reasons that led to your decision?
3) What would have needed to change for you to stay?
4) Is there anything else you'd like us to know?

After the exit meeting, the director of people provides the employee's direct manager, the department's EVP/C-level officer, and me with the departing employee's feedback. We listen to their feedback and put any constructive suggestions into place that we feel would benefit our company, team members, and/or clients.

> *Tip:* If you want the most honest feedback from your outgoing employees, I suggest you consider conducting your exit interviews verbally.

Benefits options

During the exit meeting, the director of people also talks with the outgoing employee about their options regarding benefits.

> *Tip:* Under the Consolidated Omnibus Budget Reconciliation Act (COBRA), if your company employed 20 people in the previous year, you're required to offer employees (and their families) the opportunity to keep (and pay for) their medical, dental, and vision insurance coverage for up to 18 months.[176] Some states have adopted similar laws (so-called "mini-COBRA" laws), which may apply to even smaller companies, so it's a good idea to check with your attorney on local laws.

If your company offers other benefits, such as an HSA, an FSA, and/or a 401(k), now's the time to discuss with your outgoing employee their options for keeping, transitioning, or terminating those benefits. For example, our departing employees have three options regarding their HSA: They can (1) keep their account with our provider and pay a quarterly fee, (2) roll the account over to their new employer's plan, or (3) simply cash out the account.

> *Tip:* Your HRIS should allow former employees to continue to access their pay stubs and W-2 forms indefinitely.

Equipment purchase

If the outgoing employee's company-supplied laptop is several years old (which it usually is because people tend to stay with us for many years), the director of people will ask if they want to purchase it for fair market value. If they decide they want the computer, we have them delete all proprietary information from it and deduct the cost of it from their final paycheck. If they're not interested in purchasing their laptop, we ask them to send it back after their last day; see "Returning their computer" below.

Final paycheck

The email from the director of people also tells the outgoing employee when they'll receive their final paycheck. Unless their state requires their final wage payment to be provided earlier, they'll receive it as they always have, at the end of the month when we run our payroll. Their final paycheck includes their regular pay as well as payment for any unused vacation (if applicable).

> *Lesson learned:* Some states require you to provide exiting employees with their last paycheck on their final day at work. Years ago, when we implemented our previous HRIS, we assumed we could run a payroll any time we needed at no extra cost. However, we found we'd be charged a fee of $1,500 whether we were paying 80 people or one person. So, keep in mind your HRIS may charge you a fee to run the employee's last paycheck.

Last day of work

Returning their computer

If the outgoing employee doesn't want to buy their computer, we ask them to do a factory reset on it and return it to Mark, our equipment specialist. (We've found that the easiest way to do this is to provide the outgoing employee with our FedEx number.) We don't have employees ship back monitors or all-in-one printers due to cost. We also don't ask them to send us their external hard drives either, but we do ask that they delete any proprietary information from any storage devices they keep.

> *Lesson learned:* We used to have all departing employees send their Fire Engine RED-provided

laptop back to their direct manager. However, we stopped that practice after an employee, who had been involuntarily terminated by her manager, rigged her computer to display a continuous loop of photos of fire engines crashing. As a result, we now have all employees return their computer to a "neutral" person (our equipment specialist).

We stopped asking departing employees to return their headsets and earbuds several years ago. That's because all we did was toss them in the trash (after sterilizing them); we weren't about to pass along "used" headsets and earbuds to new employees. And I'll spare you the details about the disgusting condition of a few of the keyboards and mice that employees sent back to us.

Offboarding tasks

After the employee leaves, there are a variety of exit tasks that must be completed by our director of people, director of operations, and tool administrators.

Our director of people

- Deactivates the outgoing employee's HRIS user account.
- Removes the outgoing employee from recurring departmental meetings and events on our company calendar.

- Uses our SaaS management tool to identify which tools the outgoing employee was using and then asks our tool administrators to remove their access. (We created an offboarding checklist to help our administrators keep track of which tools have been deactivated and make sure no tool is overlooked.)
- Removes the outgoing employee from our internal email lists.
- Removes the outgoing employee's name from any advisory group (if applicable).
- Archives their job description.
- Removes their name from our organizational chart.
- Deletes their name from our playbooks.
- Removes their intranet user account.
- Removes the outgoing employee's profile from our website.
- Updates our team metrics on our intranet and website.

14.2 Terminating an employee, virtually

As the leader of your all-remote company, you'll inevitably be faced with having to let an employee go at some point. You may have to part with people for any number of reasons, including bad cultural fit, poor performance, or unwillingness to learn important new skills.

In nearly 20 years, we've only had to fire two people for being missing in action. Not surprisingly, they were also MIA on the day we tried to let them go! It took us hours to track them down.

Being mindful of the remote aspect

It's never easy to go through the process of terminating an employee, and this is especially true when it comes to letting a remote employee go.[177]

At a bricks-and-mortar company, terminations usually occur in person. At a virtual company, that's simply not possible, which makes an already-uncomfortable situation even more difficult. So, we have a phone call instead, during which we observe many of the same HR best practices that organizations do with non-remote workers.

Generally, there are two people on the call: the department's EVP/C-level officer, who delivers the news, and the director of people, who serves as a witness. We keep the meeting short, notifying them that their employment has been terminated. One thing we don't do during the termination call is provide a reason for the person's dismissal. As an at-will employer, we're not required to do so.

Tip: Remember to remove the person from the company email system (and Slack) while they're on the termination call. You don't want the departing employee to let other team members know that they've been terminated; you want to be the one to inform your team.

On this call, we also let them know when they'll receive their final paycheck (and severance pay, if applicable).

Tip #1: You should always confirm the terminated employee's personal email address. You'll need it for follow-up communications, such as their exit letter/email.

Tip #2: As a courtesy, we ask the exiting employee whether or not they would like to make their final contribution to their 401(k) and HSA (if applicable). Some people prefer not to make these contributions once they've been terminated so they can have more money in their paycheck.

Sending the exit letter

Immediately after the termination call, we email the former employee their exit letter. This email includes the official notice of their termination, information regarding transitioning off their benefits, and a severance agreement for them to review.

Tip: If you're providing severance pay that's not otherwise required, you should obtain a release from the employee as a condition to the severance payment. Federal and some state laws impose timing and other conditions on severance and release arrangements, so check with your attorney on this.

Finally, depending on the age of their computer, we may offer the departing employee the option to purchase it.

Providing the final paycheck

As with voluntarily departing employees, you should be aware of your state's requirements for providing a terminated employee with their final paycheck. For example, in California, if an employee is terminated, employers are required to provide the final paycheck *immediately*. We do so by running an additional payroll on the employee's last day.

Transitioning off benefits

It's much more likely that terminated employees will want to continue their benefits until they find another job. So, as with voluntarily departing employees, we offer COBRA benefits (see requirements above).[178]

Performing offboarding tasks

Once the employee has been terminated, we immediately perform the same offboarding tasks as we do with employees who've left voluntarily. The only addition is that, unlike with voluntarily departing employees, we remove terminated employees from recurring meetings on our company calendar.

Communicating with your team

Because of your all-virtual work environment, your employees will most likely be surprised when someone is terminated. That's because they don't have the visual cues like body language and closed-door meetings, which can feed speculation that a termination is imminent at a bricks-and-mortar company.

We send a standard email to the entire company, which lets everyone know that the employee is on the move. We don't ever address the reasons for the termination or answer questions about it, which we believe is in the best interest of both the former employee and the company.

> *Tip #1:* Before you send an email to the entire company, consider if anyone (such as team members on leave) should be contacted with the news first. For example, depending on the situation, their manager, EVP/C-level officer, and director of people and/or I may meet with anyone

who's worked closely with the terminated team member.

Tip #2: I suggest that you never let anyone go on a Friday. You don't want your team members to end their week on an unsettling note.

Chapter 15
Tax credits: Like scholarships for remote businesses

Our business operations manager, Joanna, says, "Tax credits and grants are like scholarships for businesses. The money is out there if you have the time and patience to track it down." And, she's absolutely right.

How valuable are tax credits? Well, they're much more valuable than tax deductions. For example, tax credits reduce the amount of your business's tax liability, dollar for dollar. Therefore, a $1,000 tax credit would lower your tax bill by $1,000. In contrast, tax deductions lower your business's taxable income by a percentage based on your marginal tax bracket.[179] For example, if your business is in the 24 percent tax bracket, a $1,000 deduction saves you $240 in taxes.

I encourage you to take a look at state and federal tax credits.

15.1 State tax credits

The best place to start looking for state tax credits is on your state government's website. Most states provide tax credits to businesses as incentives to pursue a variety of activities that benefit the economy, the environment, or another business purpose. Tax credits for Research and Development (R&D) are among the most popular.

While science- and technology-oriented companies are among the most likely types of businesses to take advantage of R&D credits, nearly any company that's actively developing new products or processes may qualify.

As an all-remote company, the more states you have a presence in, the more opportunities you'll have to receive state tax credits. Criteria for eligibility varies from state to state, but can include the size of your company (based on revenue, net assets, and/or number of employees), the number (or percentage) of employees you have within the state, and the nature of the R&D you're conducting (creating new products or processes).

States typically set aside a specific amount of R&D tax credits each year. For example, my state, Pennsylvania, caps its total R&D credit at $55 million (with $11 million set aside for small businesses that qualify). Since 2014, we've received between $50,000 and $105,000 annually in R&D tax credits, making the time-consuming application process well worth it![180]

To take advantage of state tax credits in a given year, you'll need to track your R&D expenses for the *previous* year then submit an application to your state department of revenue (or its equivalent in your state), along with your prior year's financial statement and related federal and state tax returns.

> *Tip #1:* We tag our R&D spending in QuickBooks on an ongoing basis to ensure we don't miss any expenses.

> *Tip #2:* I recommend that you work with your CFO or accountant on completing your tax credit application. Calculating tax credits can get pretty complex.

Now, let's say your application is successful and your business is awarded tax credits. Does that mean you're out of luck if you aren't profitable or don't have a large enough tax liability to take full advantage of your tax credits? No, it doesn't. You have two options:

- **Carry your unused tax credits forward.** For example, in Pennsylvania, R&D tax credits can

be carried forward for 15 years, which gives
companies a good amount of time to become
profitable and run up a sizable enough tax bill
to exhaust all of their tax credits!

- **Sell your tax credits.** If your company needs a
  fast influx of cash, as do many companies, you
  can actually sell your tax credits (at a discount)
  to another company. How? By working with a
  company that specializes in selling state tax
  credits. We use MVM Associates
  (www.mvmgrants.com/).

15.2 Federal tax credits

As mentioned above, the federal government also offers
tax credits. Let's take a look at what your distributed
company may be eligible to receive.

Research and development tax credit

In 2017, the federal government began offering its own
R&D credit. Qualifying businesses can now claim up to
$250,000 per fiscal year and apply it against their Social
Security taxes. A company has to have less than $5 million
in gross receipts (over fewer than five years) to qualify.[181]
As with state tax credits, any federal tax credit a company
claims in the current fiscal year is based on R&D costs for
the previous fiscal year.

Paid family leave tax credits

For tax years 2018 and 2019, companies were able to receive tax credits for paid family and medical leave provided to workers who earned up to $72,000 in 2017. (Although this tax credit is only in effect for tax years 2018 and 2019, it could be extended by Congress.)[182] To qualify, a company must have a written policy that:

- Covers all workers who've been employed by the company for a year or more.
- Provides at least two weeks of leave to qualifying full-time employees (and a proportionate amount to part-timers).
- Pays at least 50 percent of the employee's wages during the leave.

I recommend that you, with the help of your CFO and your accountant, explore federal, state, and local tax credits to see which, if any, may be available to your business.[183] If you're not looking to take advantage of state and federal tax credits, you could be leaving money on the table!

Chapter 16
Tax time: Filing your virtual company's taxes

When it comes to filing and paying business taxes for your fully remote company, you probably won't be surprised to hear that I strongly recommend you work with your accountant on this; things get pretty complex when you have employees in multiple states.

With that in mind, let's take a high-level look at what you'll need to consider with regard to filing your business taxes.

16.1 Federal taxes

Your company's legal structure will affect when, how, and what you pay with regard to your business taxes.[184]

Sole Proprietor or single-member LLC. You pay business taxes based only on your personal income and report your business income or loss on a Schedule C (or Schedule C-EZ), which attaches to your personal Form 1040 tax return.

Partnership or multiple-member LLC. You file a separate business tax return (Form 1065) and provide a form to your partners (Form 1065, Schedule K-1) to show income, deductions, gains, and losses from the business. However, the business itself isn't taxed; income "passes through" and is reported on your personal income tax return.

C Corporation. If you choose to incorporate as a C Corporation, you pay taxes on the business's income (using Form 1120) and on your income from the business (Form 1040). This is where the dreaded double taxation comes in.

S Corporation. Similar to a partnership, an S Corporation's income "passes through" to shareholders' personal taxes. You file a separate business return (Form 1120S), provide shareholders with information on their income from the business (Form 1120S, Schedule K-1), and report your income from the S Corp on your personal 1040 return. Note: With an S Corporation, you'll need to file your tax return with the IRS by March 15, not April 15 as with the other legal structures above.

Estimated taxes

As a business owner, you'll also need to keep other tax-related dates in mind besides April 15. Once you've begun turning a profit, you'll have to pay estimated taxes at the end of every quarter.[185] For example, in 2019, for businesses with a tax year beginning January 1, those dates were April 15, June 17, September 16, and January 15 of the following year.[186]

Again, I turn to my accountant for help with calculating and filing our estimated taxes, but you can use tax software (such as TurboTax) if you prefer to go it alone.

16.2 State taxes

Here's a "fun" fact: In 2018, we filed tax returns in all 25 states where we had employees.

No matter which legal structure you choose, you'll need to file state tax returns and pay state taxes in every state where you have a nexus. (For tax purposes, "nexus" means where you have an employee or other operating assets in the state.)

States calculate business taxes in different ways. Some states use a percentage of net income, others use a percentage of the revenue your company billed (or recognized), and still others have a minimal fee or "franchise tax" if you have a nexus in their state. For example, California has a minimum franchise tax of $800, while my state, Pennsylvania, recently eliminated their franchise tax.

In addition, in most states, your company will be required to pay income tax based on the sales revenue attributable to that state. To keep track of the state taxes we owe, we apportion our income across all the states where we have a nexus and track our billings by state in QuickBooks.

16.3 Other taxes

But wait, there's more. Depending on where your company does business (see definition of "nexus" above) you may also be on the hook for city, county, and township taxes. Therefore, I recommend you summarize for your accountant where (by state, then by county, then by township) you have revenue, clients, and employees, and have them determine if and where you might have a tax liability. Of course, every jurisdiction is different, so you could owe a percentage of your revenue, a percentage of your payroll amount, or a fixed amount. Depending on the size of your business, QuickBooks (or whatever accounting software you're using), should be able to summarize this information for you.

Chapter 17
Succession planning: Making sure your all-remote company is built to last

I've spent nearly 20 years building a company that I'm proud of. I believe Fire Engine RED's best and most exciting days are ahead, and I wouldn't want to miss them for "all the money in the world." (That's right, I don't have a price.) In fact, several years ago, I wrote a blog article titled, "Why I Haven't Sold When Everyone Else Has,"[187] and nothing's changed; money isn't why I started Fire Engine RED, and it won't be why I decide to sell it. Rather, I'll step aside or sell the business when I feel I'm no longer the right person to lead and grow the company.

However, just like "real companies," a fully remote company needs a succession plan, too. In fact, I believe it's even more important for the CEO of an all-remote company to have such a plan in place because there are very few people today that have experience in leading a 100 percent virtual company.

Even though I have no plans to step aside or sell the company any time soon, last November, as I turned 60, I felt it was the right time to begin developing a formal succession plan—one that ensures that Fire Engine RED, including our special culture, is built to last.

Here's what I've decided: when it comes time for me to step aside or sell the company, I plan to name Sarah (our VP of products) as the company's CEO and Katrina (our VP of projects) as the company's president. I believe both Sarah and Katrina are uniquely suited to lead Fire Engine RED into the future. As part of our technology leadership team, Sarah is currently focused on vision and strategy, while Katrina is focused on people, costs, and operations. In their future roles as CEO and president, they'll have many of the same responsibilities, but at the highest level, company-wide.

Sarah and Katrina also share a deep understanding of the challenges facing the education market, having worked at colleges before joining our company in 2011. I believe their experience in our industry will help ensure Fire Engine RED's long-term success. Finally, because both Sarah and Katrina share my personal values as well as the company's, I'm confident they will help Fire Engine RED maintain its people-centric, values-driven culture.

My plan is to work closely with Sarah and Katrina over the next several years to ensure that when I'm ready to step aside or sell the company, it'll be a natural transition for them and the rest of my team.

So, I would encourage you to develop a succession plan as soon as possible. Without one, it may be more difficult to exit your company when you're ready to step aside or sell.

Chapter 18
Conclusion

As I've discussed throughout this book, remote working is a win-win for companies and employees. Companies benefit from a broader talent pool, increased productivity, higher employee retention, and all the cost savings related to not having an office. Employees benefit from the lack of a commute, a better work-life balance, and all the cost savings related to not going to an office!

Put simply, the world has changed, and remote work is here to stay.

It's the way people want to work

People of all ages want the flexibility that comes with remote work, including the opportunity to travel, exercise, pursue hobbies, and spend more time with family and friends. And when they move, they want to take their jobs with them. In fact, fewer Americans are willing to uproot their lives and relocate to a new job.[188]

The train—rather, the fire engine—has left the station

I believe the number of fully remote companies will grow as more entrepreneurs and other businesspeople discover the benefits of going remote. Not surprisingly, some states and cities have recognized the benefits to attracting remote businesses and workers and are actively trying to capitalize on the remote work trend.

For example, in 2018, Tulsa, Oklahoma, began offering remote workers $10,000 (and a desk in a coworking space) to relocate to and live in their city for a year. And in 2019, the state of Vermont started offering $10,000 in tax credits to full-time employees working for companies based *outside* of Vermont. Other cities and states, including Utah and Virginia, aren't far behind.[189] I believe that in the future, incentives like these will become commonplace as more and more companies and individuals embrace remote work.

As far as the high-profile leaders and companies bringing their employees back into the office, I predict these companies will prove to be the exception.

Of course, there will always be a few naysayers who'd have you believe fully remote companies can't be innovative, collaborative, and productive. The growth and success of Fire Engine RED proves them wrong. In fact, we're confident that our 100 percent virtual structure will continue working to our advantage, by enabling us to hire the top talent that's crucial to growing our business.

As I hope I've shown you in *Fully Remote*: Hire the right people and put the right processes into place, and the success of your company will speak for itself.

It's better to go all-in on remote

Is it "better" to be 100 percent remote than just partially remote? In my opinion, it's simply much easier to make it work when all of your processes and policies are created for a fully remote workforce, rather than having two sets of employees who work differently. As I wrote earlier, being a 100 percent distributed workplace ensures a level playing field for your entire team. Work-from-home managers understand the challenges work-from-home employees face (and vice versa).

In addition, I believe there's less opportunity for isolation at an all-remote company than a partially remote one. The key is to have everyone at your fully remote company work in well-defined departments and/or teams. (Isolation is more likely to occur when people work independently, say, as freelancers do.) And of course, a 100 percent remote company needs a very engaged CEO to tie everything together and lead the way.

I'm not saying bricks-and-mortar companies that hire remote workers can't be effective. In my opinion, it's just easier to make it "work" with a 100 percent virtual company, especially one (like Fire Engine RED) which is 100 percent remote from the very beginning.

Now, it's your turn

Before you start a fully distributed company, here's the most important question to ask yourself: *Are you able and willing to trust the people who work for you?*

If your answer is "yes" (and after you've read this book, I hope it is), I say go for it, and I'll be cheering you on … from my virtual office to yours!

P.S. If you have questions or want help along the way, I invite you to visit the *Fully Remote* website (www.fully-remote-book.com). There, you'll find helpful resources, a community of kindred spirits, and a forum where you can ask questions and get answers about how to set up, lead, and manage your own all-remote company. (Use the passcode **100virtual** to access the bonus resources available with your *Fully Remote* book purchase.)

Afterword

With gratitude

I want to thank each and every one of my team members for all they've done and continue to do for our company … and for their contributions to this book.

Akber Pabani
Alaina Dougherty
Albany Muria
Amanda Frisch
Amber Paul
Amy Simmonds
Ashley Riser
Ben Shoemaker
Ben Spiegel
Bill Preble
Blake Fitzhugh
Boris Fontaine
Brendan Hawk
Brian Claridge
Caroline Paulic
Chad Gregory
Chad Talbert
Chris King
Chuck Vadun
David Conly
Deb Wright
Dinora Orozco
Drew Johnson
Elizabeth Bross
Emily Rolfe
Emma McAneny
Erica Gooding

Erika Anderson
Ferrell Armstrong
Flavio Medeiros
Glenna Ryan
Greg Deutelbaum
Jaclyn Everett
Jamie Levick
Jared Ray
Jason Bray
Jason Friedberg
Jason Frost
Jeff McLaughlin
Jennifer Hauxhurst
Jess Sandlin
Jim Slavin
Joanna Everett
Justin Hamm
Justin Levine
Katrina Masiak
Keith McCusker
Laura Kitslaar
Lisa Ruscitelli
Mandy Nagel
Maria Remington
Mark Kieran
Matheus Esteves
Mathi Essenwanger

Meaghan Conly
Megan Tvedt
Melissa Waclawik
Micah Vilmar
Michelle Cook
Mike Matthews
Molly Erker
Morgan Frederick
Naveena Aratikatla
Nichole Eisenzopf
Nick Tillman
Nicole McCarthy
Pedro Faria
Perry Tryfonas
Pete Mueller
Rachel Epstein
Ray Regimbal
Robert Fitzhugh
Ron Vocal
Russell Schroeder
Sam Yousefi
Sarah Kozay
Shalon Kegg
Shannon Callihan
Tarize Ribeiro
Will Spiegel
Zach Beerger

I'd also like to thank the following former team members for agreeing to be part of this book. The RED door will always be open for you!

Emily Serrell Smith
Joe Genaro
Matt Maguire
Matt Razi

And again, a special thanks to Andrew Meslow, my investor and friend, who put the "angel" in the term "angel investor."

About the Author

Shelly Spiegel has been described as a "dreamer AND a doer," a compassionate visionary, a charismatic leader, and a creative force in the education market. In 2001, she founded Fire Engine RED, one of the first fully remote companies in the U.S. Before Fire Engine RED, she was the founder and president of Search By Video, which duplicated and distributed admissions recruitment videos to prospective students and their parents.

Shelly has her B.A. in Journalism from the University of North Carolina at Chapel Hill, and her law degree from the Catholic University of America, Columbus School of Law, in Washington, D.C., where she specialized in communications law. She lives and works in downtown Philadelphia.

You can follow Shelly @ShellyJSpiegel.

Reader Bonus: Valuable Templates

As a token of thanks for your purchase of *Fully Remote*, **I'd like to offer you a free bonus ... valuable templates** that can save you time AND money, right when you need them the most!

These resources can help you get your 100 percent remote company up and running faster. They're uniquely designed for founders of fully remote businesses ... and they're all included with your purchase of the *Fully Remote* book:

- **Employee Handbook**
- **Job Descriptions**
- **Security Policy**
- **And more**

Access your reader bonus at www.fully-remote-book.com. Simply download each encrypted PDF and enter the passcode provided at the end of Chapter 18.

Notes

[1] Susan Caminiti, "The Dream Job That's All the Rage across America," *CNBC*, April 3, 2018, https://www.cnbc.com/2018/04/03/virtual-companies-answer-demand-for-better-quality-of-life.html.

[2] Brie Weiler Reynolds, "26 Virtual Companies That Thrive on Remote Work," *FlexJobs*, March 14, 2014, https://www.flexjobs.com/blog/post/25-virtual-companies-that-thrive-on-remote-work/

[3] Joseph Grenny and David Maxfield, "A Study of 1,100 Employees Found That Remote Workers Feel Shunned and Left Out," *Harvard Business Review*, November 2, 2017, https://hbr.org/2017/11/a-study-of-1100-employees-found-that-remote-workers-feel-shunned-and-left-out.

[4] Liz Coffman, "What is Remote Work? Distributed vs. Telecommuting vs. Remote Teams," *Remo*, accessed September 3, 2019, https://remo.co/blog/what-is-remote-work/.

[5] "Virtual Team," *Wikipedia: The Free Encyclopedia,* accessed October 17, 2018, https://en.wikipedia.org/w/index.php?title=Virtual_team&oldid=863866015.

[6] "Definition of Virtual Company," *PC Magazine Encyclopedia*, accessed July 6, 2018, https://www.pcmag.com/encyclopedia/term/53904/virtual-company.

[7] Jessica Howington, "Is There a Difference Between Distributed Teams and Remote Teams?" *Remote.co*, March 3, 2016, https://remote.co/is-there-a-difference-distributed-remote-teams/.

[8] The Muse Editor, "The Latest Stats on Women in Tech," *The Muse*, accessed July 22, 2019, https://www.themuse.com/advice/the-latest-stats-on-women-in-tech.

[9] "Internet/Broadband Fact Sheet," *Pew Research Center*, June 12, 2019, http://www.pewinternet.org/fact-sheet/internet-broadband.

[10] "The IWG Global Workspace Survey," *International Workplace Group*, March 2019, http://assets.regus.com/pdfs/iwg-workplace-survey/iwg-workplace-survey-2019.pdf

[11] Laura Vanderkam, "Will Half of People Be Working Remotely by 2020?" *Fast Company*, August 14, 2014, https://www.fastcompany.com/3034286/will-half-of-people-be-working-remotely-by-2020.

[12] Adrianne Bibby and Brie Weiler Reynolds, "The Complete History of Working from Home," *FlexJobs*, October 30, 2017, https://www.flexjobs.com/blog/post/complete-history-of-working-from-home/.

[13] Michael Dimock, "Defining Generations: Where Millennials End and Generation Z Begins," *Pew Research Center*, January 17, 2019, https://www.pewresearch.org/fact-tank/2019/01/17/where-millennials-end-and-generation-z-begins/.

[14] Laura Shin, "At These 125 Companies, All or Most Employees Work Remotely, " *Forbes*, March 31, 2016, https://www.forbes.com/sites/laurashin/2016/03/31/at-these-125-companies-all-or-most-employees-work-remotely/#4d20cf06530c.

[15] Jessica Howington, "25 Virtual Companies without Headquarters," *Remote.co*, July 16, 2018, https://remote.co/virtual-companies-without-headquarters/. Emily Moore, "100% Remote! 13 Cool Companies to Apply to Today," *Glassdoor*, June 22, 2018, https://www.glassdoor.com/blog/100-percent-remote-companies/.

[16] Stephanie Vozza, "How a Company Works When 100% of the Staff Is Virtual," *Fast Company*, May 20, 2015, https://www.fastcompany.com/3046333/how-a-company-works-when-100-of-the-staff-is-virtual.

[17] Scott Keller and Bill Schaninger, "Focus on the Five Percent," *McKinsey & Company*, January 11, 2018, https://www.mckinsey.com/business-functions/organization/our-insights/the-organization-blog/focus-on-the-five-percent.

[18] Rama Dev Jager and Rafael Ortiz, *In the Company of Giants: Candid Conversations with the Visionaries of the Digital World*, (New York: McGraw-Hill, 1997).

[19] Dana Wilkie, "When Remote Work 'Works' for Employees, but Not the C-Suite, " *Society for Human Resource Management*, April 10, 2017, https://www.shrm.org/resourcesandtools/hr-topics/employee-relations/pages/remote-work-.aspx.

[20] "2015 AfterCollege Career Insight Survey," *AfterCollege*, accessed December 21, 2018, https://www.aftercollege.com/cf/2015-annual-survey.

[21] "Costs and Benefits," *Global Workplace Analytics*, accessed September 21, 2019, https://globalworkplaceanalytics.com/resources/costs-benefits.

[22] Bill Conerly, "Companies Need to Know the Dollar Cost of Employee Turnover, " *Forbes*, August 12, 2018, https://www.forbes.com/sites/billconerly/2018/08/12/companies-need-to-know-the-dollar-cost-of-employee-turnover/#20c8d063d590.

[23] Dan Marzullo, "Why Employee Retention Should be a Top Priority for Small Business," *Zenefits*, January 24, 2019, https://www.zenefits.com/blog/why-employee-retention-should-be-a-top-priority-for-small-business/.

[24] "Advantages of Agile Work Strategies for Companies," *Global Workplace Analytics*, accessed June 6, 2019, http://globalworkplaceanalytics.com/resources/costs-benefits.

[25] "State of Remote Work 2017," *Owl Labs*, accessed July 17, 2019, https://www.owllabs.com/state-of-remote-work-2017.

[26] Jessica Howington, "15 Stats about Telecommuting in the U.S.," *FlexJobs*, April 4, 2016, https://www.flexjobs.com/blog/post/stats-about-telecommuting-in-the-us/.

[27] "2017 Human Capital Benchmarking Report," *Society for Human Resource Management*, December 2017, https://www.shrm.org/hr-today/trends-and-forecasting/research-and-surveys/Documents/2017-Human-Capital-Benchmarking.pdf.

[28] "What Leaders Need to Know about Remote Workers," *TINYpulse*, accessed July 22, 2019, https://cdn2.hubspot.net/hubfs/443262/pdf/TINYpulse_What_Leaders_Need_to_Know_About_Remote_Workers.pdf.

[29] Matt Perry, "Engagement around the World, Charted," *Harvard Business Review*, May 15, 2019, https://hbr.org/2019/05/engagement-around-the-world-charted.

[30] Nicholas A. Bloom, James Liang, John Roberts, and Zhichun Jenny Ying, "Does Working from Home Work? Evidence from a Chinese Experiment," *Stanford Graduate School of Business*, March 2013, https://www.gsb.stanford.edu/faculty-research/working-papers/does-working-home-work-evidence-chinese-experiment.

[31] Kari Paul, "Remote Employees Are Way More Productive Than Office Dwellers," *New York Post*, March 22, 2017, https://nypost.com/2017/03/22/remote-employees-are-way-more-productive-than-office-dwellers/.

[32] Jessica Howington, "2018 Annual Survey Finds Workers Are More Productive at Home," *FlexJobs*, September 9, 2018, https://www.flexjobs.com/blog/post/2018-annual-survey-finds-workers-more-productive-at-home/.

[33] "Udemy In Depth: 2018 Workplace Distraction Report," *Udemy*, March 2018, https://research.udemy.com/wp-content/uploads/2018/03/FINAL-Udemy_2018_Workplace_Distraction_Report_links.pdf.

[34] "Udemy In Depth: 2018 Workplace Distraction Report," *Udemy*, March 2018, https://research.udemy.com/wp-content/uploads/2018/03/FINAL-Udemy_2018_Workplace_Distraction_Report_links.pdf.

[35] "Advantages of Agile Work Strategies for Companies," *Global Workplace Analytics*, accessed June 6, 2019, http://globalworkplaceanalytics.com/resources/costs-benefits.

[36] Alexander Kunst, "Number of Sick Leave Days U.S. Adults Took Last Year as of 2017, by Age," *Statista*, February 2017, https://www.statista.com/statistics/682924/sick-leave-days-among-adults-us-by-age/.

[37] "Advantages of Agile Work Strategies for Companies," *Global Workplace Analytics*, accessed June 6, 2019, http://globalworkplaceanalytics.com/resources/costs-benefits.

[38] Jason Fried and David Heinemeier Hansson, *Remote: Office Not Required* (New York: Crown Publishing Group, October 29, 2013).

[39] Alexandre Mas and Amanda Pallais, "Valuing Alternative Work Arrangements," *Princeton University*, March 2017, https://www.princeton.edu/~amas/papers/vaw a.pdf.

[40] "Nearly One-Quarter of Workers Have Left a Job Due to a Bad Commute, According to Robert Half Survey," *Robert Half*, September 24, 2018, http://rh-us.mediaroom.com/2018-09-24-Nearly-One-Quarter-Of-Workers-Have-Left-A-Job-Due-To-A-Bad-Commute-According-To-Robert-Half-Survey.

[41] Amar Hussain, "4 Reasons Why a Remote Workforce Is Better for Business," *Forbes*, March 29, 2019, https://www.forbes.com/sites/amarhussaineurope/2019/03/29/4-reasons-why-a-remote-workforce-is-better-for-business/#a04b2481a644.

[42] PGi Collaboration Software, Collaborative Advantage, "Telecommuting by the Numbers: Gains, Losses, and Everything in Between," *FlexJobs*, February 27, 2013, https://www.flexjobs.com/blog/post/telecommuting-by-the-numbers-gains-losses-and-everything-in-between/.

[43] Ana Marie Begic, "4 Ways to Easily Reduce Your Carbon Footprint by Eating Differently," *Elite Daily*, October 2, 2016, https://www.elitedaily.com/wellness/reduce-carbon-footprint-eat-better/1625654.

[44] Jude Gonzalez, "Working from Home Could Make You Happier—Especially If You're Married," *Horizon*, February 26, 2018, https://horizon-magazine.eu/article/working-home-could-make-you-happier-especially-if-youre-married.html.

[45] Brie Weiler Reynolds, "6 Ways Working Remotely Will Save You $4,000 Annually, or More," *FlexJobs*, January 9, 2018, https://www.flexjobs.com/blog/post/6-ways-working-remotely-will-save-you-money/.

[46] "Latest Telecommuting/Mobile Work/Remote Work Statistics," *Global Workplace Analytics*, updated August 16, 2019, http://globalworkplaceanalytics.com/telecommuting-statistics.

[47] Drake Baer, "The Scientific Reason Why Barack Obama and Mark Zuckerberg Wear the Same Outfit Every Day," *Business Insider*, April 28, 2015, https://www.businessinsider.com/barack-obama-mark-zuckerberg-wear-the-same-outfit-2015-4.

[48] John Kador, "Trust and Leadership in the World of Remote Work," *Chief Executive*, April 10, 2018, https://chiefexecutive.net/trust-and-leadership-in-the-world-of-remote-work/.

[49] Aliah D. Wright, "Wanted: Managers Who Trust Their Teleworkers," *Society for Human Resource Management*, October 10, 2017, https://www.shrm.org/resourcesandtools/hr-topics/technology/pages/wanted-managers-who-trust-their-teleworkers.aspx

[50] John Kador, "Trust and Leadership in the World of Remote Work," *Chief Executive*, April 10, 2018, https://chiefexecutive.net/trust-and-leadership-in-the-world-of-remote-work/.

[51] Scott Carey, "Why Did Yahoo's Marissa Mayer Fail? Five Reasons Why Marissa Mayer Failed to Perform a Turnaround," *Techworld*, June 14, 2017, https://www.techworld.com/picture-gallery/careers/what-went-wrong-for-marissa-mayer-at-yahoo-5-reasons-ceo-failed-perform-turnaround-3655968/.

[52] Daniel Thomas, "Yahoo – Where Did it All Go Wrong?" *BBC News*, January 7, 2016, https://www.bbc.com/news/technology-35243407. Adrienne LaFrance, "Yahoo's Demise Is a Death Knell for Digital News Orgs, *The Atlantic*, April 20, 2017, https://www.theatlantic.com/technology/archive/2017/04/yahoos-demise-is-a-death-knell-for-digital-news-orgs/523692/.

[53] Geoffrey James, "The Real Cost of Aetna's Work-From-Home Reversal," *Inc.*, July 5, 2017, https://www.inc.com/geoffrey-james/aetnas-no-more-work-from-home-policy-cost-them-1-.html.

[54] Francesca Levy and Rebecca Greenfield, "Is Working from Home Too Good to Be True?" *Bloomberg Business*, June 14, 2017, https://soundcloud.com/bloomberg-business/is-working-from-home-too-good-to-be-true.

[55] Rex Crum, "IBM Tells Remote Employees to Get Back to the Office," *Mercury News*, May 18, 2017, https://www.mercurynews.com/2017/05/18/ibm-tells-remote-employees-to-get-back-to-the-office/.

[56] Gabrielle M. Blue, "Where Virtual Is the Best Policy," *Inc.*, May 23, 2011, https://www.inc.com/winning-workplaces/articles/201105/where-virtual-is-the-best-policy.html.

[57] Billie Anne Grigg, "Does Every Small Business Need an Accountant, or Can You Sometimes Wing It?" *Fundera*, April 30, 2019, https://www.fundera.com/blog/do-you-need-an-accountant-for-a-small-business.

[58] "How Much Does a Lawyer Cost: Everything You Need to Know." *UpCounsel*, accessed July 25, 2019, https://www.upcounsel.com/how-much-does-a-lawyer-cost.

[59] Daniel Herndon, "How Much Should I Pay a Marketing Consultant?" *MilesHerndon*, December 21, 2018, https://milesherndon.com/blog/how-much-should-i-pay-a-marketing-consultant.

[60] "The 20 Worst Acronyms Ever," *World Wide Interweb*, accessed June 6, 2019, https://worldwideinterweb.com/20-worst-acronyms-ever/.

[61] "5 Legal Issues to Know about before Designing Your First Business Logo," *YouBlawg*, November 12, 2018, https://www.youblawg.com/ip-technology/5-legal-issues-designing-business-logo.

[62] Jane Haskins, "How Much Does It Cost to Trademark a Business Name?" *LegalZoom*, accessed October 19, 2018, https://www.legalzoom.com/articles/how-much-does-it-cost-to-trademark-a-business-name.

[63] "Sole Proprietorship," *Entrepreneur*, accessed July 22, 2019, https://www.entrepreneur.com/encyclopedia/sole-proprietorship.

[64] Andrew Bloomenthal, rev., "General Partnership," *Investopedia*, April 1, 2019, https://www.investopedia.com/terms/g/generalpartnership.asp.

[65] "How to Create a General Partnership Agreement," *LegalNature*, accessed June 6, 2019, http://help.legalnature.com/articles/how-to-create-a-general-partnership-agreement.

[66] "4 Most Common Business Legal Structures," *Pathway Lending*, accessed December 17, 2018, https://www.pathwaylending.org/news-and-blog/news/business-legal-structures/.

[67] Laura Acevedo, "The Advantages of an S Corp over a C Corp in a Very Small Corp," *Chron*, accessed June 6, 2019, https://smallbusiness.chron.com/advantages-s-corp-over-c-corp-very-small-corp-4185.html.

[68] Priyanka Prakash, "S-Corp vs. C-Corp: How They Differ (and How to Decide)," *Fundera*, updated July 25, 2019, https://www.fundera.com/blog/s-corp-vs-c-corp.

381

[69] "2017 Year-End Economic Report," *National Small Business Association*, February 2018, https://nsba.biz/wp-content/uploads/2018/02/Year-End-Economic -Report-2017.pdf.

[70] Jean Murray, "How to Determine Your Company's Fiscal Year," *The Balance Small Business*, updated September 18, 2019, https://www.thebalancesmb.com/ how-do-i-determine-my-company-s-fiscal-year-397563.

[71] Kelly Main, "3 Rules to Choosing a Professional Email Address," *Fit Small Business*, July 30, 2019, https://fitsmallbusiness.com/professional-email-address/. Kelly Main, "How to Set Up a Free Business Email Address in 5 Minutes," *Fit Small Business*, August 12, 2019, https://fitsmallbusiness.com/free-business- email-address/.

[72] Jones, Jessica. "How to Start a Company in the Virtual Workplace," *Chron,* accessed October 19, 2018, http://smallbusiness.chron.com/start-company-virtual -workplace-11800.html.

[73] Christopher Carter, "Can a Corporation Be a DBA?" *Bizfluent*, September 26, 2017, https://bizfluent.com/info-7742243-can-corporation-dba.html.

[74] Jackie Zimmermann, "DBA (Doing Business As): What Is It and How Do I Register?" *NerdWallet*, August 29, 2017, https://www.nerdwallet.com/blog/small- business/dba-doing-business-as/.

[75] Rachael Pasini, "Do I Need Special Permits to Work from Home?" *Virtual Vocations*, April 24, 2018, https://www.virtualvocations.com/blog/telecommuting-survival/special-permits- remote-work/.

[76] "Business Owner Policy (BOP) Cost," *Howmuch.net*, accessed October 19, 2018, https://howmuch.net/costs/business-owner-policy.

[77] "E&O Insurance," *Insureon*, accessed October 23, 2018, https://www.insureon.com/products/errors-omissions.

[78] "Commercial Umbrella Policy," *General Liability Shop.com*, accessed October 19, 2018, https://www.generalliabilityshop.com/about-general-liability-insurance/ umbrella-coverage/.

[79] "Commercial Umbrella Liability Insurance," *Insureon*, accessed October 23, 2018, https://www.insureon.com/small-business-insurance/umbrella-liability.

[80] John Boitnott, "7 Types of Insurance You Need to Protect Your Business," *Entrepreneur*, December 30, 2014, https://www.entrepreneur.com/article/241026.

[81] "Are Telecommuters Covered Under Workers' Compensation?" *Society for Human Resource Management,* accessed July 22, 2019, https://www.shrm.org/resourcesandtools/tools-and-samples/hr-qa/pages/wcandtelecommuting.aspx.

[82] "Workers' Compensation Insurance," *Insureon,* accessed October 23, 2018, https://www.insureon.com/products/workers-compensation.

[83] "What Posters Do I Need, and How Do I Comply with These Requirements?" *Society for Human Resource Management,* November 14, 2018, https://www.shrm.org/resourcesandtools/tools-and-samples/hr-qa/pages/determinetheirpostingrequirements.aspx.

[84] Jerry Kalish, "The ERISA Fidelity Bond," *401khelpcenter.com,* accessed October 19, 2018, http://www.401khelpcenter.com/401k/kalish_erisa_bond.html.

[85] Julia Kagan, rev., "Key Person Insurance," *Investopedia,* updated February 23, 2018, https://www.investopedia.com/terms/k/keypersoninsurance.asp.

[86] "QuickBooks Setup," *JMM & Associates,* accessed June 6, 2019, http://www.jmmcpa.net/quickbookssetup.php.

[87] Amy Hardison White, "How Are B2B Payments Different from Consumer Payments?" *Invoiced,* October 13, 2017, https://invoiced.com/blog/how-are-b2b-payments-different-from-consumer-payments.

[88] Steve Nicastro, "Credit Card Processing Companies: 5 Factors to Consider," *NerdWallet,* August 28, 2017, https://www.nerdwallet.com/blog/small-business/credit-card-processing-company-choose/.

[89] Adam Rowe, "The Secret to Security in the Age of Remote Working," *TechCo,* April 25, 2018, https://tech.co/the-secret-to-security-in-the-age-of-remote-working-2018-04.

[90] Zeljka Zorz, "Losses Due to BEC Scams Are Escalating," *Help Net Security,* June 25, 2018, https://www.helpnetsecurity.com/2018/06/25/2017-internet-crime/.

[91] David Matthews, "Scammer Sent Phony Bills to Facebook and Google Companies and They Paid Out $122 Million," *New York Daily News,* March 25, 2019, https://www.nydailynews.com/news/national/ny-news-scam-facebook-google-122-million-phony-bills-20190325-oorzinnz3jc7bmo2jhxm5oljgi-story.html.

[92] Forbes Human Resources Council, "Why Your Business Needs a Social Media Policy and Eight Things It Should Cover," *Forbes,* May 25, 2017, https://www.forbes.com/sites/forbeshumanresourcescouncil/2017/05/25/why-your-business-needs-a-social-media-policy-and-eight-things-it-should-cover/#b30a28452649

[93] "Advantages of Agile Work Strategies for Companies," *Global Workplace Analytics*, accessed June 6, 2019, http://globalworkplaceanalytics.com/resources/costs-benefits.

[94] Stephen Miller, "2019 Payroll Taxes Will Hit Higher Incomes," *Society for Human Resource Management*, October 12, 2018, https://www.shrm.org/resourcesandtools/hr-topics/compensation/pages/fica-social-security-tax-2019.aspx.

[95] "Which States Require Employers to Have a Short-Term Disability Plan?" *Society for Human Resource Management*, February 11, 2019, https://www.shrm.org/resourcesandtools/tools-and-samples/hr-qa/pages/stateswithstd.aspx.

[96] Kerry Jones, "The Most Desirable Employee Benefits," *Harvard Business Review*, February 15, 2017, https://hbr.org/2017/02/the-most-desirable-employee-benefits.

[97] Amy Pennza, "3 Health Insurance Options for Companies with Employees in Multiple States," *PeopleKeep*, March 16, 2017, https://www.peoplekeep.com/blog/3-health-insurance-options-for-companies-with-employees-in-multiple-states.

[98] "High Deductible Healthcare Plan (HDHP)," HealthCare.gov, accessed August 29, 2019, https://www.healthcare.gov/glossary/high-deductible-health-plan/.

[99] "The QSEHRA: A New Health Benefit for Small Businesses," *PeopleKeep*, accessed June 6, 2019, https://www.peoplekeep.com/qsehra.

[100] "Family and Medical Leave Act," *U.S. Department of Labor*, accessed June 6, 2019, https://www.dol.gov/whd/fmla/.

[101] "Family and Medical Leave Act," *U.S. Department of Labor*, accessed June 6, 2019, https://www.dol.gov/whd/fmla/.

[102] "Family and Medical Leave Act," *U.S. Department of Labor*, accessed June 6, 2019, https://www.dol.gov/whd/fmla/.

[103] "FMLA Frequently Asked Questions, *U.S. Department of Labor*, accessed August 29, 2019, https://www.dol.gov/whd/fmla/fmla-faqs.htm.

[104] "Is an Employee Who Works Remotely (75 Miles or More from the Employer's Office) Eligible for Family and Medical Leave Act (FMLA) Leave?" *Society for Human Resource Management*, December 4, 2018, https://www.shrm.org/ResourcesAndTools/tools-and-samples/hr-qa/Pages/telecommutingandfmla.aspx.

[105] "Health Savings Account (HSA)," *HealthCare.gov*, accessed June 7, 2019, https://www.healthcare.gov/glossary/health-savings-account-hsa/.

[106] Karen Pallarito, "Dental, Vision Plans Shifting to What Employees Want," *Business Insurance*, June 19, 2016, https://www.businessinsurance.com/article/20160619/CBO/160619981/dental-vision-plans-shifting-to-what-employees-want.

[107] Barbara Marquand, "Accidental Death and Dismemberment Insurance Explained," *NerdWallet*, February 5, 2016, https://www.nerdwallet.com/blog/insurance/accidental-death-and-dismemberment-insurance/.

[108] "IRS Announces 2019 FSA Contribution Limit Increase," *DataPath*, accessed September 22, 2019, https://dpath.com/2019-fsa-contribution-limits/.

[109] Ben Werschkul, "Nearly a Quarter of Workers Are Missing out on Retirement Savings: Survey," *Yahoo Finance*, July 11, 2019, https://finance.yahoo.com/news/nearly-a-quarter-of-workers-are-missing-out-on-retirement-savings-new-survey-133818581.html.

[110] Matthew Frankel, "The Retirement Mistake That Could Cost You $100,000 or More," *CNN Money*, July 11, 2018, https://money.cnn.com/2018/07/11/pf/retirement-fund-fees/index.html.

[111] Trent Gillies, "Warren Buffett Says Index Funds Make the Best Retirement Sense 'Practically All the Time,'" *CNBC*, May 14, 2017, https://www.cnbc.com/2017/05/12/warren-buffett-says-index-funds-make-the-best-retirement-sense-practically-all-the-time.html.

[112] Alex Goldberg, "Key 401(k) Statistics: Retirement Plans by the Numbers," *ForUsAll*, October 29, 2017, https://www.forusall.com/401k-blog/401k-statistics/

[113] Todd Campbell, "Average Americans' 401(k) Contributions, by Age and Income," *The Motley Fool*, January 15, 2017, https://www.fool.com/retirement/2017/01/15/average-americans-401k-contributions-by-age-and-in.aspx.

[114] "Which Employer Benefits Do Small Businesses Offer the Most?" *HealthMarkets*, December 15, 2016, https://www.healthmarkets.com/resources/small-business-health-insurance/most-common-employer-benefits-for-small-businesses/.

[115] "Tax Planning Tips: Disability Insurance," *Ameriprise Financial*, accessed October 19, 2018, https://www.ameriprise.com/research-market-insights/tax-center/tax-planning/taxation-of-disability-insurance/.

[116] "How to Develop and Administer Paid Leave Programs," *Society for Human Resource Management*, October 25, 2016, https://www.shrm.org/resourcesandtools/tools-and-samples/how-to-guides/pages/howtodevelopandadministerpaidleaveprograms.aspx.

[117] "Thriving in the New Work-Life World: MetLife's 17th Annual U.S. Employee Benefit Trends Study 2019," *MetLife*, accessed September 24, 2019, https://www.metlife.com/content/dam/metlifecom/us/ebts/pdf/MetLife-Employee-Benefit-Trends-Study-2019.pdf.

[118] Sachi Barreiro, "California Rules on Vacation and Paid Time Off," *Nolo*, accessed November 19, 2018, https://www.nolo.com/legal-encyclopedia/california-rules-vacation-paid-time-off.html.

[119] Alexander Kunst, "Number of Sick Leave Days U.S. Adults Took Last Year as of 2017, by Age," *Statista*, September 3, 2019, https://www.statista.com/statistics/682924/sick-leave-days-among-adults-us-by-age/.

[120] Kerry Jones, "The Most Desirable Employee Benefits," *Harvard Business Review*, February 15, 2017, https://hbr.org/2017/02/the-most-desirable-employee-benefits.

[121] Emily Dreyfuss, "Will Others Follow Microsoft's Lead on Paid Parental Leave?" *Wired*, August 31, 2018, https://www.wired.com/story/will-others-follow-microsoft-on-paid-parental-leave/. Drew DeSilver, "Access to Paid Family Leave Varies Widely across Employers, Industries," *Pew Research Center*, March 23, 2017, http://www.pewresearch.org/fact-tank/2017/03/23/access-to-paid-family-leave-varies-widely-across-employers-industries/.

[122] Emily Peck, "Mitt Romney Joins Republican Push for Terrible Family Leave Bill," *HuffPost*, March 28, 2019, https://www.huffpost.com/entry/mitt-romney-family-leave-marco-rubio_n_5c9bdccde4b08c450cd0664b.

[123] Howard Gleckman, "Will Paid Leave for Family Caregivers Catch On in the U.S.?" *Forbes*, September 5, 2018, https://www.forbes.com/sites/howardgleckman/2018/09/05/will-paid-leave-for-family-caregivers-catch-on-in-the-us/#5864836e110a.

[124] Howard Gleckman, "Will Paid Leave for Family Caregivers Catch On in the U.S.?" *Forbes*, September 5, 2018, https://www.forbes.com/sites/howardgleckman/2018/09/05/will-paid-leave-for-family-caregivers-catch-on-in-the-us/#5864836e110a.

[125] "Temporary Disability/Caregiver Insurance," *Rhode Island Department of Labor and Training*, accessed June 7, 2019, http://www.dlt.ri.gov/tdi/.

[126] "DC Paid Family Leave," *DC.gov: Department of Employment Services*, accessed July 23, 2019, https://does.dc.gov/page/district-columbia-paid-family-leave.

[127] "Workers: Support for Employees, Stability for Companies," *Washington Paid Family and Medical Leave*, accessed June 7, 2019, https://paidleave.wa.gov/workers.

[128] "Department of Family and Medical Leave," *Mass.gov*, accessed June 7, 2019, https://www.mass.gov/orgs/department-of-family-and-medical-leave.

[129] Lisa Tucker, "California Maternity Leave: Everything Expectant Parents Need to Know (Including Big Changes in 2018)," *Working Mother*, January 10, 2018, https://www.workingmother.com/california-maternity-leave-everything-expectant-parents-need-to-know.

[130] "Paid Family Leave," *Employment Development Department: State of California*, accessed July 23, 2019, https://www.edd.ca.gov/Disability/pdf/PFLNewMotherTrainingDeck.pdf.

[131] Sachi Barreiro, "How Much Are California Paid Family Leave Benefits?" *Nolo*, accessed September 25, 2019.

[132] "New York Paid Family Leave Updates for 2019," *New York State Workers' Compensation Board*, accessed July 23, 2019, https://paidfamilyleave.ny.gov/2019.

[133] "Paid Family Medical Leave for Employees FAQ," *Mass.gov*, accessed September 25, 2019, https://www.mass.gov/info-details/paid-family-medical-leave-for-employees-faq#how-much-is-the-benefit?-.

[134] "Washington Paid Family and Medical Leave: 2019 Employment Infographic," *Employment Security Department: Washington State*, July 2019, https://paidleave.wa.gov/files/Documents/2019.Employee.Infographic.pdf.

[135] Howard Gleckman, "Will Paid Leave for Family Caregivers Catch On in the U.S.?" *Forbes*, September 5, 2018, https://www.forbes.com/sites/howardgleckman/2018/09/05/will-paid-leave-for-family-caregivers-catch-on-in-the-us/#5864836e110a.

[136] "Oregon Family Leave Act and Federal Family and Medical Leave Act Overview," *Oregon Bureau of Labor and Industries*, accessed September 25, 2019.

[137] Richard V. Reeves, "Let Workers Decide Who Counts as 'Family' for Paid Sick and Family Leave," *Brookings*, February 20, 2018, https://www.brookings.edu/blog/social-mobility-memos/2018/02/20/let-workers-decide-who-counts-as-family-for-paid-sick-and-family-leave/

[138] "Fact Sheet #28A: Employee Protections under the Family and Medical Leave Act," *U.S. Department of Labor*, accessed June 7, 2019, https://www.dol.gov/whd/regs/compliance/whdfs28a.pdf.

[139] Howard Gleckman, "Will Paid Leave for Family Caregivers Catch On in the U.S.?" *Forbes*, September 5, 2018, https://www.forbes.com/sites/howardgleck man/2018/09/05/will-paid-leave-for-family-caregivers-catch-on-in-the-us/#5864 836e110a.

[140] Ed Frauenheim and Sarah Lewis-Kulin, "Giving Workers Paid Time Off to Volunteer Will Help Your Company Succeed," *Fortune*, April 26, 2016, http://fortune.com/2016/04/26/giving-workers-paid-time-off-to-volunteer-will-help-your-company-succeed/.

[141] "Definition of *Vacation* in English," *Lexico.com*, accessed September 25, 2019, lexico.com/en/definition/vacation.

[142] Eric Krell, "Weighing Internal vs. External Hires," *Society for Human Resource Management*, January 7, 2015, https://www.shrm.org/hr-today/news/hr-magazin e/pages/010215-hiring.aspx.

[143] Nikoletta Bika, "The Advantages and Disadvantages of Internal Recruitment," *Workable*, accessed June 7, 2019, https://resources.workable.com/tutorial/adva ntages-disadvantages-of-internal-recruitment.

[144] Shelly J. Spiegel, "Why I Haven't Sold When Everyone Else Has," *Fire Engine RED: WellRED Blog*, September 22, 2015, https://fire-engine-red.com/why-i-hav ent-sold-when-everyone-else-has/.

[145] Alison Doyle, "Can Employers Ask for Salary History?" *The Balance Careers*, updated March 14, 2019, https://www.thebalancecareers.com/can-employers-find -out-how-much-you-made-at-your-last-job-2063396.

[146] Matt Burgess, "How Frequently Do Private Businesses Pay Workers?" *Beyond the Numbers* 3, no. 11 (May 2014), https://www.bls.gov/opub/btn/volume-3/how-frequently-do-private-businesses-pay-workers.htm.

[147] "Employee Agreement: Everything You Need to Know," *UpCounsel*, accessed October 26, 2018, https://www.upcounsel.com/employee-agreement.

[148] Richard Harroch, "Negotiating Employment Agreements: Checklist of 14 Key Issues," *Forbes*, November 11, 2013, https://www.forbes.com/sites/allbusiness/2 013/11/11/negotiating-employment-agreements-checklist-of-14-key-issues/#575 bc9c924c6.

[149] "Independent Contractor vs. Employee: What Can These Workers Offer Your Business?" *Paychex*, January 9, 2019, https://www.paychex.com/articles/payroll-taxes/independent-contractor-vs-employee-comparison.

[150] Janet Berry-Johnson, "Canada Tax 101: What Is a W-8BEN Form?" *FreshBooks*, accessed July 21, 2019, https://www.freshbooks.com/blog/w-8ben-form-canada-tax.

[151] Paul Oliveira, "Reporting U.S. Business Payments to Foreign Individuals for Services Performed Outside the U.S." *KLR*, updated December 17, 2018, https://www.kahnlitwin.com/news/articles/Reporting-U.S.-Business-Payments-To-Foreign-Individuals-for-Services-Perfor. "About Form W-8 BEN-E," *Internal Revenue Service*, updated March 27, 2019, https://www.irs.gov/forms-pubs/about-form-w-8-ben-e.

[152] "U Dreamers Program," *University of Miami Undergraduate Admission*, accessed September 9, 2019, https://admissions.miami.edu/undergraduate/financial-aid/scholarships/daca/index.html.

[153] Roy Maurer, "How to Comply with I-9 Requirements for Remote Workers," *Society for Human Resource Management*, November 8, 2017, https://www.shrm.org/resourcesandtools/hr-topics/talent-acquisition/pages/how-to-comply-i9-requirements-remote-workers.aspx.

[154] Greg Kratz, "What Office Equipment Should You Give Remote Workers?" *FlexJobs*, April 14, 2017, https://www.flexjobs.com/employer-blog/office-equipment-give-remote-workers/.

[155] Chuck Vadun, "Does Your Remote Team Need a Child-Care Policy?" *Remote.co*, August 7, 2015, https://remote.co/does-your-remote-team-need-a-child-care-policy/.

[156] "2017 Human Capital Benchmarking Report, *Society for Human Resource Management*, December 2017, https://www.shrm.org/hr-today/trends-and-forecasting/research-and-surveys/Documents/2017-Human-Capital-Benchmarking.pdf.

[157] "Scrum Master and Product Owner: Understanding the Differences," *KnowledgeHut,* May 30, 2017, https://www.knowledgehut.com/blog/agile/scrum-master-and-product-owner-understanding-the-differences.

[158] Brian Evje, "Want HR to Matter? Start with the CEO." *Inc.*, December 4, 2013, https://www.inc.com/brian-evje/want-hr-to-matter-start-with-the-ceo.html.

[159] Karen Higginbottom, "Why Empathy Matters in the Workplace," *Forbes*, May 31, 2018, https://www.forbes.com/sites/karenhigginbottom/2018/05/31/why-empathy-matters-in-the-workplace/#3da530141130.

[160] Adam Edelman, "Trump Ends DACA Program, No New Applications Accepted," *NBC News*, September 5, 2017, https://www.nbcnews.com/politics/immigration/trump-dreamers-daca-immigration-announcement-n798686.

[161] Max Greenwood, "Poll: Nearly 9 in 10 Want DACA Recipients to Stay in US," *The Hill*, January 18, 2018, https://thehill.com/blogs/blog-briefing-room/news/369487-poll-nearly-nine-in-10-favor-allowing-daca-recipients-to-stay.

[162] "U Dreamers Program," *University of Miami: Undergraduate Admission*, accessed October 1, 2019, https://admissions.miami.edu/undergraduate/financial-aid/scholarships/daca/index.html.

[163] Rhonda Abrams, "Strategies: 9 Steps to a More Motivated Workforce," *USA Today*, July 25, 2014, https://www.usatoday.com/story/money/columnist/abrams/2014/07/25/small-business-motivation/13072073/.

[164] Ravi S. Gajendran and Aparna Joshi, "Innovation in Globally Distributed Teams: The Role of LMX, Communication Frequency, and Member Influence on Team Decisions," *Journal of Applied Psychology* 97, no. 6 (November 2012): 1252-1261 http://dx.doi.org/10.1037/a0028958.

[165] Thomas J. Peters and Robert H. Waterman, Jr., *In Search of Excellence: Lessons from America's Best-Run Companies* (New York: HarperCollins Publishers Inc., 1982, 2004).

[166] Sebastian Lambert, "2018 SaaS Industry Market Report: Key Global Trends & Growth Forecasts," *FinancesOnline*, accessed June 7, 2019, https://financesonline.com/2018-saas-industry-market-report-key-global-trends-growth-forecasts/

[167] Margaret Rouse, "Agile Project Management," *SearchCIO*, updated January 2018, https://searchcio.techtarget.com/definition/Agile-project-management.

[168] Tori Funkhouser, "How to Apply Agile Practices with Your Non-Tech Team or Business," *TechRepublic*, April 7, 2016, https://www.techrepublic.com/article/how-to-apply-agile-practices-with-your-non-tech-team-or-business/.

[169] Valerie Bolden-Barrett, "Report: HR Staffing Is at 1.4 per 100 Employees, an All-Time High," *HR Dive*, July 20, 2017, https://www.hrdive.com/news/report-hr-staffing-is-at-14-per-100-employees-an-all-time-high/447480/.

[170] "*Inc.*, Winning Workplaces Name 50 Small Top Company Workplaces for 2011," *Smart Business*, May 26, 2011, http://www.sbnonline.com/inc-winning-workplaces-name-50-small-top-company-workplaces-for-2011/.

[171] Jens Larson, "Higher Ed CRM Review: Fireworks by Fire Engine RED," *U of Admissions Marketing*, June 2, 2014, http://www.uofadmissionsmarketing.com/2014/06/higer-ed-crm-review-firweorks-by-fire.html [sic].

[172] Sara Sutton Fell, "How Remote Workplaces Benefit Women," *Fast Company*, January 6, 2016, https://www.fastcompany.com/3055021/how-remote-workplaces-benefit-women.

[173] Sara Sutton Fell, "How Remote Workplaces Benefit Women," *Fast Company*, January 6, 2016, https://www.fastcompany.com/3055021/how-remote-workplaces-benefit-women.

[174] Marie Hicks, "Why Tech's Gender Problem Is Nothing New," *The Guardian*, October 12, 2018, https://www.theguardian.com/technology/2018/oct/11/tech-gender-problem-amazon-facebook-bias-women.

[175] Sara Sutton Fell, "How Remote Workplaces Benefit Women," *Fast Company*, January 6, 2016, https://www.fastcompany.com/3055021/how-remote-workplaces-benefit-women.

[176] "Health Plans & Benefits: Continuation of Health Coverage - COBRA," *U.S. Department of Labor*, accessed June 7, 2019, https://www.dol.gov/general/topic/health-plans/cobra. Barbara Marquand, "What You Need to Know about COBRA Insurance," *Insurance.com*, October 23, 2018, https://www.insurance.com/health-insurance/health-insurance-basics/what-you-need-to-know-about-cobra.html.

[177] Lisa Nagele-Piazza, "5 Tips for Terminating Remote Workers," *Society for Human Resource Management*, June 19, 2017, https://www.shrm.org/resourcesandtools/legal-and-compliance/state-and-local-updates/pages/5-tips-for-terminating-remote-workers.aspx.

[178] "Health Plans & Benefits: Continuation of Health Coverage - COBRA," *U.S. Department of Labor*, accessed June 7, 2019, https://www.dol.gov/general/topic/health-plans/cobra. Barbara Marquand, "What You Need to Know about COBRA Insurance," *Insurance.com*, October 23, 2018, https://www.insurance.com/health-insurance/health-insurance-basics/what-you-need-to-know-about-cobra.html.

[179] "Tax Credits vs. Tax Deductions," *IRS.com*, accessed December 17, 2018, https://www.irs.com/articles/tax-credits-vs-tax-deductions.

[180] "Tax Credits and Programs," *Pennsylvania Department of Revenue*, accessed December 17, 2018, https://www.revenue.pa.gov/GeneralTaxInformation/IncentivesCreditsPrograms/TaxCredits/Pages/default.aspx.

[181] Michael Nierstedt, "The $250,000 Tax Credit You Could Be Using for Your Business," *Entrepreneur*, September 20, 2017, https://www.entrepreneur.com/article/299991.

[182] Stephen Miller, "IRS Answers Questions on Paid Family Leave Tax Credit," *Society for Human Resource Management*, September 28, 2018, https://www.

shrm.org/resourcesandtools/hr-topics/benefits/pages/irs-answers-on-paid-family-leave-tax-credit.aspx.

[183] Marcy Gordon, "Employers Can Now Receive Tax Credits for Giving Their Workers Paid Time Off," *Inc.*, September 14, 2018, https://www.inc.com/associat ed-press/new-law-gives-tax-credits-to-employers-who-offer-paid-leave.html.

[184] Georgia McIntyre, "Small Business Taxes: The Complete Guide," *Fundera*, updated July 8, 2019, https://www.fundera.com/blog/small-business-taxes.

[185] Jean Murray, "How Do I Calculate Estimated Taxes for My Business?" *The Balance Small Business*, updated June 25, 2019, https://www.thebalancesmb. com/how-do-i-calculate-estimated-taxes-for-my-business-398001.

[186] "Publication 505 (2019), Tax Withholding and Estimated Tax," *IRS.gov*, accessed September 6, 2019, https://www.irs.gov/publications/p505#en_US_2019.

[187] Shelly J. Spiegel, "Why I Haven't Sold When Everyone Else Has," *Fire Engine RED: WellRED Blog*, September 22, 2015, https://fire-engine-red.com/why-i-havent-sold-when-everyone-else-has/.

[188] Rachel Feintzeig and Lauren Weber, "Fewer Americans Uproot Themselves for a New Job," *The Wall Street Journal*, August 20, 2018, https://www.wsj.com/ articles/fewer-americans-uproot-themselves-for-new-jobs-1534690800?mod=e2li.

[189] Rachael Pasini, "Remote Work States: 7 Locations That Incentivize Telecommuting," *Virtual Vocations*, March 20, 2019, https://www.virtualvocations.com/blog/telecommuting-news/7-remote-work-states/

Made in the USA
Las Vegas, NV
10 July 2022